EVENTS AND THEIR AFTERLIFE

EVENTS AND THEIR AFTERLIFE

THE DIALECTICS OF CHRISTIAN
TYPOLOGY IN
THE BIBLE AND DANTE

BY

A. C. CHARITY

Fellow of Trinity College, Cambridge
Lecturer in English at the University of York

CAMBRIDGE
AT THE UNIVERSITY PRESS
1966

Published by the Syndics of the Cambridge University Press
Bentley House, 200 Euston Road, London, N.W. 1
American Branch: 32 East 57th Street, New York, N.Y. 10022

© Cambridge University Press 1966

Library of Congress Catalogue Card Number: 66-18116

Printed in Great Britain
at the University Printing House, Cambridge
(Brooke Crutchley, University Printer)

FOR MEG

CONTENTS

vii

PREFACE

THE subject and aims of the present work are defined in the Introduction. Here it may be enough to say that it is concerned with a particular view of history and with its workings in literature and (if 'life' is too large a term) in ethics. The argument therefore has something to do with the philosophy of history, critical theory and ethics, and the field of study includes, besides the Bible and Dante, such studies as are ancillary to our subject in the realms of patristic, medieval and, of course, modern theology.

With a subject so large it is impossible for an author to base his statements solely upon detailed research of his own into each aspect of it. He must often rely upon others, more competent than himself and more learned, who have studied and written about the particular questions at issue. Any virtue that this book may have will be owed very largely to the lucidity with which so many scholars have been able to make the fruits of their labours intelligible to a dilettante among them. My notes do their best to acknowledge such debts individually, but in the last resort the task is beyond them.

It is correspondingly clear that there will remain areas of ignorance. There are so many more-or-less relevant works that world enough and time to read them all would be, if not infinite, at least quite inconceivable. Among works which I especially regret not having had the opportunity to read, mention must be made of L. Goppelt's book *Typos* (Gutersloh, 1939) in particular. For the rest, the list is too long.

Among my debts there are others, more personal. The Rev. Professors R. P. C. Hanson and G. W. H. Lampe, Rev. Dr Norman Snaith, Fr B. Lindars, S.S.F., Mr D. H. Green, Dr Walter Ullmann and Dr A. C. Gibbs have been kind enough to read most or all of my manuscript at one stage or another of its preparation, and I have benefited enormously from their comments. I have been assisted in the reading of proofs by Miss Vivienne Taylor, Miss Ann Sinclair, Mr Michael Greasley, and my wife, who also, with my mother, assisted in the preparation of the index of scriptural references. To Fr Kenelm Foster,

O.P., who began as my research supervisor and continued to offer advice, criticism and encouragement well beyond the expected or temporal bounds of that duty, I owe a special debt of gratitude, 'e'n la mente m'è fitta'. And finally I should like to express my thanks to Trinity College, Cambridge, for electing me to the Prize Fellowship which enabled me to complete this book's preparation, and to my wife, without whose bread-winning labours it could never have been begun.

Quotations from the Old Testament are normally taken from the *Revised Standard Version of the Bible*, copyrighted 1946 and 1952, by kind permission of the publishers, Thomas Nelson and Sons Ltd, and New Testament quotations from the *New English Bible*, published jointly by the Oxford and Cambridge University Presses. Those from the *Divine Comedy* are taken from the text of the Società Dantesca Italiana, and the translations are my own. An earlier version of part of chapter 14 was published in *Blackfriars* (Nov. 1963), and I wish to thank the editor of that journal for allowing its republication here.

University of York   A. C. C.
March 1966

ABBREVIATIONS

AKG	*Archiv für Kulturgeschichte*
BK	*Biblischer Kommentar*
BKW	*Bible Key Words* (translated from *TWNT*)
BZNW	*Beihefte zur Zeitschrift für die neutestamentliche Wissenschaft*
CHL	*Commentationes Humanarum Litterarum* (Societas Scientiarum Fennica)
CQR	*Church Quarterly Review*
DDJ	*Deutsches Dante-Jahrbuch*
DThC	*Dictionnaire de Théologie Catholique*
ET	English translation
EvTh	*Evangelische Theologie*
Exp.T	*Expository Times*
IB	*The Interpreter's Bible*
JBL	*Journal of Biblical Literature*
JTS	*Journal of Theological Studies*
KD	*Kerygma und Dogma*
PAH	*Probleme alttestamentlicher Hermeneutik* (ed. C. Westermann)
PMLA	*Publications of the Modern Language Association of America*
RB	*Revue Biblique*
RechSR	*Recherches de Science Religieuse*
RHPR	*Revue d'histoire et de philosophie religieuses*
SCG	*Summa contra Gentiles*
SJT	*Scottish Journal of Theology*
SNTS	Bulletin of the *Studiorum Novi Testamenti Societas*
ST	*Studia Theologica*
STh	*Summa Theologiae*
TLZ	*Theologische Literaturzeitung*
TWNT	*Theologisches Wörterbuch zum Neuen Testament* (ed. G. Kittel, 1933 continuing)
TZ	*Theologische Zeitschrift*
VT	*Vetus Testamentum*
ZAW	*Zeitschrift für die alttestamentliche Wissenschaft*
ZThK	*Zeitschrift für Theologie und Kirche*

INTRODUCTION

'Délimiter un sujet,' writes the Jesuit scholar Henri de Lubac,[1] 'c'est abstraire'; and to sum up one's delimitation is to refine the process still further. In these introductory pages clarity demands that I set down no more than the bare bones of this work's whole intention, and leave it to the essay itself to give these bones sinews and flesh.

'Typology' is my subject, and the first task is that word's definition. But even for the present purposes it would be an unnecessarily astringent process of abstraction to reduce the various usages which the word has in practice to a single quite unequivocal definition. For its senses are not wholly distinct, and a degree of peaceful (if tense) co-existence between current meanings has attendant advantages, strategic and diplomatic. It provides a condition which, because it necessitates some account of the usages' interrelations, facilitates, too, an approach to a more basic question, about the broader relations between this whole subject and others. It is right to raise this matter here; for to delimit is also to set in a context, and the route round the boundaries gives new views of the neighbouring fields.

The discussion revolves, however, for the most part around only two definitions, neither of which applies commonly to the use of the word in non-theological writing. Typology, in the first of these senses, may be defined as either the broad study, or any particular presentation, of the quasi-symbolic relations which one event may appear to bear to another—especially, but not exclusively, when these relations are the analogical ones existing between events which are taken to be one another's 'prefiguration' and 'fulfilment'. The second definition is a comparatively dogmatic and idealistic one, intended to apply only to Christian typology, though, with only the last two words omitted, it might serve the same dogmatic purpose for the Old Testament as for the New: according to this definition, Christian typology is 'the science of history's relations to its fulfilment in Christ'.

Clearly, of these definitions, the first is the more non-committal

---

[1] *Exégèse Médiévale: Les Quatre Sens de l'Écriture*, II, 2, p. 125.

and more comprehensive. It is by the same token perhaps less suggestive and less optimistic, certainly less directly related to the formulation of theological statements. In the present work, most often, it is the actual presentation of the idea of prefiguration in biblical and non-biblical literature, rather than the discursive theoretical study of this idea, that I intend to characterize by it. In this sense we may usefully speak, without implying any dogmatic or evaluative bias, of the 'use' of typology in both testaments and outside them: wherever, in fact, a writer has attributed significance to an apprehended analogy between different events. And, though it lies outside the main scope of this study, 'typology' as thus defined may be taken to include also the practice of those forms of exegesis which are commonly called 'typological': for example, the Epistle of Barnabas's discovery of a prefiguration of Christ's crucifixion in Exod. 17. 8–11, where it tells how when Israel fought the Amalekites Moses stretched out his arms—'and whenever Moses held out his hands, Israel prevailed';[1] or the no less amazing and no less traditional interpretation of the harlot Rahab's scarlet cord, which, having originally guaranteed the safety of her household at the fall of Jericho, represents already in I Clement (early in the second century) the blood of Christ which ensures salvation to the Church.[2] In such interpretations as these at least the interpreter, if only he, regards the Old Testament event as a 'type' or 'prefiguration' of what was to come, and his exegetical labours must therefore fall within the general scope of typology as my first definition describes it.

No less clearly, the second definition will not fit these examples. Possibly they purport, though by implication alone, to make manifest their particular story's relation to its fulfilment in Christ; but their manner of doing so cannot be called 'scientific'. J. R. Darbyshire, therefore, in his article on typology in the *Encyclopaedia of Religion and Ethics*, though he too defines typology first of all as a 'science', wisely and warily adds, 'or rather, only too often, the curious art...'.[3]

---

[1] Barnabas 12. 2–5. [2] I Clement 12. 7; cf. Josh. 2. 18.
[3] Reflections of this kind cause J. D. Smart to doubt the propriety of using the word 'typology' for those features in the term's area of reference which we, in our day, can accept, for 'once anything that goes by (this name) is vindicated, the impression is created that typology...has been at least in some measure validated as an exegetical method' (*The Interpretation of Scripture*, p. 98). But the objection

Typological exegesis, then, even in its most arbitrary forms, falls under only one, but at any rate one, of our definitions of 'typology'. Nevertheless typology as an exegetical process or system, either ancient or modern, is only occasionally and marginally our concern in this study. Today it should go without saying that as a process generally applicable to biblical or other texts such exegesis is illegitimate; and only in so far as the texts themselves can be reasonably viewed as expressing, or involving, or presenting, in agreement with their author's intentions, a typological concept, that is, a concept of prefiguration and fulfilment, are they the real subject-matter of this essay.

But the comprehensive character of the first definition gives it other, less dubious, advantages than that of including the idea of a typological exegesis. For though it does comprehend virtually everything that is properly called 'typology' in the biblical and Christian traditions, the apparently arbitrary as well as the genuinely suggestive, there is no categorical necessity for it to comprehend only the Christian and the biblical, and the concept may be used, I hope profitably, as a basis for conversation between the Christian and the 'humanist' writer or scholar. I make mention here of only two ways.

Alan Richardson suggests one such conversational starting-point in his book, *History, Sacred and Profane*. He invokes the case of the secular historian who, finding something in common between a number of events which brings them together in his mind, uses, to express this relation and as a vital part of his interpretative task, an essentially analogical term, such as 'revolution'—and attempts thereby to make the infinite particularity of the historical order susceptible to treatment in the necessarily general and conceptual order of thought.[1] The idea of 'prefiguration' and 'fulfilment' is usually absent here.[2] But

does not seem to me very serious. There is enough similarity, I believe, between our objectives and those of the Fathers for us to be sure that we and they are both concerned to clarify the principles of 'fulfilment'. And if, in this same pursuit, the later age disagrees even very profoundly with the assumptions, methods and conclusions of the earlier age, as would (let us say) modern with Aristotelian physics, there is no reason why we should cease to call the pursuit by the same name, 'typology', just as we call physics 'physics'.

[1] See A. Richardson, *History, Sacred and Profane*, pp. 185-7.

[2] But cf. *ibid*, pp. 175-83 and 221 f.: 'All historical interpretation, and therefore all historical writing as such, necessarily involves the seeing of the significance of the beginning from the end. This is the very character of the biblical writings as historical documents; the NT itself is a viewing of Israel's story in the light of

it would be worth asking whether the borrowing of such concepts for one event from another (in so far as the terms applied to historical happening derive from historical happenings) may imply that certain seminal or climactic events acquire, in the historian's mind, a kind of semantic status which is comparable as such, though distinguishable in other ways, to the status of the climactic events of 'salvation history' (*Heilsgeschichte*) in the mind of Hebrew or Christian man. In this case, and I must put it tentatively, the secular historian may be said to have his own form of 'typology' in constant use.

G. von Rad and others have also pointed in connection with biblical typology to the fundamental analogical process in poetry whereby, in the most everyday things, 'in the passing of the years and the days, in the most elementary relationships of man with man, in simple mechanical performances—in everything regularity "reveals" itself' to the poet, 'and hints at an order that dwells deep within things'.[1] It is with reference to aspects of this process that the literary critic most often uses the word 'typology', in a sense quite different from the theologian's meaning, or mine, to denote, according to *O.E.D.*, 'symbolic significance, representation, or treatment'.

At first sight it is doubtful whether a comparison between the specifically historical typology of the Bible and so general and multiform a phenomenon as the element of representativeness in literature would prove very pointed or fruitful if carried on only or mainly in general terms. In any case there are reasons for believing that a more direct and more generally useful comparison with 'typology' in its literary-critical sense exists in the field of primitive religion, in the archetypal fictions of mythology. But there is, at least, in all three spheres (literary, mythological, biblical) a common empirical basis in human experience, and in all three spheres an act of faith raises from its experience of the individual happening an affirmation of some

"those matters which have been fulfilled among us" (Luke 1. 1). This is what is meant in theological language by typology. It is essentially what all history "in the full sense" unavoidably is. It is not something which makes biblical history different in kind from secular history; for, as we have seen many times, historical judgments of significance can be made only in the light of the end of the process: Bismarck, for instance, can be historically appraised only in the light of 1933 and 1945.' This, though suggestive, as it stands clearly papers over some cracks.

[1] 'Typological Interpretation of the Old Testament', *Essays on Old Testament Interpretation*, ed. C. Westermann, p. 17.

4

kind of normativeness. Nevertheless, the relating of the uncontrollable multiplicity of particular happenings to the comparatively or absolutely normal or normative is only one function of biblical typology—a fact which, one suspects, differentiates it too from the kind of typology involved in the historian's employment of analogical concepts. This study should amply confirm the at present somewhat mysterious statement that it is exactly with the locating of an *absolute* existential norm in the idea of an event of historical fulfilment—and subsequently with faith's affirmation that it has discovered such an event—that biblical typology is concerned. This concern distinguishes it from all other forms of typology. And this, indeed, is part of what is meant by the more 'dogmatic' definition of Christian typology which I offered just now—history's relations to its fulfilment in Christ—or by the corresponding definition which would apply to Old Testament typology, where the norm is still qualified, rather than absolute, but envisaged, still as 'event': history's relations to the Old Testament's vision of its promised fulfilment. For in both Testaments, and in contradistinction to the literary sense of 'typology', the norm is taken to be not a general idea but an event, in history, and indeed in history at its apparently least general and least representative moment: that is, at the moment which stands in relief for the witnesses as that of an act of God. To God's acts, or at least to his fulfilling act, whether promised or past, Christianity claims, all events are related and related historically. They have the same ultimate causes as it, and they all share together with it in the one order of contingent cause and effect, in the same history of act and response. For its part, the event of fulfilment is regarded as their perfecting and judging, the consummation in history of all God does and all that man does.

Now such considerations as these, necessarily contracted and rationalized here as they are, are relevant at this stage essentially, for the sake of something more than the search for a basis of conversation between different 'humanities'. For it is our aim to show in the essay itself how what falls, in the Bible, empirically, under the head of the first definition of typology, through its connection with just these features (normativeness, action, response, fulfilment and judgement), points by and large, in the biblical faith, to the justice of the second. It is this aim which determines the structure and method of our study: the case virtually presented itself in its present form, a comparatively detailed literary-critical analysis of representative passages and relevant motifs being incorporated in a framework largely controlled by the process of discursive argument.[1]

But the scope, as distinct from the method and form, needs a little more explanation. So far as its subject-matter is concerned, all I have mentioned would conventionally fall within the province of theology, and a theologian (of a sort only, I fear, and *pro tem.*), almost despite myself, I have, to the best of my ability, had to be. But it is fair and right to point out that I am, in my own capacity and by training, more properly a literary critic; and as such come to the subject also with aims and an interest similar to those with which I believe we should approach any 'humane', any 'secular' literature—with the care that the word should be heard, and heard rightly; and with the desire to allow it, or in the case of a word that is at first alien, as a critic to help it, to be heard rightly, that it may do whatever work its creator had summoned it for, and do it on us, in our generation. My excursion into the Bible may still seem, and be, over-ambitious, but in the context of this task it is not incongruous. So far as the word of the poet is, as it is in the Bible intensely, in its task existential, spoken, that is to say, out of human experience and to it, the hermeneutical task is the same for both literary critic and theologian: to assist the word to be heard, still today, existentially.

These reflections, of course, are not equally relevant for every literary work. Nor do they directly concern every labour of criticism. If they are more relevant here than elsewhere, this is because of the character of the texts we are studying, both of which, Bible and *Comedy*, imply an intrinsic *pro nobis* within the events they record, and confront us with this *pro nobis* almost wherever we turn. This fact, which in the case of the Bible at least may be said to be generally recognized, virtually creates and controls—and this, by and large, is *not* recognized—their

---

[1] This method, which the work's fundamentally argumentative unity made compulsory, has one disadvantage which I particularly regret. There has been too little room for discussion of the very individual uses of typology in the Fourth Gospel and Hebrews, and even Pauline typology is, I am aware, given less than its due attention.

use of typology. Our critical findings have highlighted this, and the essay exists largely to give it due emphasis.

So, if we call typology a 'science', we should make clear at once that it will turn out to be an 'applied' science rather than a 'pure' one. The danger to which G. E. Wright draws attention with regard to the 'systematic elaboration' of typological theories is that they may do less than justice to the fundamentally existential nature of the biblical faith;[1] and it is a real danger, one that is actualized in a high proportion of otherwise useful treatments of typological ideas by modern scholars.[2] For example, the contemporary treatment of typology almost exclusively in terms of 'patterns' of divine activity has to be read very generously indeed if, from the point of view of our study, it is not to be taken as constituting on the one hand a misreading of the Bible's empirical use of typology, and on the other what amounts to a dissolution of the fundamental biblical category, 'history', into certain component formal patterns or event-structures without vital continuity or interaction.[3] It might be unjust to such treatments to see in them a return to the idea behind 'myth' in the primitive religions, with its own basic concept of 'archetypes'. But one can see how such a view is encouraged by the incautious and misleading character which, in Roman Catholic and a great deal of English theology especially, the defence of typology at present assumes. To be satisfactory for the contemporary world the interpretation of typological texts must make use of historical criticism, to begin with, and then must appropriate certain features, if not of 'the existentialist', at least of 'an existential' hermeneutic corresponding as closely as possible to the existential character of

---

[1] G. E. Wright, *God Who Acts*, pp. 65 f.

[2] R. P. C. Hanson's question, in his review of Lampe's and Woollcombe's *Essays on Typology* (*Theology*, LX, Sept. 1957), is highly pertinent to the present debate: 'Are we not today, in so far as we accept typology, accepting it from motives quite different from those which induced the ancient writers to accept it? They saw in typology a witness to God's wonderful activity in causing both extraordinary prediction and extraordinary fulfilment; we see it simply as witnessing to God's character without taking very seriously either prediction or fulfilment.'

[3] See in this connection W. Pannenberg, 'Heilsgeschehen und Geschichte', *KD*, V (1959), 227–9 (reprinted in abridged version in *PAH*, ed. Westermann, pp. 309–11); H. W. Wolff, 'Das Geschichtsverständnis der alttestamentlichen Prophetie', also in Westermann, *PAH*, esp. pp. 327–9; and now also J. M. Robinson, 'The Historicality of Biblical Language', in *The Old Testament and Christian Faith* (ed. B. W. Anderson), esp. pp. 128 f.

typology's witness to history.[1] It must take account of the essential reference of typological writing in the Bible to the life of its hearer or reader. It must show how typology is, in the Bible, 'applied', how the historical analogies are not grasped, nor at all amenable to being grasped, unless the interpreter sees himself as faced with and caught up within them. For man is at all times a part of the history which he interprets: he is involved inescapably in it. And when history as a whole, or the part of it which he studies, is presented, as by the Bible, as the action of God, he can go no distance at all towards understanding it as such unless he begins to confess the action of God upon him. To this end the Bible's use of typology is, it seems to me, geared. Till this end is accomplished it confronts us with the critical question, 'Can you believe?' Once this end is accomplished, it confronts us with the demand, no less critical, 'Then act as God's action allows you!' This whole dialectic[2] is what is meant in the present study by the term 'applied typology'.

My concern with this dialectic for its own sake makes it not inappropriate to conclude with a discussion of typology in Dante's *Divina Commedia*. Here again, 'conversation' is surely a desirable end in itself; and the extent to which the two fields of study illuminate one another should sufficiently justify their juxtaposition. The conception of the *Comedy* which underlies its present treatment was what prompted the whole investigation, and in this last chapter my presentation of the existential character of typology in Christianity is filled out dialectically with arguments which, though they conform with and confirm the exposition of the strictly biblical material, could not be included within it without either losing their comprehensiveness or parting company with the literary and exegetical area of reference which I had set out to illuminate. For nothing in the canonical writings provides so full a picture of Christian man's appropriation of God's activity in his own situation: Jesus is not,

---

[1] We agree here with H. W. Wolff, *art. cit.*, at the end of the long note (14) to p. 327: 'Present-day typology must no longer succumb to a naïve objectivising. It thus appropriates to itself the idea of existential interpretation.'

[2] 'Dialectic', which the dictionaries generally define as the process of logic or argument, in theological and philosophical contexts since the times of Hegel and Kierkegaard, often involves the idea of 'dialogue' too, implying that historical or existential argument is properly carried on 'dramatically', as interaction, and not only, as it were, 'monologically' or 'unilaterally'.

after all, in historical or in theological strictness, a Christian, but a Jew—'born under the law', as Paul says (Gal. 4. 4). There are indeed New Testament passages, to some of which no doubt Dante himself implies a reference, in St Paul especially, which, by confirming the dialectic of typology's existential 'application', provide the occasion for such a depiction (e.g. the ideology of conformity with Christ, and the language of 'dying' and 'rising' 'with' or 'in' him). But except as it were in miniature (cf. the Acts' treatment of Stephen's death and Paul's captivity),[1] the depiction itself is lacking; and without it the whole dialectic—though not losing coherence—would lose, and quite properly, some force. For I present it as a possible view of a possible human existence—specifically, as a view which Christianity has embodied. I conceive, therefore, that I should be prepared to show this view *as* embodied, in works both admittedly and centrally (as distinct from canonically) Christian. The *Divine Comedy* is such a work, and I know of no other so fully suited to the purpose.

So we return, with the mention of 'embodiment' to the dictum with which we began. 'Délimiter un sujet, c'est abstraire.' It is my hope that in the course of the necessary abstractions, past and future, I may not only differentiate our subject from others, but also give an idea how vital the relations are between it and them. It is the hardest but most useful task of this essay if it can make these relations more lively.

[1] See below, pp. 150–52.

9

PART I

TYPOLOGY IN THE OLD TESTAMENT

CHAPTER I

THE FIELD OF EXISTENCE

A. MYTH

IT is reasonable to begin with a contrast: the view of existence involved in the Old Testament's understanding of history stands in clearer light when it is set side by side with the view of existence which is implied by myth, the view of archaic religion, of primitive man. Two considerations make this comparison useful. First, it was from a culture saturated with myth, in the ancient Near East, that Israel grew up: the world of mythopoeic thought was in actual historical fact the context and environment from which the religion of Israel differentiated itself. And secondly, it has become apparent from modern research that, despite the obvious paradox, 'myth' is a term more strictly comparable with 'history' than was ever before imagined.

In 1923 Malinowski stated this impressively, by saying that in its primitive form 'myth...is not merely a tale told but a reality lived'.[1] Still frequently quoted, the dictum is fundamental to a study of comparative religion, and it lives on 'in the spirit' in a more elaborate recent statement by B. M. G. Reardon:

The truth is that myth appears as an organic function of the culture within which it occurs... In the beginning myth is a *mode of existence*, an integration of thought, feeling and action. It may acquire expression in words, but only as these are pointers to a concrete reality. For myth is lived—and projected ritually—before ever it begins to be clearly thought about..., (being) in its primary state ...not so much the object of thought as its condition.[2]

The objective, empirical myth of the mythologies, therefore, becomes a secondary form of the myth, 'an expression', as B. S. Childs says, 'of man's understanding of reality',[3] but by means of an 'objective correlative' which only stands *for* the people's view of existence. The existence itself of primitive man, as

---

[1] B. Malinowski, *Myth in Primitive Psychology*, p. 21.
[2] 'Philosophy and Myth', *Theology*, LXV (April 1962), 135 (Reardon's italics).
[3] *Myth and Reality in the Old Testament*, p. 17.

M. Eliade points out, is lived out 'in myth', not only through ritual but throughout all the actions of his life that are done in pursuit of reasonable ends,[1] just as ours, to our own minds, is thought of as being lived out 'in history'. Myth, therefore, for him, as history for us, is the perspective in which he sees and understands the reality of his existence. The converse of this is true, and will gain in significance: what reality and intelligibility any form of existence may have depends upon its conforming with myth. For this, according to Eliade, is the structure of 'primitive ontology'.[2]

Immediately we look more closely at the view of life which myth embodies, however, it is clear that the comparison with history discovers little mutual between them beyond this general proposition of their shared status as 'fields' and 'perspectives' of existence. For 'the man of archaic cultures', to quote Eliade once again, 'tolerates "history" with difficulty'.[3] In both senses of 'history' this is true, either in the sense of 'the remembered past', historic and epoch-making events (events which are in the terms of the 'demythologizing' controversy 'geschichtlich'),[4] or in the wider sense of the word as one uses it to comprehend the continuous process of happening which, among other things, brings man into being and forever after confronts him. Primitive man has little conception of either. His sense of the past is limited to the unparticular, the typical, which from its perceived and rhythmical recurrence is accepted as archetypal and normative, and becomes the basis of myth. The empirical fact as such is of no interest to him. Originality, alteration, eccentricity, novelty, disturb him, are suggestive of chaos, and to chaos, by means of ritual, they are relegated: they are, so to speak, abolished; they are sent to 'non-being' as 'sins'. For they distress the order of cosmos, and if that order is to be re-established a new creation must be effected by a ritual cos-

---

[1] E.g. in *The Myth of the Eternal Return*, p. 28. He lists: 'hunting, fishing, agriculture; games, conflicts, sexuality' (*loc. cit.*); 'nutrition' (p. 4); 'the occupation of territory' and 'building' (pp. 9 f.) and, of course, ceremonies. All these 'participate in the sacred' (pp. 27 f.) and by living in such typical actions man is in harmony with the order and coherence of the cosmos.

[2] *Ibid.* p. 5.   [3] *Ibid.* p. 36.

[4] Cf. R. H. Fuller, 'Translator's Introduction' to vol. 1 of *Kerygma and Myth* (p. xii): 'By *historisch* Bultmann means that which can be established by the historian's criticism of the past; by *geschichtlich* he means that which, although occurring in past history, has a vital existential reference to our life today.'

mogony which repeats and participates in the original, archetypal cosmogony which the myth posits. Implicit in such a view is an abolition of past time, of history. For time is made 'reversible' and development becomes an impossibility.[1]

Thus, for example, the Babylonian New Year festival, the *akîtu*, is to be understood as attempting on the one hand a rehearsal, an imitation, of the cosmogony, with the aim of ensuring the regeneration of nature, and on the other, as a necessary preliminary to that, the effecting of an abolition of past time by the re-evocation of primordial chaos. Eliade's summary of this stage of the ritual is worth quoting:

> The first act of the ceremony represents the domination of Tiâmat and thus marks a regression into the mythical period before the Creation; all forms are supposed to be confounded in the marine abyss of the beginning, the *apsu*. Enthronement of a 'carnival' king, 'humiliation' of the real sovereign, overturning of the entire social order and hierarchy, 'orgy', chaos. We witness, one might say, a 'deluge' that annihilates all humanity in order to prepare the way for a new and regenerated human species.[2]

Eliade's interpretation is corroborated by others, among whom we may quote Ivan Engnell: 'Before cosmos comes chaos, its height, the "death" of the god-king.'[3]

Thus—and this festival has its counterpart in other parts of the Near East—are the antinomies to harmony abolished, and among them 'change'; and myth 'secures a practical harmony between man himself and an environment otherwise impenetrably mysterious and menacing; and by reducing time to the pattern of a rhythmic ritual it delivers him from what we ourselves find so disturbing—the unpredictable changes and chances of history'.[4] To say that this is 'unhistorical' thinking comes too short; it is, as Eliade says, positively 'anti-historical'. For if nothing new is confessedly real, there is no sanction in human life for anything but the most extreme form of conservatism. The memory tolerates only the traditional archetypes, and only the traditional archetypes will be visible in the 'good' life of man or nation. All other events, events which to our mind

---

[1] Cf. Eliade, *op. cit.* pp. 35–6.   [2] *Ibid.* p. 57.
[3] See I. Engnell, *Studies in Divine Kingship in the Ancient Near East*, pp. 33–6.
[4] Reardon, *loc. cit.*

make 'history', the details, the personal event, the unusual, are subsumed under 'sin' or 'disorder' whose mythical archetype is chaos. Alteration is thus simplified into the constricting category of 'alternation', for fundamental to all mythical thought is the idea of eternal recurrence, the repetition of primordial archetypes.

It will be seen by this that mythical thought gives no prominence to man's moral responsibility. 'The Egyptian', says H. Frankfort, 'viewed his misdeeds not as sins, but as aberrations.'[1] They are not therefore absolutely distinguished from ritual lapses, and if, indeed, as Eliade says, 'every responsible activity in pursuit of a definite end is, for the archaic world, a ritual',[2] the distinction is wholly alien. Communal or personal purification is effected by magical rites. The *akîtu* festival once again will serve for example.[3] By the god-king's cultic humiliation he atones for the sins of his people, whom he 'incorporates'. The sins coalesce with the chaos in which he, for the time, is submerged. And with his eventual victory over Tiāmat (chaos) the sins, which Tiāmat embodies, are done away with, and order restored.[4]

To summarize: just as on the wider scale myth or the mythi-

---

[1] *Ancient Egyptian Religion*, p. 73.   [2] *Op. cit.* p. 28.
[3] Cf. I. Engnell, *loc. cit.*

[4] Albright, however, finds in the 'Negative Confessions' of Egypt and Mesopotamia signs of a developed sense of responsibility. These confessions, one of which is recited by the king in the *akîtu*, attest the confessor's innocence by an extensive enumeration of sins with, each time, an avowal that he (or those represented by him) has not committed them. It is true that, as Albright says, among these protestations—'aside, of course, from some having exclusively to do with religious observance'—'there is not a single intelligible declaration which could not be conscientiously repeated by a member of the Society for Ethical Culture today' (W. F. Albright, *From Stone Age to Christianity*, pp. 226–7: he is speaking particularly of the form(s) of confession found in ch. 125 of the Egyptian *Book of the Dead*). But even when 'we recall that every Egyptian was supposed to submit to trial before Osiris and to strive for justification if he wished to enjoy a happy life in Elysium', Albright's conclusion, that 'the moral force of the Negative Confession becomes evident' (*loc. cit.*), is not inescapable. For the *Sitz im Leben*, or, in this case, *im Tod*, is ritual, and in that context there is little doubt that the confessions are a way of effecting the release from sin, not a 'true' declaration of innocence. Since, as Albright says, they include 'practically every important type of transgression against religious obligations and the rights of others' (*loc. cit.*) as well as faults of character and petty misdemeanours, Pettazzoni is surely right to conclude that such declarations are not expected to be objectively true but to create truth by the magical power of the spoken word. (R. Pettazzoni, *La Confessione dei Peccati*, II, 18–21, 94). Moral discrimination, therefore, there may be, but moral responsibility is evaded.

cal view of existence involves, by myth's very nature, an avoid-
ance of contact between man and history, a prevention of man's
confrontation with novelty, irreversibility, change, so on the
personal level man is freed from his personal history and its
consequences by evolving a technique of evasion, establishing,
thus, in his ritual, a reunion between him and the order of
cosmos, a harmony between him and nature. Implied, on both
levels, is 'a terror of history'—the phrase is taken from Eliade—
which is not something merely archaic. It was when faced by
this terror in all its immediacy that Israel provided a wholly
new means of surmounting it, by demanding faith in the God
of Abraham, in Yahweh, the God of Moses, the Lord of history.

B. HISTORY

The self-understanding of Israel differs most radically from the
view just outlined in being provoked and created by the particular, the new, the historic, happenings of such a kind being
now for the first time given value, even ultimate value, and
declared to be irreversible.[1] The event especially 'provocative'
in this respect is certainly the Exodus. It took place, and more
important is affirmed by the biblical writers as taking place,
not in mythical time, but at a specific time, in history. This
event had no archetype (Deut. 4. 32–4), and, lacking that, was
mythically inexplicable and therefore, to the mythopoeic mind,
unacceptable.

[1] It is as a witness to this that we should take the biblical writers' new interest in
chronology—an interest especially characteristic of the priestly narrative (P), and
at times almost irritatingly over-present there—whether it be found purely in the
enumeration of years or also in the long genealogies. For the irreversibility of events
means that in theory at least it is possible for the Hebrew to see history as an
unbroken order of succession reaching from Creation down to the present. The
discussion of Biblical concepts of time cannot, however, be undertaken here. There
are valuable comments in Childs, *op. cit.* pp. 74–6, but for a fuller discussion the
reader is referred to J. Marsh, *The Fulness of Time*, pp. 19 ff. etc.; Pedersen, *Israel*,
I–II, 486 ff.; Cullmann, *Christ and Time*, esp. pp. 37–68; Boman, *Hebrew Thought
Compared with Greek*, pp. 129 ff. and esp. pp. 141–3, and the criticism of these
authors made by Eichrodt, 'Heilserfahrung und Zeitverständnis im Alten Testament', *TZ*, XII (1956), 103 ff., and above all by James Barr, *Biblical Words for
Time, passim.* See also the important discussion by von Rad, 'Les idées sur le
temps et l'histoire en Israel et l'eschatologie des prophètes', *Hommage à Wilhelm
Vischer*, pp. 198–209, or the fuller treatment in his *Theologie des Alten Testaments*, II,
112–32.

And yet, Israel realized, it was upon this event that she depended for her creation, for there she was brought into being. And in consequence, to affirm her deliverance from Egypt, her constitution and creation as a nation, she must deny the mythical cosmos of her neighbours, with its concomitants of eternal repetition, manipulative magic, manipulative ritual.[1] She had to deny as illusory all belief in gods who ensured the world-order only in response to man's works of appeasement or sacrament and who never surpassed or could ever surpass expectation. To affirm her own being Israel had to affirm that she existed beyond all expectation, beyond all explanation in terms of nature or human endeavour, simply out of the hand of a transcendent God who delivered her with no cause but his own abundant grace, 'for the sake of his name' (cf. Ezek. 16. 3–7a). For God had kept them alive, in the wilderness, at a time when the ways in which man believed he could keep himself in existence (e.g. sacrifice, ritual, magic) were no longer feasible or relevant. 'You followed me in the wilderness', God tells Israel, centuries later, 'in a land not sown' (Jer. 2. 2), and the single epithet of the poet 'seizes at once the essential feature of the desert' in the Hebrew tradition, 'its oblivion of human effort, a land where none would ever speak of mother earth and where man remains a stranger and a wanderer'.[2]

Neither their magnitude ('for you were the fewest of all peoples', Deut. 7. 7), nor yet their righteousness ('for you are a stubborn people', Deut. 9. 6), caused God to act on their behalf. Neither their own *savoir-vivre* (Deut. 8. 3), nor the power of their hand (Deut. 8. 12–18; Ps. 55. 3), was able to give them their subsistence, but only

Yahweh your God, who brought you out of the land of Egypt, out of the house of bondage, who led you through the great and terrible wilderness, with its fiery serpents and scorpions and thirsty ground where there was no water, who brought you water out of the flinty rock, who fed you in the wilderness with manna *which your fathers did not know*, that he might humble you and test you, to do you good in the end. (Deut. 8. 14–16)

[1] A gradual process is simplified here. As to ritual, it should not need saying that the stress falls on 'manipulative' (cf. the further discussion in chapter 3 below). With regard to magic, cf. G. von Rad, *Old Testament Theology*, I, 34–5.
[2] H. E. W. Fosbroke, 'The Prophetic Literature', *IB*, I, 205–6.

And therefore, conversely, to turn to other gods, to deny the Exodus-history or attempt to reverse or abolish it, to murmur, for example, against Moses the servant of Yahweh and so wish oneself back in Egypt (Exod. 14. 12; cf. 15. 24; 16. 2–3; 17. 2–3; Deut. 1. 26–7, etc.) was always a temptation of the utmost gravity and consequence. It was a pressing one, for it seemed to alleviate the unmitigated requirement of faith in, and sense of dependence on, an uncontrollable and utterly demanding God, to take one from a terrifyingly free and resourceful history back into the tolerable and predictable sphere of myth. But at bottom such a step was self-murder; for, at whatever period in Israel's history this murmuring and apostasy revived, its denial of the God of history in favour of the gods of myth constituted, given the particular aetiological and existential situation of Israel, a denial or refusal of her own existence.[1] If Israelite man reverts to the natural plane he is 'unmade' on the plane of election. And for this reason unbelief is attacked by the prophets and linked with an unmaking: 'If you do not believe surely you shall not be established' (Isa. 7. 9).[2]

The conversion, then, of the Hebrew tribes which came to call themselves Israel, to faith in Yahweh, the God of Moses, may be seen as a translation, almost, an emigration, to existence in history from an existence interpreted by and in some degree conceived of as myth. The categories of myth not only failed to comprehend the coming into existence of Israel, they were, in the original autonomy which they held in primitive culture, positively contradicted by it. To do justice to what Eichrodt well calls 'the *élan* and audacity of a level of life with still unexhausted possibilities',[3] new categories were needed, and to

---

[1] The narrative of the golden calf in Exod. 32 (and cf. I Kings 12. 28–33) is rightly seen by U. Mauser as 'the culmination of the exodus stories in this respect' (*Christ in the Wilderness*, p. 29). 'Israel, called by Yahweh in the wilderness, in her attempt to exchange the worship of her God with a godhead of nature, radically impairs the foundation to which she owes her existence' (*ibid.* p. 32).

[2] Unbelief of this kind being the root of all sins against Yahweh, sins of all kinds will involve this unmaking; and because, continually, Israel falls short of the covenant, there is something equivocal about all the nation's existence, a dialectical tension between 'my people' and 'not my people' (cf. Hos. 1. 9 f.; 2. 23). Even the prophet exists in this ambiguity, and confronted by Yahweh he knows it: 'Woe is me, for I am undone' (i.e. as Hooke notes, 'deprived of existence', *Alpha and Omega*, p. 55) 'because I am a man of unclean lips and I dwell in the midst of a people of unclean lips' (Isa. 6. 5).

[3] *Man in the Old Testament*, p. 18.

these, the categories of 'history' and 'fulfilment', we must now turn.[1]

[1] I do not intend to deny, by the above remarks, that the Old Testament, and the Israelite cult in particular, continues to make some use of myth. This would be foolish as well as exegetically untenable, for it is hard to see how certain aspects of faith could be expressed without mythological forms. But the question as to the relation which the cultic use of myth bears to the historical categories in which Israel came to see herself is a vexed one. In general, my own view accords with that of G. von Rad: cf. G. E. Wright, 'Archaeology and Old Testament Studies', *JBL*, LXXVII (1958), 49: 'Whereas among Scandinavian scholars there is a tendency to reconstruct the Israelite culture along the lines of the contemporary pagan festival in which mythical renewal by dramatic action is central, von Rad, followed by his fellow German, Hans-Joachim Kraus, emphasizes in Israel the centrality of Word and History. Myth in the polytheistic sense is excluded, except as an element adopted to enhance or communicate something already given in the historical tradition. We do not, then, have to do with historicized myth, as Mowinckel would express it, but with the cultic use of historical traditions which on occasion could be mythically portrayed.' With some of von Rad's views of more specific aspects of this subject, however, I am less inclined to agree. See further, pp. 46–56 and esp. pp. 51–5 below.

CHAPTER 2

GOD AND HISTORY:
THE NEW AND THE STEADFAST

UP to a certain point the treatment of 'history' in the Old Testament necessarily involves and goes hand in hand with the treatment of the divinity, for it was almost impossible for the Israelites to conceive of them in separation. At least, this is true of the Old Testament orthodoxy, normative Yahwism, about which statements like the following are common among modern scholars: 'The essential thing about God was not his essence but his activity'; 'God exists for the Hebrew primarily in his actions'. For the activity of God in history was certainly the chief object of Israel's religious witness from the very earliest times. Ancient confessions like that contained in the statement, 'Yahweh thy God who brought you up out of the land of Egypt', more extended confessional summaries like those found in Deut. 26. 5–10a (believed to be the oldest of them), Deut. 6. 20–5, and Josh. 24. 2–13, ancient hymns such as the Song at the Red Sea (Exod. 15) and the one now found as Ps. 68, all deriving from the period of the Judges, speak almost in credal form about God's activity, not his 'nature'. What E. Jacob has said about one of these 'creeds' may with slight adaptation be said of them all: they are purely historical confessions of faith to which any metaphysical affirmation about God is foreign.[1] Much later Psalms (especially 77. 11–20; 78; 106; 111; 114; 149; and cf. psalms of praise like Pss. 33; 65; 103; 115; 135; 136; 146; 147; 148) and the festivals up to much later times, besides the narrative form into which so large a part of the Old Testament itself is cast,[2] witness to the continuity of this mode of theological

---

[1] Cf. E. Jacob, *Theology of the Old Testament*, p. 184.

[2] We recall that the whole Pentateuch is called *Torah*, which means not 'law' only but 'divine revelation'. As I shall try to show in the next chapter, this is not so much a case of 'double-entendre' as an expression of the close connection between two aspects of the same thing. The New Testament 'gospel' also expresses itself most naturally in historical terms; and there too the 'law' reveals itself as being, at bottom, an 'aspect' of history, history in the imperative. See, for example, pp. 92 f. below.

thought (for such, at bottom, it is) in Israel.[1] Eichrodt's words serve as a summary—they carry all the more weight for their caution:[2]

From the very beginnings of Israel's religion it is easier for the observer to detect the main outlines of the divine activity than those of the divine being. The latter...remain essentially outlines, and never undergo any more profound speculative or metaphysical development; but the description of the divine activity is couched in precise and concrete terms.[3]

We have only to add what perhaps is sufficiently obvious, that this concreteness and precision spring directly from the factual and historical nature of Israel's encounters with God, for from such encounters their whole view of history and Yahweh derive. The closeness of interrelation between the concepts of 'history' and 'God' meets us at every point in the Old Testament because of the real involvement of the facts of history and God. A concept of history which does not take account of Yahweh is not the Old Testament concept, and an idea of God which is not connected with history has nothing to do with Yahweh, the God of the Exodus.

So much can be learnt even from the characteristic self-designations of Yahweh in the Old Testament such as 'Yahweh,

[1] With regard to the writing of history in the Old Testament see G. von Rad, 'Der Anfang der Geschichtsschreibung im Alten Israel', *AKG* xxxii (1944), 1–42, now reprinted in his *Gesammelte Studien zum Alten Testament*, pp. 148–88. Von Rad here points out that it was in fact precisely 'theological' thought that led to the writing of history: 'das Vermögen, eine blosse Aufeinanderfolge von Einzel-ereignissen überhaupt als Geschichte zu sehen und zu verstehen, verdankt das alte Israel der Eigenart seines Gottesglaubens' (p. 6, *Ges. Stud.* p. 153).

[2] The attempt of some scholars, notably T. Boman (in *Hebrew Thought Compared with Greek*), to comprehend under 'the Hebrew concept of being' almost nothing but 'activity', 'the dynamic' and causative, has been severely criticized, largely on methodological grounds, by James Barr (*The Semantics of Biblical Language*, Oxford, 1961). The Hebrews did not think of the divine being *only* in terms of activity, nor, if they had, could the structure of the Hebrew language, as Boman hopes, be used to demonstrate it. The statement of Eichrodt which we were on the point of quoting, however, and the whole paragraph, shows how the attempt could come to be made: the attempt, though misguided, yet witnesses to a clear fact, that *normally* God (and, to a great extent, man) is thought of in the Old Testament as existing in action and acting in history, and interest in God's nature, apart from history, is both rudimentary and rare.

[3] W. Eichrodt, *Theology of the Old Testament*, i, 228, cf. also G. von Rad, *Old Testament Theology*, i, 106.

your God out of Egypt' (Hos. 12. 10; 13. 4).[1] Even 'Yahweh, the God of your fathers, of Abraham, of Isaac, and of Jacob' (Exod. 3. 6) and its shortened forms (e.g. 'God of your fathers') show that God makes himself known and reveals his 'character' in the Old Testament not by discourse, primarily, but by reference back to a whole series of long-past events known to the auditor from tradition, a history of guidance, blessing and promise. Similarly based on events, too, is the promise of further revelation, through deeds not yet accomplished:

I am Yahweh, and I will bring you out from under the burdens of the Egyptians, and I will deliver you from their bondage, and I will redeem you with an outstretched arm and with great acts of judgement. . ., and you shall know that I am Yahweh your God, who has brought you out from under the burdens of the Egyptians (Exod. 6. 6 f.; cf. 3. 16 f.; 7. 17; 14. 4, 18; Gen. 15. 7, etc.)

The fundamental structure of all these sayings might be paraphrased roughly:

I am Yahweh, who did this for you, and I shall do more. Thus you will know who I am: your God, the God who makes you, acts for you, and acts upon you, in history.

Now, certain aspects of this interrelation between the conceptions of 'God' and 'history' are germane to the whole subject of typology, and we must concentrate on them.

In clear contrast to the idea in myth of 'eternal return' stands the 'scandal of particularity' involved in the manner of God's gift of 'existence' to Israel. To this contrast we have already referred. The history into which God had introduced Israel was the realm of the unexpected, the radically new. The God to whom the events of the Exodus introduced Israel was the God of the unconditioned; transcending expectation, beyond the reach of human or natural influence, he was the God who brought forth, as it were 'out of nothing', a new possibility.

So all the strands of the Old Testament witness to the wonder of a God who could from the historical encounters of Israel produce the (generally) unforeseeable outcome, and would do so for the furtherance of his purposes. If, for example, 'undoubtedly it was Yahweh's warlike activity, affording as it did sensible

---

[1] Cf. R. Rendtorff, 'Die Offenbarungsvorstellungen im Alten Israel', *Offenbarung als Geschichte*, ed. W. Pannenberg (*KD*, Beiheft 1), pp. 33 f.

experience of his power, which evoked the most powerful response in ancient Israel',[1] throughout it is the note of amazement in the power of God which can give them the victory in the face of superior numbers which sounds most commonly. The narratives of Holy War in the books of Joshua and Judges no doubt have intentionally exaggerated the numerical disparity between the contenders, but the intention is only to lay stress on the wonder of God's achievement, a wonder which they had felt then.[2] Thus von Rad quotes with approval W. Caspari's allocation of the cry, 'Yahweh is a man of war' (Exod. 15. 3), to the moment of astonishment called forth by a discovery, a new experience of Yahweh which Israel had been allowed to make.[3] In later times, other experiences and encounters, as well as the new impulse which derived from the great prophets, led to a generalizing and more comprehensive stress on the element of wonder in God's power as manifest in other contexts than war, so that the martial imagery, where it remains (as, for example, in Isa. 25. 1–6), no longer has such specific reference to war. The wonder of his world-interest, the faithful carrying-out of his commitment to the world, is perceived by Israel in all his actions toward them. So when the writer of Ps. 107 thanks the Lord 'for his steadfast love, for his wonderful works to the sons of man', this refrain alternates with another, which shows that the works in question are now not primarily warlike but simply gracious:

> Then they cried to the Lord in their trouble,
> and he delivered them from their distress.

So pervasive is the note of awe and amazement, so significant its cause, that it comes about that at times God is almost defined —and certainly distinguished from the gods of other nations— as 'the God who workest wonders' (Ps. 77. 14), 'the God of Israel who alone does wondrous things' (Ps. 72. 18; cf. Ps. 136. 4). Ps. 86 makes the distinction between Yahweh and the gods of their neighbours in just these terms:

> There is none like thee among the gods, O Lord,
> nor are there any works like thine...
> For thou art great and doest wondrous things—

---

[1] W. Eichrodt, *Theology of the Old Testament*, I, 228.
[2] Cf. G. von Rad, *Studies in Deuteronomy*, pp. 47–8.   [3] *Ibid.* p. 46.

and we can imagine the question occurring naturally to his mind, 'can these gods then *be* gods?' It is answered before it is formed—

thou alone art God.   (Ps. 86. 8, 10)[1]

It is in these terms—i.e. in terms of an unconditioned ability to act *mightily* and bring forth the truly new—rather, perhaps, than in the less specific terms of activity generally, that we should see the distinctive character of Yahweh. The gods of the pagans were powers, if only natural powers, and could be appealed to, as J. Bright sees,[2] to restore the *status quo*, to repair disorder, to regenerate and restore the cosmos. But Yahweh was a God who comprehended and transcended these powers. His power was not limited to the maintenance and servicing of a given order of nature. On the contrary, it was '*from the status quo* of dire bondage' that he had called his people, and 'into a new future' that he had led them.[3] There is nothing here of the newness of mere repetition. It is a newness qualitatively different from anything in the past, and has therefore in the last resort a fundamentally eschatological character, for it is the entry of God's newness into time.[4] This usage of the idea of newness is found, as Brevard S. Childs remarks, chiefly in Deutero-Isaiah.

Isa. 48. 6 speaks of 'new things' (hădhāšôth), unknown before, which were 'created now, not long ago'. Isa. 42. 9 and 43. 18 contrast the new thing(s) with former things (rī' šôn). The former things, in parallel to 'things of old' (43. 18) and in contrast to 'things to come' (41. 22), are previous temporal events. The future [this

---

[1] Cf. also Deut. 4. 32–5.

[2] *History of Israel*, pp. 141–2.

[3] Quotations from Bright, *ibid.* p. 142.

[4] The importance of this element of 'newness' for Israel's consciousness of 'historicality' (Geschichtlichkeit) is seen by W. Pannenberg ('Heilsgeschehen und Geschichte', *KD*, v (1959), pp. 218–37. 'The presuppositions of the historical consciousness in Israel lie in its concept of God. The reality of God for Israel is not exhausted by his being the origin of the world, that is, of normal ever self-repeating processes and events. Therefore this God can break into the course of his creation and initiate new events in it in an unpredictable way. The certainty that God again and again performs new acts (*immer wieder Neues wirkt*), that he is truly a 'living God', forms the basis for Israel's understanding of reality as a linear history moving towards a goal' (translation slightly adapted from that found in the abridged version in English appearing in *Essays on Old Testament Interpretation*, ed. by Claus Westermann, and translated by J. L. Mays, pp. 316 f.).

writer concludes] is to bring new things never before appearing in history. The new is not a mere renewal, but the entrance of the unexpected.[1]

And when, as happens in the developing eschatology of the prophets, the pattern of Urzeit-Endzeit makes its appearance in Israelite thinking 'these two times cannot be simply identified' as they would be in myth. For 'according to the Biblical scheme the new can be described as a return and a continuance of the old while bringing, at the same time, a totally different element into being'.[2]

God, then, was the God most particularly of the radically new act, and it was this lesson—learned, of course, not automatically but in response and commitment—a lesson of their history, which led Israel, when at about the time of the Exile they began to show a lively interest in the Creation, to think of that act as *creatio ex nihilo*,[3] or, at any rate, as a sovereign act of power on the part of God, the materials of which act were, so to speak, immaterial: for their God alone had shown himself capable of such activity.[4]

[1] *Myth and Reality in the Old Testament*, pp. 78–9.
[2] *Ibid.* p. 80. Cf. J. Muilenburg, *The Way of Israel*, pp. 134 ff. and G. von Rad, 'Typologische Auslegung des Alten Testaments', *EvTh*, XII (1952), 17–33, now available in English translation in *Essays on Old Testament Interpretation*, ed. C. Westermann, pp. 17–39.
[3] See Eichrodt, *Theologie des Alten Testaments*, II–III, 63–6, and his essay 'In the beginning', *Israel's Prophetic Heritage* (Muilenburg Festschrift), pp. 1–10, esp. 9 f.
[4] The view of Albright, *From Stone Age to Christianity*, p. 261, Bright, *History of Israel*, p. 137, and Wright, *The Old Testament Against its Environment*, p. 29, n. 35, that the divine self-designation, 'I am who I am', of Exod. 3. 14, is a causative form and thus means 'I cause to be what comes into existence', would argue, and is taken by these scholars as doing so, an implicit doctrine of creation in Mosaic times. I would stress that 'implicit' is the most that can be said of the doctrine's existence so early, even if the Exodus text is rightly interpreted in that way. Despite the central place of the creation idea in the 'enthronement festival of Yahweh' during the pre-exilic kingdom (see S. Mowinckel, *The Psalms in Israel's Worship*, I, ch. 5), the question of the cosmogony does not seem to have been a pressing one until the Exile. The Jahwist's version 'represents the beginning of his historical account' (T. Boman, *Hebrew Thought Compared with Greek*, p. 172) and though this in itself is undoubtedly significant—for it implies the 'historicization' of Creation—the fact remains that it is transmitted 'by way of the barest outline... Here clearly, in contrast to P, the indifference in narration is striking. The creation of the actual cosmic system is loosely referred to only in an introductory clause' (G. von Rad, *Genesis*, p. 74). Cf. also C. R. North, *The Old Testament Interpretation of History*, pp. 76–8.

For those readers unacquainted with the mysteries of Pentateuchal criticism, it may be well to explain at this point that 'P', in the quotation from von Rad (and elsewhere in the present work), is the conventional symbol for the latest of

As vital to Israel's faith, and as significant for the subject of typology, as the idea of divine initiative which we have sketched here, is another instance of the interrelation of God and history. It would, indeed, be a serious misrepresentation of Old Testament belief to speak of the former idea and leave out the other.

For the emphasis on 'newness', the peculiar quality of the 'Creator', his ability to do in history what is (mythically) incomprehensible and unexpected, must not be taken as implying mere wilfulness in the character of Yahweh. Complementary, and not contradictory, to this 'newness' is 'steadfastness', at least in this instance; and indeed we have already had occasion to notice how Israel's wonder in one act of God—or in acts of one kind (e.g. victories)—tended later to become more general in its object, became wonder in a whole series of God's mighty acts, which they had been permitted to witness and of which they had been beneficiaries. This 'later', in fact, need not be taken too far. For although the documentary evidence is by no means contemporary with the events described in it, there remains still a reasonable assumption that from the very time of the Exodus this sense of continuity and purpose was present in Israel. The 'scandal of particularity' met them as grace, and was confirmed as such, as 'steadfast love' therefore, by the experience of the continuing presence of Yahweh with them in the wilderness. Some such experience, at all events, was undeniably looked on in Israel as the basis of her faith, and the unanimity of the narrative sources in placing it here is very impressive.[1]

the four main sources which, according to the generally accepted hypothesis, lie behind the Pentateuch: it refers to the so-called 'Priestly Code'. With regard to the others (all of which will be met in due course), there is no need to be more specific than to say that 'J' (the 'Jahwistic' source) is considered to be in all probability the oldest (c. 900–850 B.C.) and to derive from the southern part of Israel; that 'E' (the 'Elohistic' source) may be dated 800–750 B.C. and seems specially interested in the northern part; and that 'D' (which is virtually confined to Deuteronomy and named after it) comes from the seventh century, and is in many respects closely related, at least as an influence, to the books (Joshua–Kings) which follow it. All of these sources, or traditions, however, contain some older material, and the work of editing and combining them into their present form, which must have been completed soon after Ezra's promulgation of the Law of P (Neh. 8; 444 or 397 B.C.), naturally involved insertions and alterations to the existing works. Fuller information can be found in any good introduction to the Old Testament, such as H. H. Rowley's article of that name in the second edition of T. W. Manson's *A Companion to the Bible*, which I have followed in this account.

[1] R. H. Pfeiffer contends that Israel's God was conceived as capricious until the great reforming prophets (*Religion in the Old Testament*, pp. 137–8, 139–140). His

The dialectic, in history, of the divine initiative and the divine steadfastness deserves to be looked at a little further. The fact of its existence is, I take it, not in dispute. Its implications, however, for our discussion are so fundamental that it is essential to bring them out a little more clearly than has sometimes, even generally, been done.

Two such implications are specially vital. First is the relevance of this dialectic for faith. In the narratives of the wilderness-journey it is the divine steadfastness which from day to day justifies Moses' faith in face of the unbelief and fear of the people. The people are hungry. They complain against Moses. Fundamentally, their terror in the face of the future is a forgetting (cf. Ps. 106. 13). Moses remembers the mighty act of deliverance. He has no means of *knowing* that God's love is still upon them, but believes that it is. He is prepared to act on, to live in, his belief. But the people insist that they will only act upon what has been proved to them, and that they have no means of knowing God's present disposition as love. They put Yahweh to the proof:

> They tested God in their heart
> by demanding the food they craved.
> They spoke against God, saying,
>   'Can God spread a table in the wilderness?
> He smote the rock so that water gushed out
>   and streams overflowed.
> Can he also give bread,
>   or provide meat for his people?'   (Ps. 78. 18–20)

Apart from faith, therefore, the past provides no encouragement to present action. God's acts in the past can do no more than present themselves to the judgement as 'possibly true' to his eternal nature. Meanwhile, obedience to his call repeatedly leads to what seems an impossible situation: pursued by the Egyptians, they are faced with the sea; then the desert threatens to starve them. The whole Exodus is 'a precarious expedition',[1] and it repeatedly forces the question: is God's gracious act in the

---

evidence is not impressive. The verse he quotes from Ezekiel: 'I, Yahweh, have spoken it and it shall happen, and I will do it, I will not slacken, nor will I spare and repent' (Ezek. 24. 14), does not witness to something irreconcilable with the repenting God of, for example, Exod. 32. 14, as Pfeiffer assumes (p. 139). Rather, the words assume the possibility of such repentance, to which, after all, Ezekiel himself witnesses (ch. 20, 8*b*–9, 13*b*–14, 17, etc.).

[1] U. Mauser, *Christ in the Wilderness*, p. 21.

past a 'tragic irony', or true self-disclosure? Each time they will wait and see, repeatedly 'testing' God. Yet this way God's steadfastness is never known; for it is the discovery of faith rather than its incentive. It is known only as it is believed in.

Thus the world has been, for Israel, deprived of all objective inevitability. God's 'truth', his trustworthiness, steadfastness, upon which all things depend, is known only to faith.

This brings us close, in certain respects, to the position outlined by R. Bultmann in his *Jesus Christ and Mythology*.[1] 'The action of God', he writes, 'is hidden from every eye except the eye of faith.'[2] It cannot be proved, nor objectified.[3] The genuine confession of its existence is possible only on the basis of a present decision to surrender oneself to its power as it here and now bears upon one.[4] 'God as acting does not refer to an event which can be perceived by me without myself being drawn into the event as into God's action, without myself taking part in it as being acted upon',[5] that is, 'addressed, asked, judged, or blessed' by him.[6] And this leads Bultmann to say:

The affirmation that God is creator cannot be a theoretical statement about God as *creator mundi* in a general sense. The affirmation can only be a personal confession that I understand myself to be a creature which owes its existence to God. It cannot be made as a neutral statement, but only as thanksgiving and surrender.[7]

This, according to Bultmann, is because 'statements which speak of God's actions as cosmic events are illegitimate'.[8]

Here, though, we come to the crux. Recognition of this hidden action (in faith) is for Bultmann a personal, an individual response. But as Weiser, Bultman's co-author of the *TWNT* article Πίστις points out, faith in Israel was at first primarily a communal response,[9] and its object, accordingly—but at all times!—was in the first place always the action of God upon Israel. Thus the action of God which the faith even of the individual within Israel finds to be bearing upon him and drawing him in is understood from the first as more general in

---

[1] Ch. v, 'The Meaning of God as Acting' (pp. 60–85).
[2] *Ibid.* pp. 61 f.   [3] *Ibid.* pp. 61 f. and 72 f.   [4] *Ibid.* p. 63.
[5] *Ibid.* p. 68.   [6] *Loc. cit.*   [7] *Ibid.* p. 69.
[8] *Ibid.* Nothing in those of Bultmann's writings which I have read leads me to suppose that by this statement he means to deny that God works on the cosmos. 'Cosmic' here is to be referred to the same complex of ideas as 'observable', 'objective'.   [9] *Faith* (*BKW*, 10), p. 1.

scope, more inclusive, than to involve him only. It is for God's grace towards Israel that he gives thanks, for it is in Israel's election that he finds his own.[1] That this sometimes led to a false sense of security is testified by the prophets; but it is still of *Israel's* election that they themselves speak—as an act of God it exists in spite of individual faithlessness, or widespread, or general, apostasy.[2]

But to say this is, in a sense, only to draw out the consequences for the community of believers, and for the believer in such a community, of what Bultmann says of the individual's belief as such.[3] The statement that God 'acts' is made by Israel on the basis of her communal experience of being, and having been, 'acted upon'. It is a general response of thanksgiving for action affecting them generally.

Yet if this consequence is admitted it becomes plain that Bultmann's frequently ambiguous remarks about the meaninglessness of speaking 'in general terms' of God's actions[4] need to be qualified. For even if he is right to say that God's action can never become part of a general world-view, a 'knowledge possessed once for all', but is realized only in its appropriation 'here and now' in decision,[5] yet still, as that decision is renewed

---

[1] See below, ch. 3, and cf. the peculiar view which Bultmann takes of this matter in his essay, 'The Significance of the Old Testament for the Christian Faith', *The Old Testament and Christian Faith*, ed. B. W. Anderson, pp. 29 f.

[2] Cf. Th. C. Vriezen, 'Prophecy and Eschatology', *VT* (Suppl.), I, 204 f.

[3] *Op. cit.* p. 69.

[4] Cf., for example, Bultmann, *op. cit.* p. 64. That Bultmann underestimates the value of the general assertion of God's action's *possibility* is certain, and as the question is not without consequence for our subject it is worth touching upon here, even though its fuller treatment must wait for the New Testament chapter. By denying the legitimacy of a theoretical understanding of its 'possibility' one cuts man off also from an existential realization of the *reality* of God's action even upon him. For man can truly believe only if no part of his understanding, by denying its feasibility, contradicts (which is different from 'taking offence at', 'being scandalized by', in the New Testament sense) the object of faith. 'Faith is the assent... of the whole man to the message of God' (K. Rahner, *On the Theology of Death*, p. 14), and theology exists to make possible this total response. It can do no more, but it should do, so far as possible, no less. So long as they are not treated as proved, or observable, God's acts may even, indirectly, be *preached* in disguise as a 'project for thought'—as by Kierkegaard, *Philosophical Fragments*, ch. 1. The true location of 'scandal' in the New Testament lies in the distance which has to be leapt between assent to God's acts' 'feasibility' and assent to the paradoxical reality of the concrete presence of God's act in the history of the 'One Crucified'. This is the brink to which typology leads, and no further. Cf. my remarks on 'feasibility', pp. 97 f., 100 f., and cf. Jesus-Israel (iii), pp. 130–35 below.

[5] Bultmann, *loc. cit.*

again and again and becomes, by continual renewal, the basis
of a transformed and transforming understanding of existence,
the reality of God's acts can become the *presupposition* of a world-
view specifically faith's, of a *Glaubensweltanschauung* in which
man attributes to God an existence apart from the faith which
alone apprehends him, and to the influence of God's action a
wider sphere than the individual consciousness. Such a world-
view has been seen as epitomized, in the individual's case, in
'doxology', where, though God's steadfastness is still not the
incentive of faith, faith now asserts its discovery.[1] But it is most
properly the 'possession of a community which, like Israel,
exists ideally only as a community of faith[2] and which, in so far
as it does exist thus, gives to the content of its faith the continuity, and so the stability, which is the pre-condition of a
'world-view'. As the community which confesses its dependence
upon Yahweh's action and commits itself to his purpose, Israel's
response is to say not only, ' *This* is Yahweh's doing, and it is
marvellous *in our eyes*' (Ps. 118. 23), but 'He is steadfast' (Ps.
118. 1 and *passim*), 'He accomplishes all his purposes' (cf. Isa.
46. 10), and finally, as may be deduced from Amos 9. 5–7,
'Yahweh does all things'. Thus praise and wonder in the immediately determinative past and present act or acts of Yahweh
leads Israel to the general assertion of his control over all history,
which, as von Rad rightly says, is one presupposition of her
historical thought and her history-writing.[3] 'Her conception of
the divine all-powerfulness was so total as to leave faith no
choice; a gap in this causal nexus was unthinkable.'[4] Faith in

[1] 'Doxology is a mode of personal existence...The personal experience of salvation demands a super-personal ontological statement transcending that experience itself' (E. Schlink, quoted from H. Diem, *Dogmatics*, p. 37). Bultmann's
emphasis is different, but it seems a fair inference from what he says of Luther's
terra ubique domini that he himself would allow so much: 'Luther's statement...is
not genuine as a dogmatic statement but only here and now when spoken in the
decision of my very existence' (*op. cit.* p. 63). Thus 'here and now', what is in one
sense a 'cosmic' statement may nevertheless be 'genuine'.

[2] To her own mind Israel exists as such a community even in the time of the
Judges: cf. M. Buber on 'The Song of Deborah', *The Prophetic Faith*, pp. 8–12, 19.

[3] 'Der Anfang der Geschichtsschreibung im Alten Israel', *Gesammelte Studien zum
Alten Testament*, p. 152. Cf. also H. Wheeler Robinson, *Inspiration and Revelation in
the Old Testament*, pp. 123–32, and see Isa. 45–7.

[4] Von Rad, *loc. cit.*; and cf. also R. Rendtorff, 'Geschichte und Überlieferung',
Studien zur Theologie der alttestamentlichen Überlieferungen (for G. von Rad), p. 90:
God's action 'becomes for Israel herself recognizable again and again at particular

31

God's steadfastness finds in him the guarantee of the unity and continuity of history.[1]

It is thus too that Israel can make God's past action the bearer not only of present conditions, of *Heilsgütern*, the gifts which his hand has already provided, but also of promise for the future, of coming fulfilment. It is another implication of the order of theological ideas which we have made the subject of this section, and it is the basis of typology in the prophets: Yahweh's 'steadfastness', even in creating 'new things', makes prophecy possible. I shall speak more fully of this in a later part. Here, let me just underline: it is faith's discovery of God's steadfastness (his steadfast love and mercy, his righteousness and just judgement) which makes it possible, e.g. for Deutero-Isaiah[2] in the passages quoted, not only to speak of the wonder of God's acts in general, but with assurance to prophesy their coming. Though from the point of view of the present the radical newness of these things makes them unknown and, apart from the word of God through his prophet, unknowable, yet, from the point of view of faith, they are promised by God's steadfast love as revealed in his 'mighty acts'. Before the exile, while Israel relied too complacently on her security, the prophets did not emphasize this. 'Because it was to the patriarchs that the popular ideas of a splendid future were linked', the prophets pass over the patriarchs in silence.[3] If God is to be gracious to Israel again, it will be conditional upon her repentance: then 'it may be' that Yahweh will be gracious to the remnant of Joseph, and will be with Israel 'as (Israel) has' (too easily) 'said' (Amos 5. 14 f.). But towards the end of the exile the position has changed. Once brought low, and in an apparently hopeless situation, the people may rely again on the promises made to their forefather Abraham (Mic. 7. 20; Isa. 29. 22 [both secondary]; Isa. 41. 8–10), they may trust again in God's 'steadfast, sure love for David' (Isa. 55. 3 f.), and remember

points; but it is not wholly constituted by isolated individual events. Rather, these, through the coherence in which they stand and have their meaning, make directly visible that it is the *whole* history of Israel which is the activity of God.'

[1] Cf. H. W. Wolff, 'Das Geschichtsverständnis der alttestamentlichen Prophetie', *EvTh*, xx (1960), 218–35 (reprinted in *PAH*, 319–40), esp. pp. 222–30 (= *PAH*, pp. 324–33).

[2] See pp. 77–9 below.

[3] Lindblom, *Prophecy in Ancient Israel*, p. 375.

the time, above all, of their deliverance from the Egyptians (Isa. 43. 16 f.; 51. 10). At this time, as Lindblom says, 'the typological way of contemplating history yielded guarantees of the realisation of the religious and national expectations'.[1] At this time, while Israel is helpless, the apparent impossibility of the eschatological newness is shown by history to be possible; it is indeed assured by God's word and nature. The dry bones, in Ezekiel's vision, are a powerful symbol of the impossibility of Israel either saving herself or being able, from the natural course of events, to expect her salvation. But God's past acts show nothing to be impossible for him. His word, through the mouth of the prophet, gives the bones of life.

Then he said to me, 'Son of man, these bones are the whole house of Israel. Behold, they say, "Our bones are dried up, and our hope is lost; we are clean cut off." Therefore prophesy, and say to them, Thus says the Lord God: Behold, I will open your graves, and raise you from your graves, O my people; and I will bring you home into the land of Israel.'

By these events, by God's achievement, that is, of the natural impossibility, 'you shall know', this text goes on, 'that I am Yahweh', and 'you shall know that I, Yahweh, have spoken, and I have done it, says Yahweh' (Ezek. 37. 11–14).

It is obvious that such confidence in God's power to achieve the impossible, the miraculously new, in history, sets the prophets of Israel, and for that matter the historians and psalmists, in absolute contradiction and contrast to myth's kind of confidence in the pre-posited order of nature: for the consistency of grace is totally different from that of nature. But the point is worth bearing in mind. For when, in discussing typology, one speaks, as one must, of 'repetition', one is using this term of God's acts and it therefore has to do justice both to steadfastness and to newness. Designed, I suppose, primarily to express the relationship of historical actions of God to one another in series and similarity, it appears sometimes to be less than fair to the transforming character of every such act, the newness that adds grace to nature and redeems nature by grace.[2]

[1] *Ibid.* p. 376.
[2] We agree therefore with the protest of F. Baumgärtel (see especially his essay on 'Das hermeneutische Problem des Alten Testaments', *TLZ* (1954), no. 4, cols. 199–211, reprinted in *PAH*, pp. 114–39) against a typologizing exegesis of the Old

Testament which stresses the affinities between the two testaments in such a way as to endanger the vital truth that the Old Testament differs in its self-understanding from the New Testament and can only be received as testimony to the Gospel if it is allowed to be testimony from outside the Gospel. 'In dem evangelischen Verstehen muss das Alte Testament das *Alte* bleiben' (col. 209; = *PAH*, p. 132). This emphasis seems to me wholly correct as against W. Vischer's method in *Das Christuszeugnis des Alten Testaments* (cf. Baumgärtel, *Verheissung*, pp. 91–5, and J. D. Wood, *The Interpretation of the Bible*, pp. 156–9) and to some extent also against that of A. G. Hebert in *The Throne of David* and *The Authority of the Old Testament* (cf. J. D. Smart, *The Interpretation of Scripture*, pp. 76 ff.). If typology is to be justified it must do justice to *change*—changes of self-understanding between the two testaments, and the change from which such changes of self-understanding largely derive, the change in human existence which is brought about by the 'new' act of God. Baumgärtel's assumption, however, is that typology is never able to do this: and similarly Bultmann, who considers that fundamentally 'die Typologie steht unter dem Gedanken der Wiederholung' and 'rechnet mit...dem zyklischen... Lauf der Zeit' ('Ursprung und Sinn der Typologie als hermeneutischer Methode', *TLZ*, 1950, p. 205). I contest both these assumptions as does also, recently, B. W. Anderson, 'Exodus Typology in Second Isaiah', *Israel's Prophetic Heritage* (J. Muilenburg Festschrift), pp. 177–95. Cf. also C. Westermann, 'Bemerkungen zu den Thesen Bultmanns und Baumgärtels', *PAH*, pp. 102–13; and R. Rendtorff, 'Hermeneutik des Alten Testaments als Frage nach der Geschichte', *ZThK*, LVII (1960), 27–40.

CHAPTER 3

MAN AND HISTORY: APPLIED TYPOLOGY

JAMES MUILENBURG, speaking of the Old Testament, says that there 'history is the word of God actualizing itself in events'.[1] We have found some support for this statement, and much more could be found. We have seen that in history God creates in accord with his nature and promise what could otherwise not come to pass. Even 'natural' chains of events are controlled, at their start, by his word. This is what is expressed, somewhat crudely perhaps, to our minds, but with exemplary clarity, by the Deuteronomistic history, especially in the two books of Kings. Here, for example, Ahijah the Shilonite prophesies the removal of ten tribes from Solomon's kingdom ('because he has forsaken [Yahweh] and worshipped Ashtoreth ...; and has not walked in [Yahweh's] ways'), an event which is to take place not in Solomon's reign but in the time of his son, Rehoboam (I Kings 11. 29–39). Rehoboam comes to the throne, encounters some fiscal difficulty, acts against the council's advice, and by his high-handed action antagonizes the people, thus bringing on the disastrous division of the kingdom. All this, says the Deuteronomistic writer, 'was a turn of affairs brought about by the Lord to fulfil his word spoken by Ahijah the Shilonite to Jeroboam the son of Nebat' (I Kings 12. 15). Von Rad sees in the series of similar 'prophetic predictions and exactly noted fulfilments which runs through the Deuteronomist's work' an embracing 'theological schema',[2] one, moreover, which was 'true to the tradition given to him'.[3] Yahweh's word is conceived of as creative of Judah's history, 'and that in a double capacity: as law, judging and destroying; as gospel—i.e. in the Davidic prophecy, which was constantly being fulfilled—saving and forgiving'.[4] 'Thus', von Rad concludes, 'the Deuteronomist shows with exemplary validity what saving history is in the Old Testament: that is, a process of

---

[1] *The Way of Israel*, p. 46.   [2] *Studies in Deuteronomy*, p. 78.
[3] *Ibid.* p. 89.   [4] *Ibid.*

35   3-2

history which is formed by the word of Yahweh continually intervening in judgment and salvation and directed towards a fulfilment.'[1] He speaks of the principle properly, therefore, as a 'theology of history'.[2]

The dependence of the Deuteronomic view on the prophetic understanding of history is plain enough. History is, for the prophets too, 'Yahweh's work', created by Yahweh's 'word'. God says to Jeremiah, 'I am watching over my word, to do it' (Jer. 1. 12), and Ezekiel receives the promise: 'The word which I speak will be done' (Ezek. 12. 25 and 28). In neither case does this imply two separate actions; the word of Yahweh is more or less directly creative of the event:

> For as the rain and the snow come down from heaven
>   and return not thither but water the earth,
> making it bring forth and sprout,
>   giving seed to the sower and bread to the eater,
> so shall my word be that goes forth from my mouth;
>   it shall not return to me empty,
> but it shall accomplish that which I purpose,
>   and prosper in the thing for which I sent it.
>
> (Isa. 55. 10 f.)

Zimmerli has suggestively spoken of Ezekiel's 'Worttheologie',[3] and it is a phrase that applies too to the conception of God's word in Jeremiah and Deutero-Isaiah, as von Rad points out.[4] One remembers also the Psalmist's affirmation: 'By Yahweh's word the heavens were made...He spoke, and it came to be; he commanded, and it stood forth' (Ps. 33. 6 and 9).

But the Old Testament, nevertheless, is aware that no simple equivalence between God's will and history is possible. God's acts summon man to return to him, but they do not constrain him. 'I have done these things', God says through his prophet, 'yet you would not return to me' (Amos 4, 6–11). A dialogue between God and Israel takes place in her history, a dialogue during the course of which, though the final issue is assured by

---

[1] *Studies in Deuteronomy*, p. 91.

[2] Cf. also W. Zimmerli, 'Verheissung und Erfüllung', *PAH*, pp. 77 f.

[3] *Ezechiel, BK*, p. 89 (cited from von Rad as below).

[4] *Theologie des Alten Testaments*, II, 107. Compare the whole section (pp. 93–111), but especially, for the relations between this 'Worttheologie' in the prophets and the Deuteronomistic history, pp. 107 f.

the power of God, the relationship between him and Israel, or between that future and the present Israel, is always changing, always in motion—perhaps like the tides.[1] God's direction of history has room for antinomies to his will, hindrances which are, in particular, the results of man's freedom. All this is confessed in Israel, not for the first time by the prophets, but already by the very existence, alongside the direct confessional statement of God's act and Israel's election, of the imperative mood of the Law.[2]

For the Old Testament succeeds in doing justice both to the sovereign will of God and to the freedom of man. And it makes these two factors so interdependent that to present even sketchily the whole dialectic of history as conceived there one must supplement the discussion of 'God and History' with some account of man's place in history. One must supplement the one-sidedness of Muilenburg's definition with the balancing one-sidedness of Bultmann's (which is not designed to apply particularly to the Old Testament). History, for the latter, is human actions and—since 'human life goes its way not only through actions, but also through events which encounter us through that which happens to one'[3]—reactions. The interdependence of the two sides makes the definition of each visible only in their encounter; and history is the Word of God actualizing itself in events *and* (the simple conjunction here joins tentatively the elements of a relation as yet undefined) human action and reaction *vis-à-vis* these events and this Word.[4]

If, therefore, Yahweh is scarcely conceived in the Old Testament apart from his actions and his actions are known primarily in relation to Israel, then, according always to the Old Testament, Israel and her qualities are properly apprehended and judged only when she is seen in her historical relation (past, present and future) to Yahweh. According to the way in which man responds to God, as well as according to

[1] Cf. H. W. Wolff, 'Das Geschichtsverständnis der alttestamentlichen Prophetie', *EvTh*, xx (1960), 222 = *PAH*, p. 324: 'History, for the prophets, is the purposive dialogue of the Lord of the future with Israel.'

[2] See, most recently, R. E. Clements, *Prophecy and Covenant*, pp. 22 f., 54 f., and the literature cited there.

[3] *History and Eschatology*, pp. 136 f.

[4] Cf. J. Marsh in the ecumenical symposium *Biblical Authority for Today*, p. 183.

the way in which God acts towards him, so he is.[1] It remains for us to develop this theme.

It implies the priority of God's action. Israel's existence, and man's in Israel, depends first upon that. If it were not for that fact the truth of man's existence would be different. The Psalmist's question, 'What is man?' (Ps. 8. 4), could then be answered pessimistically only: man would be subsumed in the scheme of nature and at nature's mercy. But through the inexplicable favour of God, who 'set him a little lower than the angels' at the Creation and continues to 'visit' and 'be mindful of him' in history (*ibid.*), man's existence is radically altered and such pessimism is in total error: man is what God has made him, he is as God has created him.

Thus, for Israel, the nation's existence, its true being, lay in election. For thus she was constituted by God. No other explanations were relevant or could be used. 'Israel's greatness', as G. E. Wright says, 'lay in what to the nation was a simple fact, that God had chosen her.'[2] The basis of this self-understanding was, once again, clearly the Exodus. For of that event the doctrine of the chosen people was, to quote Wright again, 'the initial and fundamental theological'—we should prefer, in our context, to say 'anthropological'—'inference'.[3] We need only refer, once again, to a passage like Deut. 26. 5–9:

A wandering Aramean was my father, and he went down into Egypt, few in number; and there he became a nation, great, mighty, and populous. And the Egyptians treated us harshly, and afflicted us, and laid upon us hard bondage. Then we cried to Yahweh, the God of our Fathers, and Yahweh heard our voice...and Yahweh brought us out of Egypt with a mighty hand and an outstretched arm...and he brought us into this place and gave us this land, a land flowing with milk and honey.

[1] Cf. J. K. S. Reid, *Our Life in Christ*, pp. 36–40 and especially p. 46: Man 'can neither be nor rightly be apart from God who created him'. It is not to cast doubt on the general correctness of this if I say that it does not seem to me that 'both truths' are expressed in the verse which Reid cites (Jer. 10. 23); there 'rightly being' alone is envisaged.

[2] *God Who Acts*, p. 50.

[3] *Ibid*. The fact that the word *bāḥar* (to choose, to elect) is not used in the technical sense until the Deuteronomistic writings is not significant here. The basic notion behind it, as R. E. Clements says, is extremely old (*Prophecy and Covenant*, p. 46 n.). The two passages which I quote (Deut. 26. 5–9; Exod. 19. 3–6) are both from sources considerably older than the canonical prophets; and both imply such a notion.

Israel explains her existence especially in terms of this act of Yahweh, simultaneously confessing her faith in this act and her dependence upon it. The act constituted them as what they were henceforth to be, peculiarly God's own:

Thus shall you say to the house of Jacob, and tell the people of Israel: You have seen what I did to the Egyptians, and how I bore you on eagles' wings to myself. Now therefore,...you shall be my own possession among all peoples...and you shall be to me a kingdom of priests and a holy nation.   (Exod. 19. 3*b*–6)

But if Israel's existence as 'holy to God' may be described by means of a categorical indicative as it is here, this implies nothing static—it is not done once for all and so done with— and it gives no grounds for complacency. What it does imply is, on God's side, a purpose, and on man's side, an unconditional obligation to God for the gift of existence, and unconditioned responsibility to the purpose inferred from the gift. The creative 'truth' of God's act demands from Israel active participation and even, as we shall see, imitation. Israel therefore is faced with an uncompromising imperative which is already behind the indicative. For 'to know the truth' (which is the same as recognizing for what it is the historical activity of God) 'is to stand under the imperative of God'.[1] God had called them to be his own; therefore they must be his own. Only by living up to the imperative could each man affirm the indicative as applying to him, and so become what, by virtue of the act of God, he already was: a member of God's chosen people, living in the new history which God had given him, according to the way which God had shown him.

Israel was called, then, to realize each moment afresh God's purpose in her election, to fulfil it in her own existence. And in the absence, at the earlier stages, most probably, of a full recognition of the ultimate and eschatological tendency of the providence of God, his purpose was almost immediately present to them as one of service. Thus 'classic expression', says Eichrodt,[2] 'is given to the purpose of Israel's election...in the recurrent formula of an old historian for God's demand of Pharaoh, "Let my people go, that they may serve me" (Exod.

[1] Hoskyns and Davey, *The Riddle of the New Testament*, p. 29.
[2] *Man in the Old Testament*, p. 41.

7. 16; 9. 13; 10. 3)'. Transposed and addressed to Israel this might read, 'serve me, for you have been freed',[1] and that this was henceforth, inescapably, the will of God for them as revealed in his actions, and so the basic *datum* of history, was recognized in their Law's attribution to 'Yahweh, your God, who brought you out of Egypt, out of the house of bondage' (Exod. 20. 2; Deut. 5. 5). The point has been well made, as often, by Walther Eichrodt:

The divine demand...was from the beginning embedded in a *history* of this God with his people. In this history the divine Lawgiver was recognized from the beginning as the divine Life-giver, and his demand was distinguished from all arbitrary tyranny as a call to a relation of grace. And the individual's obligation, in the 'Thou shalt' of the Law..., was seen, not as a heavy yoke, but as a necessary and blessed form of life, as a liberation from chaotic self-destruction.[2]

In the Law the true life of man under election comes to expression, as a gift from the hand of God:

Be careful to do all the words of this law. For it is no trifle for you, *but it is your life*, and thereby you shall live long in the land which you are going over the Jordan to possess.   (Deut. 32. 46–7)

The past act of God becomes grace to them when by service they live in accord with the purpose it manifests. The new future which God has made possible becomes their future when in obedience and faith they accept it. In its backward-looking aspect the keeping of the Law is an act of faith in the past as revealing the steadfast love of Yahweh. In its forward-looking aspect, it is an act of trust in the future, for to serve Yahweh is to trust in his purposes and his power to fulfil them. What obedience emphatically does not constitute is the grounds for the covenant. 'It is not a matter of commanding that which makes a man belong to God, but of forbidding that which abolishes this relationship...The "reward" can thus consist only in remaining in this positive relationship to Yahweh.'[3]

---

[1] Cf. Ps. 105. 43–5: 'So he led forth his people with joy...to the end that they should keep his statutes and observe his laws.'

[2] *Man in the Old Testament*, pp. 16 f.

[3] W. Gutbrod, 'Law in the Old Testament', pp. 25 f. in the *Bible Key Words* (*BKW*) series translated from *TWNT*.

For the covenant and blessing precede the demand. Obedience is the confirmation of the Covenant, 'They shall be my people, and I will be their God' (Ezek. 11. 20; cf. Exod. 19. 5, with its parallelism, '*obey* my voice, and *keep* my covenant'), and—as is made plain in the blessings which conclude the legal blocks in Leviticus (26. 3–13), and Deuteronomy (28. 1–14)—the condition of continuing blessedness: 'Yahweh will establish you as a people holy to himself, as he has sworn to you, if you keep the commandments of the Yahweh your God and walk in his ways' (Deut. 28. 9).

Such an existence would be a testimony to the holiness, righteousness and mercy of Yahweh. Thus 'all the peoples of the earth shall see that you are called by the name of Yahweh' (Deut. 28. 10).

Yet because the continued reception of blessing is dependent on man's response, there remains the possibility of its rejection. The covenant relation can be destroyed by disobedience on the part of Israel. In such case what the act of God did is—at least for the time—undone. The 'cursings' which follow and counterpoise the 'blessings' (Lev. 26. 14–39; Deut. 28. 15–68) are like them expressed in conditional form: the condition is disobedience, the consequence loss of the new conditions of life under the covenant. Graphically the Deuteronomist or his source depicts such a loss as a return to Egypt, an Exodus in reverse:[1]

The Lord will bring you back in ships to Egypt, a journey which I promised that you should never make again; and there you shall offer yourselves for sale to your enemies as male and female slaves, but no man will buy you. (Deut. 28. 68)

The promise made to Abraham (Gen. 15. 5; 22. 17) will be by man's doing undone, though God has fulfilled it (Deut. 1. 10):

Whereas you were as the stars of heaven for multitude you shall be left few in number; because you did not obey the voice of the Lord. (Deut. 28. 62)

Instead of witnessing to the mercy of Yahweh among all the nations (Deut. 28. 10 above), they will become 'a horror, a

---

[1] A motif which is earlier than Deuteronomy or the exile. See Hos. 9. 3: 'But Ephraim shall return to Egypt and they shall eat unclean food in Assyria' (and cf. 9. 6; 11. 5).

proverb, and a byword, among all the peoples where the Lord will lead (them) away' (Deut. 28. 37).

The Law, therefore, comes before man with the possibility, brought about by the act of God, of a choice between two forms of existence: 'Behold, I set before you this day a blessing and a curse' (Deut. 11. 26), 'life and death' (Deut. 30. 19). A decision is inescapable, for in the encounter with God in his act, or the 'word' of his act, man is judged by his response to it. There only, as we said earlier, is the 'definition' of man made visible. By trusting or distrusting the truth of God's act man affirms or rejects for himself the existence in the newness of grace which that act makes possible. And apart from that trust or distrust, or if trust is not renewed constantly, his existence is merely equivocal.

With the nation as a whole, according to the prophets at least, this last is precisely the case. Amos, as Vriezen points out, 'always speaks of *'ammi* (my people) in his prophecies (7. *vv.* 8 and 15; 9. 10, cf. 14), and he nowhere arrives at the verdict that God has rejected Israel, even if he prophesies that the nation shall fall and rise no more (5. 2) '.[1] Hosea sees his age's relation to Yahweh as in question: *'ammi* or *lo-'ammi,* Yahweh's people or not? (Hos. 1. 9 f.; 2. 23). Later prophets reinforce this judgement: the empirical Israel may perish, but the people of God nonetheless exists and remains, though visible only to the eye of faith.[2] The continued 'establishment' of God's people is very much an issue for Isaiah. It depends on their faith (Isa. 7. 8; 28. 16).[3] If they are to go into exile, it is because they 'do not regard Yahweh's deeds', have no 'knowledge' of them (Isa. 5. 11–13; cf. Hos. 4. 6). But still they are called God's people and God will be true to his promises ('Immanuel', Isa. 7. 10–17, is to be the sign of it, and cf. 9. 2–7). The paradoxical character of Israel's existence comes to its focus in Yahweh's 'strange work' of destruction (28. 21). Those who learn to trust in Yahweh alone will be saved (28. 16). It is not too much to say that the event is seen by this prophet as coming about for that purpose: to bring Israel once again into encounter

---

[1] Th. C. Vriezen, 'Prophecy and Eschatology', *VT* (Suppl.), 1, 204 f.

[2] *Ibid.* p. 205.

[3] Using the Septuagint reading: 'He who is firm in faith shall not be shamed.' Cf. H. W. Robinson, *Inspiration and Revelation in the Old Testament*, p. 125.

with God. In this way Hosea also had seen the menace of Assyria: it is a threat—back to Egypt! (Hos. 9. 3)—but at the same time a new auspice (Hos. 2. 14 f.). It is thus that the prophets see Israel's political destruction: it is judgement and grace, a renewed encounter with God.[1]

We must emphasize at this point, however, that when, in times, say, of peace and prosperity, there was no great act of the Lord outwardly controlling their history, no apparent need for deliverance, no 'Holy War' to be fought, the judgement and the decision could not on that account be avoided. The 'word' of his act, the recollection of the nation's origin, came with its demand of faith and obedience as critically to the judgement of Israel (i.e. for judgement or decision by Israel) as the acts and origins themselves. For Israel was still the creation of God's act of deliverance. Even to forget it involved a denial of the election, a relapse to a merely 'natural' form of existence, at the mercy of nature.

Therefore the Law and the *cultus*—not to speak, for the time, of the prophets—cultivated recollection. Both the words of the Law and the life of obedience to it stood as signs of the act of God. Striking, for example, in the Old Testament's presentation of its Law, is the frequent parallelism with *derek*, a 'way'.[2] The Law was a 'way' to 'walk in' (Exod. 16. 4; Lev. 18. 4; Deut. 5. 33; 26. 17; 28. 9; 30. 16; Josh. 22. 5; I Kings 2. 3; 6. 12; Ps. 78. 10; Jer. 7. 23; Ezek. 11. 20; etc.) or even to 'run in' (Ps. 119. 32). Obedience was the way of blessedness (Ps. 119. 1). More strikingly, it was as 'a following' of Yahweh that belief in him was conceived (cf. I Kings 18. 21) and the consequent obedience meant that the believer's ways were Yahweh's, 'his ways' (Deut. 26. 17; 28. 9; 30. 16; etc.).[3] All this, especially when added to the fact that this directional imagery is peculiar to the Old Testament (and thence to Christianity),

---

[1] Cf. W. Zimmerli, 'La nouvelle Exode dans le message des deux grands prophètes de l'exil', *Hommage à Wilhelm Vischer*, pp. 216 f.

[2] Cf. G. Ostborn, *Tōrā in the Old Testament*, pp. 33–6; Tinsley, *The Imitation of God in Christ*, pp. 33–5.

[3] The so-called 'Zadokite Document' provides an especially clear example from much later times of this relation between God's acts and the obedience of the righteous: 'Listen to me, and I will open your eyes to see and understand how God acts, so that you may choose what he has desired and reject what he has hated, walking blamelessly in all his ways and not straying...' (*Zadokite Document*, II, 14, trans. T. H. Gaster, '*The Scriptures of the Dead Sea Sect*', p. 73).

gives weight to E. J. Tinsley's contention[1] that the keeping of the commandments was fundamentally linked in the Israelite mind with the traditions of Israel's tribal journey, when they 'followed the ways of the Lord' (cf. Num. 32. 11; Josh. 14. 8) as he led them in the pillars of cloud and fire through the wilderness (Exod. 13. 21–2).[2] The commandments were God's ways and to keep them implied a following of God, a repetition, so to speak, of the historical way once taken in the footsteps of God. Obedience was an imitation of that of the 'fathers', an affirmation that, whatever the particular historical circumstances, they were under the hand of the same God and following him, and therefore that the wilderness journey was a norm or type of their own existential situation under God, under God's judgement and grace.[3]

Nor is it only the 'way' imagery which makes this conclusion inescapable. The crucial claims of God were directed to each day and age still alive in the terms and expressed in the figures which would forever recall the circumstances and occasion of their origin.[4] Whether it be an *imitatio patrum* or directly an *imitatio dei* that is in specific cases invoked, still, as several commandments make clear, the Exodus events are the norm by which to measure behaviour. The laws in Deuteronomy and elsewhere regarding the freeing of slaves and the justice and kindness due to the sojourner, the fatherless and the widow are well-known examples:

You shall remember that you were a slave in the land of Egypt, and the Lord your God redeemed you; therefore I command you this day' (Deut. 15. 15; cf. Lev. 25. 42, 55);

---

[1] *The Imitation of God in Christ*, pp. 33–5.

[2] The hypothesis of M. Noth and G. von Rad, according to which the Sinai and wilderness traditions were originally unconnected, seems to me to do less than justice to the 'fundamental link' here between journey and obedience.

[3] Interesting in this connection is Jeremiah's charge against the lawgivers of his day. They have made a lie of God's laws (8. 8f.), magnifying it out of all proportion. What the unfalsified Torah is for Jeremiah becomes plain from 6. 16: the 'good way' to walk in is found in 'the ancient paths'. Compare on these texts and on the whole subject of the 'way' of God in the Old Testament, Arnulf Kuschke, 'Die Menschenwege und der Weg Gottes im Alten Testament', *ST*, v (1952), esp. pp. 110–18.

[4] D. Daube, in *The Exodus Pattern in the Bible*, uncovers a reciprocal process, whereby legal principles and language are used by the narrators in the Old Testament to interpret the events of redemption.

'The Lord executes justice for the fatherless and the widow, and loves the sojourner, giving him food and clothing. Love the sojourner therefore; for you were sojourners in the land of Egypt' (Deut. 10. 18–9; cf. Exod. 22. 21–3; 23. 9 'for you know the heart of a stranger'; Lev. 19. 33–4 'you shall love him as yourself'; Deut. 24. 17–18, 21–2).

But in the last analysis it is in the events of the Exodus that the laws of ritual cleanness, even, find their rationale:

I am the Lord your God, who have separated you from the peoples. You shall therefore make a distinction between the clean beast and the unclean... You shall be holy to me; for I the Lord am holy, and have separated you from the peoples, that you should be mine.

(Lev. 20. 24–6)

So, for the compiler of the 'Holiness Code' (Lev. 17–26), does all holiness—again, in the last analysis: it is an imitation of the God who in history had revealed his own holiness and separated the people for himself:

You shall be holy, for I the Lord your God am holy.

(Lev. 19. 2; cf. 11. 44–5)

Even the fact that sometimes the connection between the laws and the events was an artificial and forced one (e.g. Deut. 24. 9) goes to show how fundamental to Israelite theory the connection was. The same may be said, indeed, for the attribution of all law to Moses, or rather, to God through the mediation of Moses. What E. Voegelin says of the production of the Deuteronomic Code might apply to almost the whole of Old Testament law: the compilers 'can contrive a myth' of Mosaic origin 'and at the same time believe it, for the myth embodies the truth of an experience—that the instructions of the Deuteronomic Code authentically renew the truth of order communicated by Moses'.[1] Micah's well-known verse expresses the very heart of the conception of the divine yet historical origins of law:

He has shown you, O man, what is good;
    and what does the Lord require of you
but to do justice, and to love kindness,
    and to walk humbly with your God.   (Mic. 6. 8)

[1] *Israel and Revelation*, p. 175.

45

Obedience then was a recollection, a repetition and sign of the ways of God. And conversely, of course, disobedience was a forgetting (Ps. 78. 10–11), a walking contrary to God (Lev. 26. 27) as opposed to a following.

In this way the Law, besides guarding the Covenant, had a function as the word of God's act, the discriminator of man's existence under blessing or curse. These functions are combined also in the liturgy and festivals of Israel. There too, and more clearly indeed, the acts of Yahweh in the nation's past are re-evoked in word and symbol, to confront man with crisis and provoke the decision to believe or not believe, which is to say, to be or not to be what by deliverance they were made. There too the critical relation between historical election and eternal moral demand is presented,[1] and, once again, we meet this relation in the guise of an *imitatio patrum*.

The agricultural origins of the festivals need not detain us. What matters is that the three great Hebrew feasts (Un-leavened Bread, Weeks, and Asiph—later Tabernacles) became 'historified' into a way of reliving the salvation events of 'that time',[2] of making those events 'contemporary'.[3] Pedersen's work on the connection between the Passover and Exod. 1–15 is now well known: these chapters of Exodus provide indications of the way in which the Passover mimetically recalled the critical stages of the saving events.[4] And W. D. Davies shows how the language used in the instructions for celebrating the feast tended to blur the distinction between those who were involved directly in the original events and those involved in them only aetiologically and through their participation in the feast.[5] The credal summary in Josh. 24, which also has a cultic *schema* underlying it (a festival of covenant renewal), exhibits some-what similar features in the way its pronouns change between third person and second:

Then I brought *your fathers* out of Egypt, and *you* came to the sea; and the Egyptians pursued *your fathers* with chariots and horsemen

---

[1] See A. Weiser, *Introduction to the Old Testament*, pp. 87–90.

[2] J. Marsh shows that this phrase was used in the book of Deuteronomy 'more or less as a technical term referring to the whole period of the Exodus-complex' (*The Fulness of Time*, pp. 48 ff.).

[3] See S. Mowinckel, *The Psalms in Israel's Worship*, I, 109–16.

[4] See J. Pedersen, *Israel*, III–IV, 384–415.

[5] *Paul and Rabbinic Judaism*, pp. 102 ff.

to the Red Sea. And when *they* cried to the Lord, he put darkness between *you* and the Egyptians, and made the sea come upon them and cover them; and *your eyes* saw what I did to Egypt; and *you* lived in the wilderness a long time. (Josh. 24. 6–7)

A peculiarly interesting example of the same fundamental process of 'contemporization' is found in the book of Deuteronomy. The book, once again, has the basic structure of a cultic celebration[1] and Deut. 31. 9–13 itself suggests a connection with the feast of Tabernacles. Here we find *hayyom*, 'this day', used as a kind of *leitmotiv* to involve the congregation of Israel at the time of celebration with their fathers who had travelled towards Canaan, the Promised Land.[2] The expression applies primarily, no doubt, to the period of the Exodus, but given the real *Sitz im Leben* of the book it seems no less likely that it is cast in the form of a *present* expression of time in order to stress that the past is new. 'Today and always today' is Voegelin's paraphrase;[3] and Tinsley writes that '*Hayyom* points to a present occasion...wherein through the recital of the history and law of Israel with whatever cultic and dramatic mimesis went with it, the presentness of the past was experienced anew.'[4] Three instances of the word's use in Deuteronomy will be enough to indicate the variety of ways in which it is used to produce this effect:

'Not with our fathers did the Lord make this covenant, but with us, who are all of us here alive *this day*' (i.e. *hayyom* used to underline the contemporaneity of the Covenant through the steadfastness of Yahweh, ch. 5. 2);

'Hear, O Israel; you are to pass over the Jordan *this day*' (i.e. *hayyom* used to suggest contemporaneity with past events, ch. 9. 1);

'And these words which I command you *this day* shall be upon your heart' (i.e. *hayyom* used to underline the contemporaneity of past demands, ch. 6. 6).

Once again, then, Israel is brought into existential encounter with God's act. 'This day' contemporizes the imperatives along with the promises of God, and the representation of history in

[1] Von Rad, *Gesammelte Studien zum Alten Testament*, pp. 33 ff.
[2] See G. von Rad, *Old Testament Theology*, I, 231.
[3] *Israel and Revelation*, p. 374.
[4] Tinsley, *op. cit.* p. 54. Compare again von Rad's treatment of Deuteronomy in his study of 'Das formgeschichtliche Problem des Hexateuch', *Gesammelte Studien*, 33–41, esp. pp. 36 f.

the liturgy involves the nation in a confession of faith. There is no lack of material evidence, both in the Old Testament (e.g. notably, in the Psalms) and in the Mishnah, of this essential function of the cultus in ancient Israel. But it is useless to multiply examples.

Plainly, from what we have said, the contemporizing devices such as we have quoted from Joshua and Deuteronomy are much more than simply sleight of hand. There is one point, however, not so far mentioned, which goes some way to make this plainer. This is the conception of 'corporate personality' to which H. Wheeler Robinson drew modern attention.[1] By the very fact of their having this (only semi-intellective) mode of thought the *imitatio patrum* was a natural conception to the Hebrew, for what 'corporate personality' means is that the individual is in some way identical with the tribe and *vice versa*, and the son identical with—by custom he was already imitator of—the father. Boman cites the ancient poem in Gen. 49 as an example of this,[2] where Jacob-Israel and the names of the twelve sons are at one moment individuals, at another nations and tribes; but we may suspect the same ambiguity not only in the liturgy but in the prophetic writings, not least, per- haps, in the crux-laden cycle of Servant Songs in Deutero- Isaiah.[3]

But now circumspection is necessary, for the Israelite cult, in particular, bears a real formal similarity to the rituals of mythopoeic religion. Corporate personality is a conception shared with other primitive peoples, the *imitatio dei* is a concept well known in myth, and a ritual repetition of the gestures of gods and ancestors is one of the fundamentals of primitive religious behaviour. Eliade quotes:

'We must do what the gods did in the beginning' (*Śatapatha Brāhmana*, VII, 2, 1, 4);

'Thus the gods did; thus men do' (*Taittīriya Brāhmana*, I, 5, 9, 4),

---

[1] 'The Hebrew Conception of Corporate Personality', in *Werden und Wesen des Alten Testaments*, ed. J. Hempel, pp. 49–62. M. Noth denies the relevance of this to the issue of 'contemporaneity' in the *cultus* (see the essay cited on p. 52 below, esp. p. 12 = *PAH*, p. 62). Though its importance should not be exaggerated, as com- pared with that of the other factors to which we have drawn attention, it does not seem to me by any means irrelevant here.

[2] *Hebrew Thought compared with Greek*, p. 148.

[3] See below, pp. 113–19.

and he comments: 'This Indian adage summarizes all the theory underlying rituals in all countries.'[1] Moreover, the intervening time between the archetypes and their repetition is wiped out, abolished, and the archetypes become 'contemporaneous': 'he who reproduced the exemplary gesture thus finds himself transported into the mythical epoch in which its revelation took place'.[2] And if, as we have said, it is (to some extent) by conforming to the divine acts that Hebrew man attains to the reality which has been given him in those acts, it is also true that in myth 'an object or an act becomes real in so far as it imitates or repeats an archetype'.[3]

The similarities are impressive. But it would not be right to allow the obvious kinship of the Israelite cult to those existing in the surrounding civilizations to imply identity between them. The differences, too, are significant, and if we spend the remainder of this section examining them they will help to throw light, not on the cult only, but also on the whole question of Israel's conception of history, which is the basis of an 'applied' and existential, not merely 'aesthetic' or speculative, typology.

In the first place, the imitation of the gods in mythological religion has behind it the idea of sympathetic magic:

It is one of the tenets of mythopoeic logic that similarity and identity merge; 'to be like' is as good as 'to be'. Therefore, by being like, by enacting the role of, a force of nature, a god, man could in the cult enter into and clothe himself with the identity of these powers, with the identity of the gods, and through his own actions, when thus identified, cause the powers involved to act as he would have them act.[4]

This was manifestly unacceptable to normative Old Testament religion. Von Rad speaks of Yahwism's 'unyielding inflexibility against magic from the moment that magic reveals itself as a well-tried technique for influencing the deity, or when man, with its aid, takes into his own control, to further his own needs, events or powers that belong to the deity',[5] and he calls this opposition 'unique in the history of religion'.[6] Yahweh was not

---

[1] *The Myth of the Eternal Return*, p. 21.   [2] *Ibid.* p. 35.
[3] *Ibid.* p. 34; see also p. 14 above.
[4] Thorkild Jacobsen, in *Before Philosophy*, ed. H. and H. A. Frankfort, p. 215.
[5] G. von Rad, *Old Testament Theology*, I, 34 f.   [6] *Ibid.*

subject to influence, and if, among the people, it was assumed that they could by ritual ensure his favour's continuance, whatever their way of life, the prophets at least, quite clearly, refused to have any truck with the theory.[1] In contrast, the *imitatio dei* in Israel was usually, as we have seen, solely a special expression of the people's taking upon themselves the responsibility laid upon them by the moral standard of Yahweh's acts, their normative character: 'As God treated you, so do to others.'[2]

More significant is the question of the cult's 'legend' and of the felt relation between it and the congregation. Here one difference in particular is stressed by Old Testament scholars. We have already referred to it in passing, but it repays closer attention. The Old Testament locates its cult's basic legends in past historical time. It historizes, or 'historifies', festal celebrations which were originally agricultural feasts of the kind celebrated in Canaan at the Conquest. But the gestures of gods, heroes, ancestors rehearsed by Near Eastern ritual in general took place, as Eliade says, in 'mythical time'. If, as is sometimes the case, they were based upon actual happenings, this element

---

[1] See J. Bright, *History of Israel*, pp. 242 f.

[2] The representation of God in so far as it was involved in the prophetic, priestly and kingly offices would require separate treatment. Here it must be enough to say that in none of these offices was there any idea that the office-bearer magically influences the God whom he represents. Of these offices kingship is the most closely and broadly representative of the divinity in Israelite thought as in Near Eastern religion generally. Of the king, Mowinckel, who does not often under-emphasize the connections between Israel and other ancient cultures, says: 'The king is the natural, official leader of the public cult, even if on ordinary occasions the priest officiates in his stead. He is the channel through which Yahweh's blessings flow to the people, being conveyed primarily through his cultic functions. The presupposition and condition of this is that he should be loyal to the laws and justice of Yahweh. Although in virtue of his equipment (annointing and Yahweh's spirit) he is "divine" and more than an ordinary human being, and although as leader in the cult he is the representative of the people in the presence of the Deity: he prays, intercedes, offers up sacrifice, and receives power and blessing. The covenant is concentrated in him; and through him and his line the promises are mediated. Through him the congregation stands before God and meets God' (*He That Cometh*, p. 89). In our context it is worth noticing that Mowinckel also says: 'That the king in Israel should have been regarded as identical with Yahweh, or in the cult have played Yahweh's part, is wholly improbable; nor is there any proof whatever that this was ever the case' (*The Psalms in Israel's Worship*, I, 59). See also G. A. Cooke, 'The Israelite King as Son of God', *ZAW*, N.F. 32 (1961), pp. 202–25, where the author stresses the close connection between the king's sonship and that of Israel, and the importance, for both conceptions, of the covenant promises and demands.

of actuality was without significance. Their objective status as
'happenings' was not merely, as is the case with the acts of
God towards Israel, unverifiable, incapable of scientific proof,
it was not even the object of faith. But to Israel, needless to say,
the historicity of Yahweh's acts was the vital object of faith.[1]
This is so even in the case of the creation-history which was at
the basis of the New Year festival. 'Creation', says Mowinckel,
'was no longer considered an undatable phenomenon, but a
mighty mythic-historical action taking place on a definite
occasion, later "recalled" and kept up...at the festival.'[2]

But it remains a question how far this change alters the
rationale of 'contemporaneity' in the Israelite *cultus*, and it is
an important one. Von Rad sees the 'historizing' of the feasts
only as a 'first step' in Israel's understanding of her historical
existence, and one which goes back to a time when the originally
isolated events celebrated in the particular feasts were not yet
ordered into the eschatologically orientated historical succession
presupposed by the oldest strands behind the Pentateuch, the
works of Jahwist and Elohist (J and E).[3] However, once this
ordering was, independently of the cult, accomplished—another,
'epochal', step[4]—the principle of contemporaneity in the cult
was compromised. Though the 'cultic' and 'chronological'
conceptions of history may for a while have existed side by side,
they were in tension, or even opposition, for the former is, in
its essence, 'anti-historical'. [5]

But von Rad's argument may be challenged. To begin with,
the supporting thesis (of von Rad and M. Noth) that the various
traditions of saving events were originally separate and local,
is reasonably attacked by scholars such as Weiser[6] and Bright.[7]
According to these latter, Sinai, Exodus and the other basic
traditions which the Pentateuch associates with that time, were
thought of as being linked in a chronological succession from

[1] In this case Pedersen's account of the Passover festival leaves something to be
desired, for it appears to remythologize a cult which the Old Testament has largely
demythologized. Cf. esp. *Israel*, III–IV, 409 f.
[2] *The Psalms in Israel's Worship*, I, 139 f.
[3] *Theologie des Alten Testaments*, II, 118. For the symbols, J and E, see the excursus
at the end of the note on pp. 26 f. above.
[4] *Ibid.* p. 119.
[5] *Ibid.* pp. 121 f.
[6] A. Weiser, *Introduction to the Old Testament*, pp. 83–93.
[7] J. Bright, *Early Israel in Recent History Writing*, pp. 104–6.

the very beginning of the tribal league and more or less, there-fore, from the inception of the Israelite *cultus* as such. On this view, the 'conflicting' conceptions of time and history must have co-existed longer than von Rad thinks likely. But these scholars go further. They argue that the cult itself provides evidence that the saving events were conceived as associated historically with one another. The fact that the 'Credo' of Deut. 26. 5–9, which is admitted by both parties to have come from a time soon after the Conquest, does not mention the theme 'Revelation on Sinai' (though it already links three, or perhaps implicitly four, of Noth's five original themes) does not mean, as von Rad and Noth argue, that this block of tradition was still separate. On the contrary, it is likely that the 'Credo' had its *Sitz im Leben* precisely in the regular ceremony of covenant renewal in which the Sinai tradition, according to Noth himself,[1] was at home.[2] Weiser argues a similar case with regard to the other early cultic confession, Josh. 24.[3] And he takes a further step when he goes on to say that it was precisely from the cult that the Pentateuchal sources derived the shape of salvation-history which was to be the foundation of their narratives.

In the festival of the covenant...is to be sought the original cultic environment into which all the Pentateuchal sources were com-pelled by the weight of a living tradition to fit their presentation of the history of salvation. Hence also the Pentateuch as such is not to be judged merely as a literary precipitate of tradition long since detached from the cult (von Rad), but as a fixation of tradition intended for liturgical recitation which sprang directly out of the cult and still stood in active relationship with it.[4]

If Weiser's argument is correct, it would follow that, far from conflicting with Israel's 'historical' understanding of her existence, the cult had a large part in shaping it. But there are independent grounds for believing that von Rad has exagger-ated this conflict.[5] If we take seriously the 'historic' character

---

[1] *History of Israel*, p. 127.   [2] Bright, *op. cit.* p. 105.
[3] Weiser, *op. cit.* pp. 87 f.
[4] *Ibid.* pp. 89 f.
[5] These grounds' independence of Weiser's argument may be to some extent vouched for by citing M. Noth, who, though he shares many of von Rad's *über-lieferungsgeschichtlich* presuppositions, in his essay 'Die Vergegenwärtigung des

of God's acts there is no need to invoke a concept of eternal repetition in order to explain the basis of contemporization in the Israelite cult. Instead of the unrepeatable nature of historical occurrence being compromised, the absolute relation of the saving events to all Israel's life means that they are already, without repetition, 'at hand'.[1] Their being 'epochal' ('historic') means that precisely: they do not disappear into the past along with the 'fathers' of Israel, but bear immediately upon the continuing conditions, moral, spiritual, and material, which they created in the fathers' times.[2] Viewed in the light of this conception, the cult and the 'Überlieferungsprozess' from which the Old Testament histories developed can alike be seen as attempting the 'Vergegenwärtigung und Aktualisierung der Heilsfakten', 'as precisely the endeavour of the Old Testament witnesses to exhibit the basic saving events to each generation as also in their special situation effective and valid'.[3] In the cult Israel can realize afresh the 'wonder' of God's acts of grace and his steadfastness to the covenant. In a religious context of this sort the ostensibly 'mythical' qualities of the Israelite cult ought not to disguise the fact that 'myth' here has lost its autonomy, the rationale of its ritual having been by Israel naturally adapted to the controlling categories of history.[4]

Alten Testaments in der Verkündigung', *EvTh*, xii (1952–3), 6–17 (= *PAH*, pp. 54–68), defends 'contemporization' on grounds similar to those adopted here. It is particularly worth noticing that Noth can say: 'Zur Vergegenwärtigung' (which is, after all, primarily a cultic phenomenon) 'gehört...notwendig die erzählende Weitergabe der geschehenen Wundertat Gottes' (p. 11). Instead of conflicting with the principles of contemporaneity in the cult, in other words, the narratives furthered their effectiveness.

[1] May we interpret in this way what W. Pannenberg says in the long footnote-appendix to his article 'Kerygma und Geschichte'? 'To speak of an act of God (*Handeln Gottes*) with regard to a particular happening means to pronounce a judgment as to its concrete relation to the events more or less directly connected with it and to history as a whole' (*Studien zur Theologie der alttestamentlichen Überlieferungen*, for G. von Rad, pp. 139 f.).

[2] The 'materiality' and 'this-sidedness' of the Old Testament 'Heilsgütern' is stressed by von Rad who points especially to the Old Testament conceptions of 'life' (*hajjim*) and 'well-being' (*salom*) and to the accounts of land-purchase (Gen. 23; Jer. 32. 7 ff.; Gen. 33. 18 f.; II Sam. 24. 24; Ruth 4. 3 ff.) ('Typologische Auslegung des Alten Testaments', *EvTh*, vii, 1952–3, 28). Cf. also W. Eichrodt, *Man in the Old Testament*, pp. 33 f., 49 f. The real concrete historicality of the life under blessing in the Old Testament is typified in this aspect of it.

[3] W. Pannenberg, *art. cit.* p. 137.

[4] Approaching the question from a different direction B. S. Childs reaches similar conclusions. See his *Memory and Tradition in Israel*, pp. 81 ff.

The change which myth's loss of autonomy involved can be seen most clearly, perhaps, in the New Year Festival. Though much of the material of the cult is, beyond question, adopted from the original Canaanite festival, the latter's central conception (which it shared with the analogous festivals in Egypt and Babylonia–Assyria) was excluded from the Israelite version.[1] This was the idea that the defeat, death, and resurrection of the god precede his final victory. This, plainly enough, was 'wholly incompatible with Yahweh's essential character', as Mowinckel says:[2] not only was Yahweh not subject to death or defeat, 'his own power and existence and kingship cannot (even) be threatened by any enemy'.[3] But this theology, with the change it produced, 'affects', as Pedersen observes, 'the very core of the feast. The regeneration concerned becomes, not a regeneration of God, but merely a renewal of his power, or rather of his promise to renew the exercise of that power, that is to say, the Covenant between Yahweh and Israel.'[4] In this way the historical occurrence of God's act—in this case, of his world-creation—remains, as it does not in 'myth', past; but the revelation of God's act, and hence of his nature and will and promise, is through its representation in word or mime re-experienced in all its continuing relevance and vitality. Thus, in the recital or mimetic display of God's acts, in the Israelite festivals, these acts are not brought into being, effected, or in the strictest sense of the phrase, 'made contemporary'; instead, their already existent and existential contemporaneity is proclaimed and realized as 'ever new'. Essentially, this is the 'message' of the festival,[5] and the festival's purpose is the realization of the message:

> Yahweh has 'made known' his victory,
>   he has 'revealed' his vindication...
> he has remembered his steadfast love and faithfulness
>   to the house of Israel.   (Ps. 98. 2–3; cf. 76. 1; 48. 3)

[1] Cf. Mowinckel, *op. cit.* I, 136–40, and Pedersen, *Israel*, III–IV, 440–3.

[2] *Op. cit.* I, 136.

[3] *Ibid.* p. 139.

[4] Pedersen, *op. cit.* III–IV, 442. Cf. J. Barr, 'The Meaning of Mythology in relation to the Old Testament', *VT*, IX (1959), 8 f.

[5] Cf. Mowinckel, *op. cit.* I, 142 f: 'In the festal experience it is first of all through his works, his "saving works"' (I should wish to add, 'in history')...'that Yahweh reveals himself, manifesting to all the world who and what he is. They are the "message" of the festival'.

54

We can now see better how the change from myth to history in the cult legends affects their contemporizing. If, 'in the cultic festival, past and present are welded into one',[1] this is because, as Köhler says, 'past and present are one single act of God'.[2] In liturgy and law, in cult and in the process of development and adaptation which the historical traditions underwent, the 'epochal' and 'historic' past of God's act becomes what already inherently it is: contemporaneous.

And this in turn sends us back to the categories of history. We can see the truth now of another statement of Köhler's: in so far as 'history presupposes the past, and what is past is what has lost its reality..., the Hebrew mind hardly knows the past or history'.[3] But of history in the sense of the 'historic', where the past presupposed is that past which determines the scope of present opportunities, the Israelite is, among the ancients, uniquely aware. His mind is in this sense 'historical' through and through. Beyond this, what James Barr says is true: 'if we ask how this Hebrew interest in the historical arose we are probably forced back on Israel's own confession to the centrality of the Exodus and the events surrounding it'.[4] At all events the records of the Exodus bear witness to the kind of experience which might plausibly bring such an interest about.

What is preserved [says Buber] for us here, is to be regarded not as the 'historization' of a myth, or of a cult-drama, nor is it to be explained as the transposition of something originally beyond time into historical time: a great history-faith does not come into the world through interpretation of the extra-historical as historical, but by receiving an occurrence experienced as a 'wonder', that is, as an event that cannot be grasped except as an act of God. Something happens to us, the cause of which we cannot ascribe to our world; the event has taken place just now, we cannot understand it, we can only believe it (Exod. 14. 31). It is a holy event. We acknowledge the performer.

And Buber quotes the 'undeniably contemporary' 'Song of Moses': 'I will sing unto Yahweh, for he has verily risen, the horse and its rider he has cast into the sea.'[5]

---

[1] *Ibid.* I, 113.   [2] *Hebrew Man*, p. 139.   [3] *Ibid.*
[4] J. Barr, 'The Meaning of Mythology in Relation to the Old Testament', *VT*, IX (1959), 8.
[5] M. Buber, *The Prophetic Faith*, p. 46.

And again, on man's side, whatever 'contemporaneity' in the Israelite cult might imply, it could not, with such an event as its basis, involve, like the rituals of Egypt, a stagnating in their traditions, a perennial *status quo*. Israel is introduced to a realm of which primitive religion can, by its nature, take only limited cognizance: the future. The 'newness' of God's act meant a call to a new life, a new way of life, which the God of 'new things' brings about. 'Contemporaneity' brought man into encounter with God not to restore *status quo*, harmony, the primaeval past which makes normality normative, but to make present to him an altogether new status, which takes him away from natural into historic existence, investing him with a new freedom and a new burden of responsibility.[1] Contemporaneity was not, in other words, in the least an end in itself, as it was in myth, but a means to an end, the assumption of a responsibility before God and to him: to serve.

[1] Cf. Frankfort, in *Before Philosophy*, pp. 245 f.

CHAPTER 4

GOD AND THE FUTURE:
A TYPOLOGY WITHOUT APPLICATION

It is, I think, quite improper to separate from 'typology' those features of Old Testament thought on the nature of man's historicality *vis-à-vis* the action of God which I have just traced. For they bear upon that subject with the greatest suggestiveness. We have found an emphasis on history as the realm of encounter with God through God's activity. We have discussed the dialectic between 'newness' and 'steadfast love' in the quality of God's activity, the relation between the new possibility created by one act of God, if faith apprehends it as such, and the sense of that new possibility's *actuality* confirmed by faith's apprehension of new acts of God. If therefore God's activity reveals him to be 'steadfast' it follows that any one divine act may present itself to faith as the promise, confirmation or fulfilment of another. The qualities (grace, salvation, judgement, etc.) which each act shares with others, and through which one learns to attribute steadfastness to God, allow each act, as perceived, to be taken as a 'sign', as 'typical' and 'true' to the God of whom tradition, or the prophet, tells. That God's acts were taken as such, as 'types' therefore, I believe is sufficiently manifest.

But it was not a quality in God, merely, which his actions showed. It was also a purpose, a purpose accomplished—something in the indicative, 'done'—and yet, for each generation and individual, something imperative, to be done. This part of the purpose was Israel's service, and to make this purpose immediate to each generation the constitutive saving acts which created the opportunity of service and made its demand inescapable were represented in word, and, probably, in some kind of mime. So far as it was at all attainable, moreover, the 'fulfilment' of the demand of God by man's obedience was itself a mime, a mimesis. For it showed the 'ways' of God, was a 'following' of him, like that of the fathers. And this is so intricately connected with the foregoing belief in the steadfast-

57

ness of God, was indeed so much the intention, or at least the necessary result of that belief, that this too would vastly impoverish the whole conception of 'typology' if it were dissociated from it. I have therefore headed the last chapter with the words 'applied typology'.

Yet clearly the fulfilment of 'types' in the cult and the law—or rather, in worship and obedience—is not the whole of typology nor the chief context or most common connotation of the term. One might, indeed, reading the modern debate on the subject, have the impression, and excusably, that there is in fact no connection.[1] Partly, no doubt, this results from the extreme reaction against allegorizing the Scriptures which is to be found not only in Protestantism but at least in some measure in Roman Catholicism. A distinction was rightly drawn between allegorism and typology, but because 'typology' has in this day and age been so often defined in the terms most likely to make plain that distinction—e.g. as 'historical', 'factual', as against 'merely spiritual' and 'in terms of general moral truths'—certain elements in the phenomenon of biblical typology have been understressed or ignored. Chiefly, it is the *function* that has been ignored, the phenomenon's critical usage in the Old Testament to confront man with the action of God. Because of this, typology tends to appear somewhat wooden, a mechanical game of contrivance which may or may not have some validity in so far as it shows 'that there is a correspondence between historical realities at different stages in sacred history',[2] but which, if left merely at that, is of purely aesthetic interest. Lampe, Phythian-Adams, Hebert, Daniélou, de Lubac, almost all the contemporary defenders of 'typology' ignore its critical character as the 'word' of God's act—more exactly, of his new act—which faces the present with an existential decision and a call to a new existence.

And to this danger another is related. For when typology is limited to the correspondence between one 'sacred era' and

---

[1] Symptomatic in this respect is J. Muilenburg's discussion of contemporary biblical hermeneutics, where (as indeed the situation dictates) the author distinguishes three approaches: the new 'chastened and disciplined' typology of von Rad and others, M. Noth's appeal to the way in which Israel 'contemporized' past events, and the 'current existentialist approach to the problems of interpretation', 'Preface to Hermeneutics', *JBL*, LXXVII (1958), 20 f.

[2] J. Daniélou, 'The Fathers and the Scriptures', *Theology*, LVII (March 1954).

another,[1] typology's claim to be existentially relevant is apt to be lost along with the interim periods.[2] In face of this tendency Zimmerli's emphasis on the continuity between 'promise' and 'fulfilment' is welcome; for between these two, which are both themselves present in history, the Old Testament sets not a gap or hiatus but movement, process, development,[3] which can certainly not be described in straightforward *heilsgeschichtlich* terms as progress or regress, as upward or downward sloping lines, but in which God's grace and judgement are at work continuously.

Now although Zimmerli calls neither this 'interim process' nor the relationship between 'promise' and 'fulfilment' by the name of 'typology', it will be seen from what has already been said that I believe it legitimate to do so. Certainly, if one is to call the historical correspondence 'typology' one should use the word also for the interim. For in this interim too the historical correspondence exists, even if, as the Old Testament makes plain, it exists only equivocally. For in the period following the election of Israel, the nation lives in ambiguous actualization of the promise inferred from God's act. Man in Israel is in general both blessed and rejected. His fulfilment of the way of Yahweh is never complete, but always in promise. Like his forebears in the wilderness, he both 'wanders' and 'follows Yahweh', existing on the border-lines of faith. He thus also foreshadows total fulfilment, and foreshadows total rejection. Either way, forwards or back, he is 'typical' of man's response to the action of God. The past involves him; the future calls him to a closer imitation of God, to a more complete 'sonship' of Yahweh.[4]

[1] See, for example, W. J. Phythian-Adams, *The Way of At-one-ment*, pp. 5, 17, 19, etc., where the one 'sacred era', the Exodus, is said to be recapitulated by the other, the Incarnation. I do not think it affects the point about 'recapitulation' to say that this limitation of the 'sacred' to 'eras' is untenable. Cf. R. Rendtorff, 'Geschichte und Überlieferung', quoted on p. 31 n. above.

[2] Cf. R. Rendtorff, 'Hermeneutik des Alten Testaments als Frage nach der Geschichte', *ZThK*, LVII (1960), 33; von Rad, *Theologie des Alten Testaments*, II, 381 f.

[3] W. Zimmerli, 'Verheissung und Erfüllung', *EvTh*, XII (1952/3), 34–59, reprinted in *PAH*, pp. 69–101.

[4] Cf. G. Cooke, 'The Israelite King as Son of God', *ZAW*, N.F. 32 (1961), 225: as well as being 'actual' Israel's sonship of Yahweh was 'potential'; 'the sonship of both Israel and the Davidic kings was eschatological in the sense that its fulfilment and full blessing was hoped for and could be fulfilled only by covenant faithfulness and righteousness'.

In agreement with this, the past did not, in the Hebrew cult for example, *mean* the present, but involved it. And the converse of this was, that the present was, so to speak, the 'subfulfilment' of the past, no more and no less.[1]

It was a 'subfulfilment' obviously and immediately in one way, of course, simply because the empirical Israel was still afflicted by sufferings. The existence of enemies, even, quite apart from the problem created by defeat at their hands, rendered Israel's life tenuous. The same could be said for any form of adversity. And the fact must have tended, quite early in Israelite history, to turn the national hope to the future, for if their God *was* God, his power and his favour could not be exhausted by the mere gift of a land. That history was not yet in perfect conformity with the will of Yahweh was observable, and that at some day it would be so was, long before the canonical prophets, an article of faith—something implied in part, perhaps, already by the early theology of Holy War, where worship of Yahweh meant sharing in his battles[2] for the fulfilment of purposes not yet accomplished. But it was more than implied, it was explicit, in the monarchical period, in the Jahwistic narrative. Here history is the bearer of promise, and as such points to fulfilment. The motif controls the whole work,[3] which sets its narrative in a frame which stretches, in principle, from creation to eschatology.[4] In this narrative the main creative basis of promise is of course the patriarch-history,[5] and the promise is one which has been at any rate to a large extent fulfilled already by the conquest following the Exodus. Yet J's purpose is not to describe the existing state of the nation as if Yahweh's aim was attained. The growth of a nation from Abraham (Gen. 12. 2), and the gift of the land to his descendents (12. 7) are only two parts of a threefold promise and the third part still awaits its accomplishment: in Abraham all the

---

[1] With this term, 'subfulfilment', we may compare the Old Testament's occasional use of to 'fill after' God—i.e. wholly to follow him: Num. 32. 11 f.; cf. also Num. 14. 24; Deut. 1. 36; Josh. 14. 8 f. and 14. 14; I Kings 11. 6. See C. F. D. Moule, 'Fulfil' in the *Interpreter's Dictionary of the Bible*.

[2] Cf. M. Buber, *The Prophetic Faith*, pp. 8–12 ('The Song of Deborah') and p. 19.

[3] See von Rad, *Genesis*, pp. 21 f.

[4] A. Weiser, *Introduction to the Old Testament*, pp. 110 f.

[5] 'Die ganze Vätergeschichte schon des Jahwisten tritt unter das Zeichen der Verheissung' (W. Zimmerli, 'Verheissung und Erfüllung', *EvTh*, XII (1952/3), 36 = *PAH*, p. 71).

nations of earth will be blessed (12. 3). Of the fulfilment of this third part the fulfilment of the other two is the guarantee. Indeed, this third part is even strengthened as promise by the fact that the other two have already, by their fulfilment, half-fulfilled *it*. Or rather, if it is true that the Jahwist added this promise to the two handed down by tradition,[1] their fulfilment itself creates this new promise, for it indicates a movement of increase in the kingdom of Yahweh, whose final scope includes all men.[2] Meanwhile, the narrator's own time is in tension. Standing in subfulfilment, or in 'the first stage of fulfilment',[3] Israel is summoned and drawn to the future.[4]

History's perfect conformity with Yahweh's will is thus still awaited. There is plenty of evidence that in popular belief a narrowly nationalist optimism confused Yahweh's will here with their own will: in this case the less than Utopian conditions of their own existence led to a concept of a future 'Day of Yahweh' when these things would not be as they were, when Yahweh would scatter their enemies once and for all and so 'justify' or 'vindicate' his people. And against this stands the outbreak of Amos:

> Woe to you who desire the day of Yahweh!
> Why would you have the day of Yahweh?
> It is darkness, and not light... (Amos 5. 18)

But still, in the classical prophets, and increasingly from the time of the Exile,[5] some kind of final triumph of Yahweh's purposes is often envisaged, a 'kingdom of God' in which there

---

[1] As for example von Rad holds: cf. his *Genesis*, p. 23 and pp. 154–6.

[2] Von Rad considers this a 'prophetic' message on the part of the Jahwist (*Genesis*, p. 23) and quotes B. Jacobs' commentary on Genesis (Berlin, 1934) where it is called 'a command to history' (*ibid.* p. 156). Certainly it was reaffirmed by the great prophets, by Isaiah (2. 2–4), Jeremiah (2. 3), and of course Deutero-Isaiah (42. 4–6; etc.): and already, possibly, it is presupposed by Amos (6. 1; cf. M. Buber, *The Prophetic Faith*, p. 99). Cf. also Isa. 19. 19–25, where the promise fulfilled for Israel at the Exodus is promised to the Egyptians in turn!

[3] Von Rad, *Old Testament Theology*, I, 175.

[4] That J's view of this matter is representative for the Old Testament generally is easily proved. We shall confirm it in passing in the course of our discussion of prophecy. Cf. also von Rad's essay in *PAH*, esp. pp. 16 f.; and W. Zimmerli in the same volume, pp. 89–92: 'All Old Testament history, in so far as it is guided and initiated by God's word, has the character of fulfilment; but in the very fulfilment of promise there lies a new promise.'

[5] Cf. Eichrodt, *Theology of the Old Testament*, I, 485–6.

would be peace among men,[1] and no more tears (Isa. 25. 8) or hunger or thirst (Isa. 49. 10), a time of vindication—but a vindication of Yahweh rather, perhaps, than the nation.[2] And so far as that goal is concerned the most that worship and service contained was a faint foreshadowing, a prolepsis.[3] Real 'fulfilment' lies in the future, and it comes from the action of God.

Thus prophet and people in Israel look first to the quarry from which they were hewn (Isa. 51. 1), and from the past draw their conclusions as to the imminent future and the last times— the Messianic Age, the day of Yahweh, and the goal of history. Alike, they look back to the Exodus and to other events in the past as manifestations of God, and in each case a confidence gained from such looking back supported their optimism. So important was it to the prophet to be able to show the congruity of his message with the revelation of the God of the Exodus that Deuteronomy seems to lay down a test of his teaching's continuity with the past as what Marsh calls the first and fundamental test of a prophet's integrity:

If there arise among you a prophet, or a dreamer of dreams, and gives you a sign or a wonder, and the sign or wonder which he tells you comes to pass, and if he says, 'Let us go after other gods', which you have not known, and 'let us serve them', you shall not listen to the words of that prophet or to that dreamer of dreams; for Yahweh your God is testing you...But that prophet or dreamer of dreams shall be put to death, because he has taught rebellion against Yahweh your God, who brought you out of the land of Egypt and redeemed you out of the house of bondage.   (Deut. 13. 1–3 a, 5 a)

---

[1] See, for example, the oracle now contained in Isa. 2. 2–4 and Mic. 4. 1–3, with its famous lines describing the changing of armour into implements.

[2] Cf. H. H. Rowley's essay 'The Day of the Lord' in *The Faith of Israel*, pp. 177–201; also Th. C. Vriezen,' Prophecy and Eschatology', *VT* (suppl.) I, 199–229; G. von Rad, *Theologie des Alten Testaments*, II, 125–37; and R. E. Clements, *Prophecy and Comment*, pp. 103–18.

[3] We do not enter here into the question of whether eschatology in Israel developed out of the cult. A convenient summary of the debate up to the war is in H. W. Robinson's *Inspiration and Revelation in the Old Testament*, pp. 138–43. Among recent discussions cf. Mowinckel, *op. cit.* I, 186–92, and Lindblom, *Prophecy in Ancient Israel*, pp. 316–22. I would espouse Lindblom's conclusion: 'The pattern of death and life, distress and salvation, typical of the prophets, did not derive from the cult; its origin is to be found in the basic religious ideas of Israel, inherited from the past and, of course..., reflected in the Yahwistic cult' (p. 321). As to the varying attitudes of the prophets to the, after all, varying cult, cf. *ibid.* pp. 351–60 and 383 f., and R. E. Clements, *op. cit.* pp. 86–102.

'The exclusive relationship of Yahweh with Israel', comments Eichrodt on this passage, 'constitutes the axiomatic standard for the prophetic message, and it is not to be questioned simply because the prophet can demonstrate signs and wonders.'[1]

Purely as a matter of mechanics, therefore, the prophetic faith, like the popular, can look to the future and see it in terms of the past, though the past is to be transcended. There is no need to multiply instances. A small book by D. W. B. Robinson provides a working collection:

There would be a new Exodus, a new redemption from slavery, and a new entry into the land of promise (Jer. 16. 14 f.);[2] a new covenant and a new law (Jer. 31. 31–4). No foe would invade the promised inheritance, 'but they shall sit every man under his vine and under his fig-tree' (Mic. 4. 4). There would be a new Jerusalem (Isa. 26. 1; Ezek. 40) and a new David to be God's shepherd over Israel (Jer. 23. 5; Ezek. 34. 23 f.) and a new temple where perfect worship would be offered, and from which a perfect law would go forth (Isa. 2. 2–4; Ezek. 40–6).[3]

Of course, the expectations here listed by Robinson cannot all be assumed to have existed in the popular faith as well as in the message of the prophets. It is, for example, extremely unlikely that the popular religion conceived of an improvement in the Law. But the significant fact remains: basically, in the prophets and among the people, prediction or expectation is typological in structure: the past provides analogical signs of the future. And probably, so far as these so to speak 'deductive' processes were concerned, there would be little tangible difference either between the oracles of degenerate nabism—which was still Yahwistic in name (cf. Jer. 14. 14; 29. 9; Ezek. 13. 6; 22. 28)—and the later oracles of the return from exile which entered the tradition as authoritative prophecy—for example the one now found in Isa. 11 (*vv.* 11 f., 15 f.): 'Yahweh will extend his hand yet a second time...';

> And there will be a highway from Assyria
>   for the remnant which is left of his people,
> as there was for Israel
>   when they came up from the land of Egypt.

---

[1] Eichrodt, *op. cit.* I, 334.
[2] Needless to say, these references are far from exhaustive.
[3] D. W. B. Robinson, *The Hope of Christ's Coming*, p. 11.

This, and similar analogical structures provided the oracles with a ready self-explanation, almost, one may say, with an apologetic.

The questions raised by this are plain enough, but important. For the prophets' use of typology is called in question, on grounds which we share with Bultmann, if, on what I have called the 'deductive' level, these predictions are not only indistinguishable from, but necessarily bound up with, the objective and *weltanschaulich* view of God's acts which we look upon as illegitimate. This point is, I think, on the logical or hypothetical level, sufficiently answered above (pp. 28–32): legitimate speech about God's future acts is no more to be absolved from the conditions of faith and commitment than is discourse about God's acts in the past. And on the empirical level this is the answer made by the prophets themselves. It was of course not in these terms, but it was in this spirit, that they distinguished themselves and their 'word' from the words and the prophets which and whom they called 'false'. The condition of faith, the self-commitment of the man to his message, is taken so seriously by the Old Testament prophets that it gains real literary-critical importance for the exposition of their work. The difference between the legitimate and the illegitimate typological prophecy rests then again, in large part, on the distinction between an 'applied' typology and a typology 'without application'. The legitimate form, at least of weal-prophecy, always demands that the people surrender themselves to God's purpose.

Thus, on the one hand, the prophets are not less concerned with history than the people. It is in history, as Lindblom has recently fully confirmed, rather than in introspection, that the prophets have the deepest source of their knowledge of God, just as it is to the well-being of the community rather than to individual mystical union that they direct their efforts.[1] And, on the other hand, their interpretation of history is, compared with that of the false prophets, less tainted with what we should today call 'historicism', a view of history as a movement leading visibly as well as inevitably towards a definite goal. Still, the prophet has a kind of assurance. Believing that God is

---

[1] Cf. Lindblom, *op. cit.* pp. 306–11. This is not to deny the charismatic nature of their office, which they themselves stress.

steadfast, eternal, faithful, he believes that the acts in which his faith sees God's hand were and are typical of God's other acts. Upon his understanding of the past, therefore, will depend his understanding of the future. He expects, or rather believes, for it may be in spite of appearances (the natural basis for expectation), that in similar circumstances God's present and future acts will conform with his past.[1] Though the mediators of God's work differ, and his instruments alter, with the historical situation, the tendency of that work is constant: salvation and judgement.[2] It is not therefore, and here we come to the other main grounds of distinction, for their reliance on history that the people and their popular soothsayers are at fault.[3] Rather, it is the fault indicated by Eichrodt when, having noted that for the prophets the whole of past history is filled with divine revelation, he goes on to say: 'So far from finding fault with their people for expecting special acts of God, they regard them as to blame for not taking sufficiently seriously God's real intervention in their destinies, both in the past and in the present, and for seeking instead to safeguard their position with all kinds of earthly assistance.'[4] Whether Eichrodt had it in mind at this stage to include under 'all kinds' not merely earthly assistance but earthly assurance, there is no means of telling. He was certainly aware it could happen, for he had already affirmed that it was precisely the historical inheritance of Israel—whose continuity the prophets deliberately affirmed—'which was capable of neutralizing, or at least weakening, the terrifying force of the divine threat to human existence—and in popular belief had in fact already done so'. 'It was just because men thought they knew this God so well', he continues, 'that they felt secure in their relationship with him, and believed that they could relax in comfortable confidence: "It is not he; neither shall evil come upon us" (Jer. 5. 12; cf. 6. 14).'[5]

---

[1] Cf. J. Marsh, *The Fulness of Time*, p. 55.   [2] Cf. Lindblom, *op. cit.* p. 311.

[3] Cf. N. W. Porteous, 'Prophecy' in *Record and Revelation*, ed. H. W. Robinson, pp. 240–1, who expresses it thus: 'While it is true...that to the prophets Yahweh was the Lord of history, their interest in history was for the most part confined to it as the sphere in which man was brought into direct relation to God in judgment and redemption, not as the sphere in which God was co-operating with man to further common interests. This is what the "false prophets" could not understand.' Cf. also E. Oswald, *Falsche Prophetie im Alten Testament*, p. 29; J. Lindblom, *Prophecy in Ancient Israel*, pp. 213 f.; Pedersen, *Israel*, III–IV, 142.

[4] *Theology of the Old Testament*, I, 370.   [5] *Ibid.* p. 349.

To this comfort Amos already opposes his message of woe: 'It is darkness, and not light' (Amos 5. 18); and until the exile this note was the prevalent one in canonical prophecy. And it leads us to ask therefore, whether, in the prophecies of doom, the prophets were departing from, even rejecting, the typological pattern of so many weal-prophecies, or if, alternatively, the typological interpretation of history upon which the doom-prophecies rely is one almost wholly at odds with popular conceptions. It is hard from the evidence so far presented to determine which case is true. But there are indications that it is the second.

> I form light and create darkness,
> I make weal and create woe:
> I, who do all these things, am the Lord. (Isa. 45. 7)

We must consider these indications, and develop the arguments arising, in the next chapter.

CHAPTER 5

MAN AND THE FUTURE:
AN EXISTENTIAL TYPOLOGY

WE have shown how fundamental to Old Testament law is its historical basis. It is not simply that the law was given in history at Mount Sinai, but that the ethical norm it establishes is based on the nature of the God whose historical self-revelation effected the new existence of Israel: of this existence the divine self-revelation provided the ideal pattern. In the covenant-concept, description and prescription were thus brought together, the imperative with the indicative. What already they *were* in the covenant, by virtue of God's act, now—in each present time—they *must* be, or forfeit the blessing.

We have also noticed how in the liturgy, as well as in the forms into which the Law often was cast, the Israelite was confronted with God's past acts so that if in faith he obeyed the call which those acts involved he partook of the new life of a man under grace, under God's steadfast love, instead of returning to a merely natural existence at the mercy of nature. In the prophecies, as in this case, the purely descriptive indicative is nothing without the response of commitment—or rather, it brings man under judgement: he refuses, by his neglect of the way of life in the blessing, to live in the blessing, and so comes under the curse.

It is the claim of the prophets, and indeed of the whole Old Testament, that this is what Israel has done. Naïve or expedient optimism among the professional prophets, like the popular distortion of the covenant-idea into a claim upon Yahweh's exclusive favour, the stipulations being forgotten, has spread in Israel a false sense of security.[1] Micah quotes the popular belief:

[1] Cf. J. Lindblom, *Prophecy in Ancient Israel*, pp. 210–15 and 329 f., where he notes that the pre-exilic prophets make little reference to the covenant, presumably because 'the juridical character of this idea led the people to make claims on Yahweh and to cherish ambitious dreams of a supposedly inevitable glorious future'. To the prophets 'the essential was not the claim of the people on Yahweh, but Yahweh's claim on Israel', to which the election-idea gave more unequivocal expression.

> Is not Yahweh in the midst of us?
> No misfortune can come upon us. (3. 11)

Confident as to God's favour, Israel's leaders pervert truth into falsehood: they have said in effect:

> We have made a covenant with death,
>   and with Sheol we have an agreement;
> when the overwhelming scourge passes through
>   it will not come to us;
> for we have made lies our refuge,
>   and in falsehood we have taken shelter. (Isa. 28. 15)

False prophets conspire to keep the true Word of Yahweh from the leaders' hearing (e.g. Amos 7. 10–17). The case of Micaiah ben Imlah (I Kings 22) foreshadows many another. Prophet and priest both deal falsely (Jer. 6. 13):

> They have healed the wound of my people lightly,
>   saying, 'Peace, peace',
> when there is no peace.
>   (Jer. 6. 14; 8. 11; 14. 13; etc.; cf. also Mic. 3. 5)

And because the blessing they prophesy is apparently quite unconditional, requiring nothing from its recipients but the status of Hebrew, no repentance, no new way of life, it is not the covenant blessing at all, say the prophets, and for that blessing Israel by its sins does not qualify. Therefore, says the God of the prophets, in the next verse of Jeremiah to that just quoted—it is one of many examples—

> 'Therefore they shall fall among those who fall;
>   at the time that I punish them,
>   they shall be overthrown',
>   says the Lord. (Jer. 6. 15 b)

It would appear then that to the classical prophets of Israel a prediction of well-being that is not grounded in covenant, or—what amounts in the last analysis to the same thing—in a true and deep understanding of history as distinct from one merely superficial, leads the people into faithlessness and brings on them well-being's opposite, woe. The nation's sufferings, in this case, acquire in the prophets a new meaning. Not merely do they make visible the plain fact that the goal of history is not yet attained, they also stand as judgements on faithlessness, they spring from the people's rejection of the existence which God's acts make possible. The prophets regard the central theme of the history of Israel since the Exodus, therefore, as that of 'God's controversy with his people for their failure to live by their credo, his destruction of the nation by successive stages',[1] for 'any nation which went so stubbornly against the will of its God as to make the entire pattern of its life, in the state, in social conditions and in cultic organization, into a conspiracy against Yahweh (cf. Jer. 11. 9), a systematic rejection of his exclusive sovereignty, had forfeited the right to exist'.[2] Still it is history that provides them with evidence for this view, and still it is history as showing man's confrontation with God. 'Throughout the nation's history this turning away from God has from the very first', they find, 'been present as the woof in the web.'

Hosea sees the mendacious character of Israel's inmost soul already prefigured in the patriarch Jacob; from Egypt onwards the nation has tried to escape from God's guidance; the entry into Canaan was synonymous with a falling away from Yahweh (cf. Hos. 12. 4, 13; 11. 1 f.; 9. 10)—in short, every incident of its history exhibits the nation's ungrateful and rebellious spirit (cf. Amos 4. 6 ff.; Isa. 9. 7 ff.). Their present disobedience is but the working out of a permanent attitude of mind (cf. Ezek. 20; Jer. 7. 24 ff.).[3]

And outside the prophets the same fundamental criticism is levelled in Pss. 78 and 106, for example.

When this view of past history is linked, therefore—as it must be, given the tenuousness of present existence—with the idea of an eschatological goal and a 'day of Yahweh', it endorses and sharpens the prediction of woe. For the nation's continual sin affronts Yahweh, as it did in the past,[4] all the more because much was given (Amos 2. 2). And by 'walking contrary' to God Israel is bound to bring judgement upon herself, for she 'walks contrary' to a history governed by him. Nor are the

---

[1] G. E. Wright, 'The Faith of Israel', *IB*, p. 351.
[2] Eichrodt, *Theology of the Old Testament*, I, 379.
[3] *Ibid.* pp. 376–7.
[4] The fact is confessed in the earliest Pentateuchal narratives (J and E), which already contain the tradition of the wilderness 'murmurings' long before it received its stress in the 'classical' prophets.

operations of this judgement confined to 'the last day'. The prophets see it in the events of their own time or in the imminent future, even if its manifestation and climax is reserved for the end, when Yahweh will remove all evil from his sight, 'for his name's sake', so that all glory in him.[1]

Clearly, therefore, such prophecies—equally with the weal-prophecies—are basically typological. They constitute a typology of man's rejection of God's act and word, and their validity, like the weal-prophecies', rests on the repeated confrontation in history of man with God's acts, and on the believed steadfastness of the God of that confrontation. And for that reason, simply, it continually happens that one and the same event, whether past or future, produces both blessing and woe, since upon man's response these depend. Pre-eminent in this respect is the wilderness-journey. In Ps. 95 that history calls to the present for a purer response and commitment than that of the fathers:

> O that today you would hearken to his voice!
>   Harden not your hearts, as at Meribah,
>   as on the day at Massah in the wilderness,
> when your fathers tested me,
>   and put me to the proof, though they had seen my work.
> For forty years I loathed that generation
>   and said, 'They are a people who err in heart,
>   and they do not regard my ways'.   (*vv.* 7*b*–10)

And in Ezek. 20, after an extensive account of the same history, of the provocation of God by the people's rebelliousness and God's withholding his hand again and again 'for the sake of his name', it is cast, at *v.* 33, into the future:

As I live, says the Lord God, surely with a mighty hand and an outstretched arm, and with wrath poured out, I will be king over you. I will bring you out from the peoples and gather you out of the countries where you are scattered...and I will bring you into the wilderness of the peoples, and there I will enter into judgement with you face to face. As I entered into judgement with your fathers in the wilderness of the land of Egypt, so I will enter into judgement with you, says the Lord God...I will purge out the rebels from among you, and those who transgress against me; I will bring them

---

[1] Cf. L. Morris, *The Biblical Doctrine of Judgment*, esp. pp. 20–5, 41–3.

out of the land where they sojourn, but they shall not enter the land of Israel. Then you will know that I am the Lord.[1] (*vv.* 33–6, 38)

Weal-prophecy or woe-prophecy, the God whose activity gives new dimensions to man's existence, with each act gives him the need to choose and the opportunity of rejecting both God and the new existence, to choose life or death, to live under judgement or grace.

It is important to note that in this prophetic typology, and the passage just quoted will instance it, the future is as critically related to the present as the past is in the liturgy and law. God's acts are critical, and the word of them, even the promising, threatening, word, is genuine only if this fact is taken seriously. The future's claims are as categorical as those of the past; and their overwhelming sense of this fact leads the prophets to present in their message a call to 'live up to' the future of God. Even in its proclamation, therefore, Yahweh's future activity, like his past, rests on the present as imperative as well as indicative. This means, in part, what we have already asserted, that prediction, and typological prediction, is not the final object of prophecy or typology.[2] They have existential objectives, they relate to the 'now' of decision. The term 'contemporaneity', therefore, applies to the future action of God as it did to his past.[3] The distinctions of past, present and future no doubt existed even to the minds of the prophets, and the identity of 'times' which have the same 'contents' has no doubt been over-stressed.[4] Nevertheless, sometimes the distinction is

[1] On this text, the only one in Ezekiel announcing a new Exodus and also, interestingly, the only one in which Yahweh is affirmed to be king, see the account by W. Zimmerli, 'Le nouvel "Exode" dans le message des deux grands prophètes de l'Exil', *Hommage à W. Vischer*, pp. 217–21.

[2] Indeed, in so far as 'prediction' is taken to be a soothsaying of future chains of material happenings, to be validated by their occurrence, it is not at all the concern of the prophets. Zimmerli makes the point admirably: 'Yahweh himself is the future of which they speak' ('Verheissung und Erfüllung', *PAH*, p. 83). 'The prophetic promise at its deepest proclaims not, in the way of a soothsayer, a coming *something*, but rather the coming of Him who comes, as he kills, and as he calls to life' (p. 85).

[3] Cf. M. Noth, 'Die Vergegenwärtigung des Alten Testaments in der Verkündigung', *EvTh*, xii (1952/3), 12 f. (= *PAH*, p. 62).

[4] We refer again to Barr's criticism of Marsh, J. A. T. Robinson and Boman, *Biblical Words for Time*, pp. 20–32. See also B. S. Childs, *Myth and Reality in the Old Testament*, pp. 78–9, and H. and H. A. Frankfort's discussion of what they call 'coalescence in time', *Before Philosophy*, pp. 33 f.

blurred, and the prophets interweave past, present, and the near and distant future in order to make all times impinge on the present to which they speak Yahweh's word.[1] In Deutero-Isaiah's picture of the ransomed returning from Babylon the present is made to seem an image of the 'end' in much the same way as, a few verses earlier, the Creation-myth stood as an image of the crossing over the Sea of Reeds. All four acts, indeed, reflect and interpret each other (Isa. 51. 9–11), and their juxtaposition gives to the present time an eschatological urgency (vv. 4–8): 'Rouse yourself, rouse yourself, stand up, O Jerusalem' (v. 17). And Marsh cites a passage in Amos:

He begins by dealing with the present condition of the nation... (2. 6–8). He then recalls what God did for them 'at that time' when he first called them... (vv. 9 f.). And then he passes to the assertion of God's action in the future: 'Hear this word that the Lord hath spoken against you, O children of Israel, against the whole family which I brought up out of the land of Egypt, saying, You only have I known of all the families of the earth: therefore I will visit upon you all your iniquities' (3. 1–2).[2]

The end-time is made to appear almost present in many passages, in order that the disobedient and complacent nation may realize her situation and, perhaps, take the opportunity of repentance. For example, Amos says in the name of Yahweh, 'The end is come upon my people Israel' (8. 2); and at the other end of prophetic period Joel links a contemporary plague of locusts with the future judgement by Yahweh, throwing, as Weiser says, 'the light of eschatology on to the present moment'[3] (chh. 1–2). We are to infer from these passages that Israel must reckon with Yahweh's wrath now, before its force breaks upon her.

Similarly, with the picture in Jer. 4. 23–6 of the return of chaos:

[1] Vriezen notes that 'in Israel no fundamental distinction was made between things to come (without any further definition), indicating the limit of the speaker's horizon, and the future taken absolutely' (art. cit. p. 202, cf. pp. 223 f.); but we should reckon with the fact that apart from prophecy we have little to go on to substantiate this as a general truth, and in prophecy, after all, it may very well be an expedient: cf. Ezek. 12. 27 f.

[2] The Fulness of Time, pp. 55 f.

[3] A. Weiser, Introduction to the Old Testament, p. 241.

I looked at the earth, and lo, there was chaos;
    at the heavens, and their light was gone.
I looked at the mountains, and lo, they were quaking;
    and all the hills swayed to and fro.
I looked, and lo, there was no man,
    and all the birds of the air had flown.
I looked, and lo, the garden land was a desert,
    and all its cities were ravaged
      before Yahweh, before his fierce anger.

According to Lindblom, we are to see in this passage not eschatology 'absolute' but a visionary picture of universal destruction used by the prophet to represent the coming devastation of Judah;[1] Judah's doom will have something of an eschatological quality: it is Yahweh's judgement on the nation being 'realized'. The prophet could not very well have uttered his warning with more sense of urgency than this method produces.

Here again the contrast with the 'false prophets' is obvious enough. The true prophets' visions are, like Ezekiel's vision of the future temple, shown to 'the house of Israel' that 'they may be ashamed of their iniquities' (Ezek. 43. 10), but the prophecies of *šalom* (peace) to which Jeremiah refers in an oracle already partially quoted have no thought that there is any such need (Jer. 6. 15). If these prophecies have any implication for the present it is not that the present should bring forth fruits meet for repentance (Ezek. 13. 4; Lam. 2. 14). By this failure they are not merely neutral in their effect upon Israel's history. By instilling an illusion of security with their weal-prophecies the false prophets hasten the inevitable judgement. When it comes, with the taking of Jerusalem and the captivity, 'This was for the sins of her prophets' (Lam. 4. 13, cf. 12). This is true in a special sense, for the false prophets have even prevented their words coming true by not demanding the one thing that might make for a restoration of the people's fortunes, repentance:

They have not exposed your iniquity
    to restore your fortunes,
but have seen for you oracles
    false and misleading.   (Lam. 2. 14)

[1] Lindblom, *op. cit.* p. 127.

73

These points are, as I said, obvious enough. But they do cast the light of contrast on to the extreme existentiality of true prophetic typology. In the false prophets neither eschatology nor history is laid before the present as challenge. As against 'applied' typology in the great prophets, their typology, such as it is, is 'unapplied', 'without application'. They speak 'peace' in Yahweh's name, creating complacency on account of his mighty acts, instead of calling the nation to surrender itself to the existence which those acts create.

Thus, in the message of God's future act, in the prophets, that act confronts man and tries him: it asks him whether he will surrender himself to the divine purpose or no. The words which the prophets had to speak, Eichrodt writes, 'did not concern God as he is, permeating all things, but God as he is to come, summoning all men to answer to himself', an 'all-questioning power'.[1] And in a situation in which a certain improvement in detail of the national *status quo* was regarded as all that was still left to come, the new vision of a future irruption of God came with both novelty and shock, judging Israel for the shallowness of her faith (cf. Isa. 29. 13–14) and calling her to shape a new life in response to the challenge of the divine will. In face of this questioning God, 'the only way in which human action (could) escape from futility, and share in the genesis of the new reality, (was) as a decision taken in view of the divine advent';[2] it is in this way that Israel is called to participate in the 'wonder' of God's new creation while it lies still in the future: by faith in the word, by response to the call, she will find herself, even in the midst of the suffering and judgement which break upon present existence, standing as a 'sign'[3] of the future, perfect, kingdom of God.

[1] *Theology of the Old Testament*, I, 345–6.
[2] *Ibid.* p. 388.
[3] It is not irrelevant to point out here that 'sign' in Hebrew (*'oth* or *mopheth*) has a more resticted sense than my usage here necessarily requires. This is well brought out by Tinsley (*op. cit.* pp. 56–9), the gist of whose remarks I here summarize. The word refers to events or realities which are self-authenticating only to the faith of the humble and obedient; in itself ambiguous, it can be truly interpreted only by the faithful; others misconstrue it. One man's sign, therefore, to adapt the adage, is another man's stumbling-block (Isa. 8. 14). This explains how 'signs' in the Old Testament came to be associated with 'temptations' or tests: on the one hand Israel tests Yahweh by demanding more and more proofs, on the other hand Israel is itself tested by its understanding or failing to understand the signs that Yahweh has given. For this reason Israel 'erred' in the wilderness and for this reason the

Here once more, but now at its profoundest, is the idea of service as 'subfulfilment' of the purpose of God. In a life such as Israel was called to, the indicatives of the covenant would be confirmed by the fulfilment of its imperatives. And at the same time the indicatives of eschatological prediction would find their foreshadowing 'types' in the community which accepts as applying to itself the prophetic imperative to 'live eschatological existence', paradoxically here in the present but pointing the way of future fulfilment, as signs of the way of God.[1]

The failure of Israel to do this, or even to perceive its necessity, led almost inevitably to the doctrine of the 'righteous remnant'. From the time of Elijah (I Kings 19. 18) onwards we see a belief growing that through the sins of the nation at large Israel's blessing is forfeited, or becomes the heritage only of the righteous of the nation. In Isaiah this remnant appears, significantly, as in some sense an eschatological, or 'proto-eschatological', community, grouped about the prophet as his disciples (Isa. 8. 2, 16) and under his influence turning away from the nation which stays unrepentant on the brink of disaster, to become, like the prophet himself and his sons, 'signs and portents in Israel from the Lord of hosts' (Isa. 8. 18).[2] An important change has come about between these two conceptions, though, emphatically, they are not contradictory. The remnant's existence is now more proleptic than retrospective: it consciously stands for the future. 'Here is Israel *kata pneuma*', says Eichrodt, 'the people of God living not by common blood but by faith in the Word, the people which God will use as the cornerstone for the new building of his kingdom (Isa. 28. 16).'[3] Meanwhile the remnant lives in 'a merely pro-

prophets were persecuted. In this same sense of 'sign' it is important to note that the prophets as well as their prophecies were signs. Increasingly, as Hooke, for example, notes, they became 'identified with their message' (*Alpha and Omega*, p. 79), not only through symbolic actions—these were present from the days of the *nebi'im*—but through their faithfulness to their calling (as, for example, in Isa. 8. 18—see below, p. 75).

[1] We may in this connection recall how J. Marsh speaks of 'those who lived A.D. in B.C.' as 'already beginning to live..., by their faith in the coming fulfilment of God in history, a new pattern of life that belonged to the time that was still to come' (*The Fulness of Time*, p. 158). This is to minimize the distinction between the two 'ages' but we shall see that the Old Testament itself does provide some support for such a formulation.

[2] Cf. note on pp. 74 f. above.

[3] *Man in the Old Testament*, p. 43.

visional form of existence, whose meaning consists in pointing towards something still to come and still veiled, towards which the will turns in tense expectation',[1] a future in which the covenant-reality, hitherto only half-lived, will be lived wholly, for the law will be written within them, upon their hearts (Jer. 31. 33).[2]

Israel, then, or the remnant, is modelled upon and pre-figures a future reality, the eschatological kingdom of Yahweh. And the exilic prophets, by applying this doctrine to the return of the exiles from Babylon, bring out its full implications without much altering its initial rationale. Even in the first Isaiah a connection was visible between the remnant and the returners: it was in the name 'Shear-Jashub' which the prophet had, with conscious symbolism, given to his son. Originally, in all likelihood, it was meant primarily for ill-omen (Isa. 7. 1–9; 10.22): 'only a remnant will return (="repent")'. But the time for that being past, with Israel defeated and captive, it was natural that the name's more hopeful rendering should be developed: 'a remnant will return'.[3] Already, indeed, in Isa. 1–39 (as we have it) this implication of the name is recognized (Isa. 10. 20 f.).[4] In *vv.* 20–1 the remnant are certainly 'survivors' whether or not of the Exile, and it is said of them that they 'will lean no more upon him that smote them, but will lean upon the Lord, the Holy One of Israel, in truth' (Isa. 10. 20).

This, once again, is prescription as well as prediction. It may be an eschatological kingdom that is prophesied here, or it may

---

[1] *Man in the Old Testament*, p. 45.

[2] The idea of the remnant, as Vriezen correctly notes (*art. cit.* p. 214), is not Isaiah's ultimate ideal. As I see it, it is only an eschatological *Vorbild*. After the judgement there will be an extension of the life which they represent before it. Similarly in Zephaniah the remnant of Judah which he pictures in 2. 7 and 3. 12 would appear to have already survived a judgement not only upon Judah but upon the world (cf. Lindblom, *op. cit.* p. 370), but they have been addressed also in the present (2. 3) and so may be taken to be as essentially prefigurative as the 'remnant' in Isaiah. 'All peoples' will ultimately share the life of pure service (3. 9 f.) which the 'remnant' represents (cf. 3. 13).

[3] On the whole I am inclined to agree with Vriezen, *art. cit.* p. 208, that the ambiguity (or double-ambiguity, for 'return' means also 'repent') is intended by the prophet. It is the paradox at the heart of his message. See also Lindblom, *op. cit.* p. 188.

[4] Since the last two verses of the four-verse unit, ch. 10, *vv.* 20–3, require the alternative, more ominous, meaning, the first two verses may have been added in the Exile. But opinion is divided, Lindblom (*ibid.* p. 367) taking the opposite stand, i.e. *vv.* 22 f. are secondary, the hopeful *vv.* 20 f. genuine.

be something more temporary and provisional. In either case, there is no doubt that a command is involved in the prediction. Israel is to lean upon the Lord in truth. And any equation, or even relation, between the empirical and the eschatological people of God is conditional still upon the former's response to his claim. Israel is required to be *now* what, in the prophet's vision, in God's will, she will be.

Above all, the same is to be said of the prophecies of the return in Deutero-Isaiah, with an account of which we may conclude this chapter. There is still the backward-looking reference, or series of references, to the Exodus and other climactic points in Israelite history which qualify these prophecies as typology. The promises to David (II Sam. 7. 8–16) and Abraham (Gen. 12. 1–3, etc.) will be fulfilled (Isa. 55. 3–5; 51. 2–3), though hitherto by her disobedience Israel has forfeited the blessing these promises contained (Isa. 48. 17–19; 42. 24). As in the past Israel's sufferings were not God's last word, not immutable, for he delivered her: promising it first, then doing it (Isa. 48. 3)—so now he promises 'new things' again (Isa. 48. 6), again it is deliverance from captivity (Deut.-Isa. *passim*) and by his hand alone (*ibid.*); the people will be led through a wilderness (Isa. 40. 3; 43. 19; etc.) and brought to their own land (Isa. 51. 11; etc.): all this is sure, for God who alone can vouchsafe such things (Isa. 44. 6–8; 46. 8–10a) vouchsafes this:

> I have spoken, and I will bring it to pass;
> I have purposed, and I will do it...
> I bring near my deliverance, it is not far off,
> and my salvation will not tarry;
> I will put my salvation in Zion,
> for Israel my glory.   (Isa. 46. 11b, 13)

Among these predictions, dominated with Exodus-imagery as they are, there is a new note and a new auspiciousness. In a passage to which we have already referred (Isa. 51. 9–11) not only is a Canaanite Creation-myth brought in to serve as a metaphor for the Exodus, but also, and with no less aptness, the Return is pictured in eschatological lineaments:

> And the ransomed of the Lord shall return
> and come with singing to Zion;

77

everlasting joy shall be upon their heads;
   they shall obtain joy and gladness,
and sorrow and sighing shall flee away.   (v. 11)

The imagery which accompanies other oracles of the return
strikes the same note: we need only refer to the transformations
envisaged as taking place in the wilderness, the levelling of its
mountains (Isa. 40. 4), its refreshment with rivers (Isa. 41. 18),
and the consequent fertility (41. 19). It would be wrong to take
such passages as 'merely hyperbolical', or 'of a typically
Oriental extravagance'; for clearly, at the very least, they mean
that the 'new' act of Yahweh will transcend all that has ever
been known (Isa. 48. 6–8). But neither, on the other hand, does
this imagery mean that the prophet expects the return to be
the eschatological act. It stands as a 'sign' of that act. The
blessing which is given to Israel in its delivering foreshadows an
everlasting deliverance (Isa. 51. 6, 8) in which all nations will
be involved (Isa. 51. 5). It is not the end yet, for it is possible
that sufferings will still be inflicted even on Israel (Isa. 54. 15),
but neither is it totally distinct from the end, for the nation that
had been 'captive of the mighty and the prey of tyrants' (Isa.
49. 24), 'deeply despised, abhorred by the nations, the servant
of rulers' (Isa. 49. 7), now by her miraculous preservation
makes visible to all people the grace of Yahweh (Isa. 52. 10),
makes conceivable a time when they will all share in it (Isa.
51. 4–5), even represents and promises such a time (Isa. 45.
20–3), even, from Israel's viewpoint most important of all, helps
to bring it about.

   And if all this was the indicative of prediction, it stands also,
all of it but above all this last phrase, as an imperative laid upon
Israel, the remnant, who exist out of miracle, stand for that
miracle, and must live up to that miracle so as to make it plain:
they live to be its witnesses, witnesses for Yahweh (Isa. 43. 10–
12; 44. 8). For 'now the Lord says' (Isa. 49. 5):

> It is too light a thing that you should be my servant
>   to raise up the tribes of Jacob
> and to restore the preserved of Israel;
> I will give you as a light to the nations,
>   that my salvation may reach to the end of the earth.
>
>   (Isa. 49. 6)

And this implies nothing merely passive. Their being forgiven (Isa. 40. 2; 43. 25; 44. 22; etc.) and made the object of mercy has indeed nothing to do with their own works, and by itself it stands as a sign of the grace of Yahweh. But the ends of that act of forgiveness include service—peace is the heritage of the *servants* of Yahweh (Isa. 54. 17)—the establishment of righteousness and justice (Isa. 42. 6; 54. 14; and compare the form of address to Israel in 51. 1 and especially 7: 'the people in whose heart is my law'), and upon that their own peace depends: '"There is no peace", says Yahweh, "for the wicked"' (Isa. 48. 22; cf. Isa. 57. 19–21). The re-creation of Israel in spite of her sins, therefore, means no lessening of the divine demands (cf. Isa. 48. 17–19). The true ends of forgiveness will be manifest only if Israel realises these demands in the service of God: the revelation will then be shown to all people (Isa. 42. 4, 6; 51. 4) so that all people may glory in Yahweh (e.g. Isa. 49. 7, and the beginning of the last Servant Song, ch. 52, *vv.* 13–15) and glorifying may serve him who offers redemption to all (Isa. 45. 22 and perhaps also 55. 6–7). Israel is commanded to show forth this eschatological purpose, the new existence of man under God, the new reality which, as Brevard Childs says, takes on form in obedient Israel.[1]

It has been my design to show how historical typology in the Old Testament has for its aims (1) the presentation of certain historical, including future, events in such relation to one another that they may be perceived to be purposive acts of God, tending towards fulfilment; (2) to present these acts of God, 'wonders' though they are, as the more or less absolute norms by which the life of Israel is judged by God and is to be understood by Israel; (3) to present the God-given existence as a 'new reality', which Israel must so fully appropriate as to represent it to others, living out in history an eschatological life. The fact that, on the Old Testament's own showing, this existence was never fully achieved within Old Testament times, despite the vitality and verve of its heralding in the prophets, means that the Old Testament 'ends in dissidence':[2] by and large the new

---

[1] Compare his excellent discussion in *Myth and Reality in the Old Testament*, pp. 96–105.

[2] *Ibid.* p. 97.

existence was rejected by Israel. But that does not alter the fact that it is outlined there, made possible; and it does not alter the fact that it is this 'making possible', visible, and real, that is the object there of 'typology'. It is characteristic of acts of God that they may be not only 'signs' but 'signs rejected'. It is the case, Christians believe, with Jesus, himself 'a prophet and more than a prophet' in this way as in others, who was 'destined to be a sign rejected' (Luke 2. 34) and, 'to the Jews, a stumbling-block' (I Cor. 1. 23).

But 'typology', as we receive the word, is generally only descriptive of the presented relation between acts of God, a statement, to be precise, that there exist certain historical correspondences between different stages of 'sacred' history.[1] Yet if, as it seems, this indicative in Israelite prophecy, as in Old Testament thought generally, is inseparable from the demand, the sign from the call to follow, and 'are' (indicative) from 'are to be' (imperative), we must coin a new phrase to include both terms of this dialectic. 'Applied typology' has served us; let us define it here as typology which is concerned much less, more or less speculatively, with the past and future states of man and God, than with the neglected demand which the divine acts imply, that man become what they make him able to be, an analogical counterpart to the analogical actions of God, a representation of God and his action to others; and thus typology which focuses, or 'applies', past and future in the present 'word' of them, and exhorts each present age to repentance.

---

[1] Thus, for example, G. W. H. Lampe, *Essays on Typology*, pp. 25–7, 30; J. Daniélou, *From Shadows to Reality*, pp. 31 f. and *passim*. A. G. Hebert, *The Authority of the Old Testament*, pp. 218 f., follows W. J. Phythian-Adams in preferring to use the term 'homology' to describe such correspondences.

PART II

TYPOLOGY IN THE NEW TESTAMENT

CHAPTER 6

THE SCOPE OF NEW TESTAMENT
TYPOLOGY

Of the motifs of the previous part that which relates typology
to the steadfastness of God has, in modern times at least, commanded general assent. It is unfortunate that the images which
dominate the expression of this motif—whereby the divine
activity has a 'rhythm' or 'pattern' (Phythian-Adams, Lampe,
etc.)[1]—gives to the unfolding of sacred history an appearance
of something as natural, as inevitable and impersonal, as the
seasons,[2] but however imperfect the imagery the fundamental
intention of these writers is sound: it is to point out that the
divine activity, its purpose and its consistency, is basic to all
genuine typology.

If, then, it is faith's discovery of God's steadfastness which
leads the Old Testament writers to regard history as something
able to be fulfilled, it is also this which leads the New Testament
writers to see in the story of Jesus Christ that fulfilment to
which the Old Testament looks forward. Fundamental to all
the discourses in the Acts is the claim that the eschatological
predictions of the prophets are fulfilled in his passion and

[1] See Phythian-Adams, *The Way of At-one-ment*; Lampe in *Essays on Typology*.
Professor Lampe has recently come closer to my point of view. See his article,
'Hermeneutics and Typology', *London Quarterly and Holborn Review* (Jan. 1965),
p. 23.
[2] F. V. Filson's verdict upon Phythian-Adams's conception strikes me as essentially sound: 'This method of stating the fact of fulfilment leads to or goes with a
priestly conception of the Christian ministry which distorts the New Testament
focus; it gives too great a place to outward form in the Old Testament, and does
not do justice to the free prophetic spirit which in both Testaments is the distinctive
and deepest strain' (*The New Testament against its Environment*, p. 60). A similar
criticism would apply to the (nevertheless in many respects brilliant) work of L. S.
Thornton, *The Form of the Servant*: its emphasis on 'mystery' seems to me a move in
the direction of a remythologizing of New Testament theology and one which
even enhances the 'mythological' element there (in our sense as well as in Bultmann's). Cf. such a statement as this (from part III, 'Christ and the Church', p. 14),
for example: 'We may think in terms of a single organism in which Christ is the
head and the Church is the body. It will then follow(?) that everything that happened to our Lord from the moment when he became incarnate has also happened
to the Church in him.'

83

6-2

resurrection. Jesus is regarded as himself God's eschatological act, the culmination of God's steadfast love in the history of Israel and man, inasmuch as he is the mediator of the new and final covenant, of the kingdom of God, the one who makes present the kingdom and offers it to all on behalf of his Father (Luke 12. 32). More supremely, therefore, than in the 'mighty acts' of God in Old Testament times God in Jesus alters the conditions of human existence, transforming them, making them 'new'. Now he offers man freedom even from his subjection to the laws of his own nature; Jew and Gentile are raised to become each a 'new creature', for 'the old order has gone, and a new order has already begun' when 'anyone is united to Christ' (II Cor. 5. 17). This then is the 'fulness of time', the time when 'God sent his own Son, born of a woman, born under the law, to purchase freedom for the subjects of the law, in order that we might attain to the status of sons' (Gal. 4. 4–5).

It is now widely agreed, however, that this picture of a 'realized' eschatology does not by itself do justice to the total conception of history and eschatology in the New Testament. Jesus' preaching of the kingdom of God relates it to both present and future, it is 'here' and yet 'not here', 'already' and 'not yet'.[1] In his study of 'the eschatological message of Jesus' W. G. Kümmel speaks of the apparently imminent eschatology in Jesus' preaching as merely a necessary form of expression designed to express the '*nearness* of the kingdom' which is already present and moving towards the complete realization of God's will for our salvation.[2] 'If therefore the imminent expectation', he continues, '...can certainly be detached from Jesus' message, the *future* expectation is essential and indispensable, because in this form alone can the nature of God's redemptive action *in history* be held fast.'[3] Other scholars (notably the one-time pupils of Bultmann, E. Fuchs, E. Käsemann, H. Conzelmann, and G. Bornkamm) disagree with Kümmel's treatment of the tension between present and future as a temporal, 'world-historical' matter. They see the tension

---

[1] The best treatment of these issues known to me is N. Perrin's *The Kingdom of God in the Teaching of Jesus*, a book which provides an excellent summary of the outstanding contemporary contributions to their discussion. R. Bultmann's treatment, too, in *History and Eschatology*, though one-sided, is profoundly engaged, and engaging (esp. pp. 31–55).

[2] W. G. Kümmel, *Promise and Fulfilment*, esp. pp. 148–53.   [3] *Ibid.* pp. 152 ff.

as existential rather than temporal; it has to do, they say, with the destiny of the individual (death or life, judgement or salvation) as determined by the decision he makes in the present when confronted by God's act in the mission of Jesus:[1] 'The future of God is *salvation* to the man who apprehends the present as God's present, and as the hour of salvation. The future of God is *judgement* for the man who does not accept the "now" of God but clings to his own present and also to his own dream of the future.'[2] Perhaps, for the preaching of Jesus, this treatment is the more correct. But in any case, the existence there of the present/future dialectic is not in dispute, and it would today seem perverse to dispute it.

Neither is this tension lost in the primitive Church of New Testament times. The New Testament, to be sure, provides evidence of a spasmodic tendency to retranslate what Kümmel calls the 'eschatological promise' of Jesus into 'apocalyptic instruction'—a tendency, that is, to treat his words as a key to the signs preceding the final world-judgement of God. It is generally recognized that Mark 13 is the result of such a process: genuine *verba Christi* lie behind this discourse, but they have been supplemented, edited, re-applied, to interests differing markedly from their own. Instead of the call (characteristic of Jesus and New Testament preaching generally—cf. for example I Thess. 2. 11 f.—as to a lesser extent of the first and second Isaiahs) to 'live eschatological existence', to participate in God's kingdom by living its life, we find the emphasis falling rather on the characteristic cry of apocalyptic, 'expect eschatological events; watch out for their coming'.[3] Where this process occurs in the New Testament the dialectical tension between present and future is relaxed; the relation then is such that they are simply consecutive.

But alongside the indulgence in the early Church of this natural curiosity, the Fourth Gospel's paradoxical 'the hour

---

[1] Cf. E. Fuchs, 'Verheissung und Erfüllung', *Zur Frage nach dem historischen Jesus*, pp. 66–78; 'Glaube und Geschichte', *op. cit.* pp. 168–218; 'Das Zeitverständnis Jesu', *op. cit.* esp. pp. 343–8; G. Bornkamm, *Jesus of Nazareth*, pp. 90–5; J. M. Robinson, 'The Formal Structure of Jesus' Message', *Current Issues in New Testament Interpretation*, ed. W. Klassen and G. F. Snyder, pp. 91–110; and N. Perrin, *op. cit.* pp. 119–24.

[2] G. Bornkamm, *Jesus of Nazareth*, p. 93.

[3] See N. Perrin, *op. cit.* pp. 177–9.

comes, and now is' (John 4. 23; 5. 25) stands in contrast; and it bears witness to a persistent attempt to do justice to the proper dialectical nature of the tension in question.[1] In the terms of 'Heilsgeschichte theology' we may say that the 'eschaton' is presented in this Gospel as appearing before the end as the end's guarantee; but we must add that this 'guarantee' is such only to faith, even if, to faith, God's act in Christ is nothing less. For faith in the Christ already includes faith in the future, whatever the future may bring—whether persecution, suffering, death—for to faith God is disclosed in the Christ-event as Lord over all, and so Lord over all of these (John 14. 1–21; I John 4. 16–5. 21; and compare the verses which flank the account of Old Testament faith in Hebrews ch. 11: 10. 39 and 12. 1–2). St Paul has the same message. Bultmann expresses it: 'Faith is faith in God "who gives life to the dead and calls into existence the things that do not exist" (Rom. 4. 17). Faith is therefore faith in the future which God bestows on man, in the coming God.'[2] Because we believe that Christ died, and was raised from the dead, we are confident that *nothing* in death or life can separate us from God's love (Rom. 8. 31–9). If this is an 'existential' expression of the tension, St Paul in this chapter, and typically, puts alongside it a temporal and historical one: the whole universe(!) is to be freed from the shackles of mortality to enter upon the liberty and splendour of the children of God (Rom. 8. 19–22). Elsewhere in St Paul the revelation of the 'fulness of time' in the advent of Christ points to a future in which not merely the history of Israel will be fulfilled but 'all things' will be 'brought into a unity' or 'fulfilled' in Christ (Eph. 1. 10; cf. Col. 1. 16, 20). In St Paul at least, the two ways of expressing the tension are not thought to be mutually exclusive: they are aspects of the same faith. He has certainly not put away the idea of a *Heilsgeschichte* as something superseded by Christ (see especially Rom. 9–11).[3] Simply, by com-

[1] See N. A. Dahl, 'The Johannine Church and History', *Current Issues in New Testament Interpretation*, ed. W. Klassen and G. F. Snyder, pp. 124–42.

[2] R. Bultmann, *History and Eschatology*, p. 100.

[3] Bultmann's almost exclusively anthropological-existential reading of Paul, which leads him to see Christ as the end of all *Heilsgeschichte* (cf. his essay, 'The Significance of the Old Testament for the Christian Faith', *The Old Testament and Christian Faith*, ed. B. W. Anderson, pp. 29–31, and his *History and Eschatology*, p. 43), has brought protests not only from outside but from inside his school. See G. Bornkamm, 'Demythologizing the New Testament Message', *Kerygma and History*,

parison with Judaism (and, to a lesser degree, with much of the Old Testament), he has, like Jesus, regalvanized the *Heilsgeschichte*'s existential reference by centring his *heilsgeschichtlich* statements not on a philosophy of history or on apocalyptic speculation but on the personal confession which authenticates such statements, 'Christ is Lord'. Such a confession does not signal the end of history, but a new beginning which Christ has disclosed and made viable, a beginning in a sharing of his death which has the sharing of his life as its end. From this basis in faith's confession, cosmic statements such as those in Romans may be justified theologically along lines we have already traversed.[1] Observably, they spring from faith in the steadfastness of God.

It is very noticeable—to take a further step—how frequently the same language is applied to the events of the passion and resurrection of Jesus, to the events of the last day, and to the present life of the Christian. Paul's references to 'resurrection' will serve as instances. For example: 'God not only raised our Lord from the dead; he will also raise us up by his power' (I Cor. 6. 14); 'Put yourselves at the disposal of God, as dead men raised to life' (Rom. 6. 13); 'Were you not raised to life with Christ?' (Col. 3. 1). What this deliberate reapplication of language expresses is recognizable as a conception basic to Pauline theology: his belief that both the existence which the Christian possesses in the present, and all that is still outstanding, still to be attained (cf. Phil. 3. 10), are related organically and dialectically to the creative 'past' of God's action in Christ. And, showing that, it shows more, and with ideal clarity; it reveals how the New Testament's 'future', like the future of the Old Testament which the gospel now to a large extent realizes, is a typological construct: what will be fulfilled is foreshadowed; what has happened will be fulfilled.[2] Christ's

ed. C. E. Braaten and R. A. Harrisville, pp. 191–6; and cf. R. H. Fuller's account in *The New Testament in Current Study*, pp. 69–76.

[1] See pp. 28–32 above.

[2] Thus 'fulfilment' in the New Testament is a more complex category than the phrase 'Christ the fulfilment of history' would suggest if by 'Christ' only the so-called 'historical Jesus' (or rather, these days, the so-called 'so-called historical Jesus') were understood. For though it is clear that the New Testament attributes to the historical Jesus (by which I mean Jesus as he was, in his historical existence) —especially if the resurrection is taken to be part of his 'history'—a prospective as well as a retrospective relation to a larger history which he 'fulfils', still there is

resurrection and death are at least 'significant', and they are that precisely: for the Christian, they represent, promise, and partly *mean* other events, whether or not these events are taken as 'world-historical'. There is thus a real similarity between the two Testaments in the relations they depict between historical and eschatological events. A shift of degree is implied by the fact that Christ is himself the beginning of God's eschatological act, the entry into the world of the event of 'fulfilment', so that from now on one may look back to him to see the coming of what remains still an eschatological kingdom of God. For in him the kingdom is not merely, as in the case of the Exodus, suggested, but, by his perfect response to his Father, really contemporized. In Christ's history God's sovereignty does not come by halves, equivocally, but *in toto*. But this shift of degrees —though it alters the course of history, makes an epoch, brings about a change from 'this age' to 'the age to come'—still leaves the terms of the typological correspondence between 'present' and 'end' noticeably similar.

And this similarity leads us back to another question, which our discussion of the nature of the present/future 'tension' also raises, the question of how far typology in the New Testament has also a similar ethical and existential scope to that of the Old Testament. Are foretelling and forth-telling, prediction and history, related to a present demand as clearly and by a similar typological structure?

This question gains in importance from its having been generally ignored; and its neglect becomes comprehensible when seen in connection with the patristic use of typology, which, whether consciously or not, has provided most modern writers with their pre-understanding of its scope. For in the Fathers, clearly, the functions of what we have called 'applied typology' are not an outstanding feature of its use. In second-century Christianity typology became quickly, though perhaps never wholly, limited to the demonstration that certain figures

something to which the New Testament looks forward which will fulfil, complement, complete the historical Jesus' work. This future 'fulfilment', which the historical Jesus may be said to 'prefigure', is taken to be the work of the exalted Lord, of Christ seated at the right hand of God—with whom the Christian's 'hidden life' will be 'manifest' (Col. 3. 1–4), and with whom 'all things will be drawn into unity' (Eph. 1. 10; Col. 1. 20; Rom. 8. 21). In interpreting my definition of Christian typology (see p. 1), it must be borne in mind that the historical Jesus is not the whole of 'Christology'.

in the two Testaments correspond to one another. Such a demonstration, while of some value and validity in contra-Jewish and, to a lesser extent, contra-pagan apologetics, and, later, also in the catechetical exposition of doctrine, involved, by being so limited, a loosening of typology's bond with the imperative of God's challenge to history—to conform with his acts. This, in the last resort, may signal a decisive misconstruction of the whole typological relation between ethics and history.

Two passages must suffice to exemplify the value of a 'separated' expository typology and the danger arising from this separation. The first is a fine piece from Irenaeus, whose argument against Marcion and his distinction between the Gods of the two Testaments was suitably conducted on lines such as these:

Sic et Deus ab initio hominem quidem plasmavit propter suam munificentiam; patriarchas vero elegit propter illorum salutem; populum vero praeformabat, docens indocibilem, sequi Deum; prophetas vero praestruebat in terra, assuescens hominem portare eius Spiritum, et communionem habere cum Deo: ipse quidem nullius indigens; his vero qui indigent eius, suam praebens communionem; et his qui ei complacebant, fabricationem salutis, ut architectus, delineans, et non videntibus in Aegypto a semetipso dans ducationem; et his qui inquieti erant in eremo, dans aptissimam legem, et his qui in bonam terram introierunt, dignam praebens hereditatem; et his qui convertuntur ad Patrem, saginatum occidens vitulum, et primam stolam donans: multis modis componens humanum genus ad consonantiam salutis...Et per omnes illos transiens Verbum, sine invidia utilitatem praestabat eis qui subiecti sibi erant, omni conditioni congruentem et aptam legem conscribens.[1]

Formally this is not typological writing, but it is typological in effect: its effectiveness wholly depends upon real historical parallels between the two Testaments. So skilfully is it composed that one is sometimes in doubt whether the author has not gone on to speak of the New Testament. In the last sentence, indeed, one could believe that he had, if it were not that he goes on to speak of the Word's bestowal of a written Law. Yet because he has not played fast and loose with the Old Testa-

[1] *Adversus Haereses*, IV. 14. 2 (Stieren ed.).

ment, but used terms to interpret it which are recognized as its own he has not illegitimately read back into its history what the Jews had not already read into or found in it. The 'Word', which, by adding its New Testament connotations to the Old Testament 'word of the Lord', he does introduce, seems therefore to fit with the rest, and Marcion is properly answered. The same God acts in the same way in both dispensations. The actions of God in both ages have the same quality.

But already this passage might warn us of the approach of the mediaeval 'doctrine' of exegesis:[1] *allegoria quid credas docet*, the typological meaning, that is to say, teaches you what to believe —what you must do is the province of the *sensus moralis*, a form of allegory often essentially similar to that met with in Philo. It is no great step from a typology addressed (though here with only a comparative urgency)[2] to the individual in his situation, exhorting him to believe in God's saving action and recognize it as grace, to a typology which merely teaches what to believe and accept as doctrines. But it is not without consequence. For meanwhile Clement of Alexandria is addressing the individual (though in necessarily general terms) in ways that almost entirely divorce faith and history, on the one hand, from ethics, on the other. Instead of 'contemporaneity' and an existential commitment to the present importance of God's past saving acts (which was the basis of Old Testament ethics) we are told what to do in this way:

'If anyone die suddenly before the priest, the head of his consecration shall be defiled; and he shall immediately shave it' (Num. 6. 9). By 'sudden death' he means an indeliberate sin, and says that it 'defiles' because it pollutes the soul. For the cure he prescribes that the head be shaved on the spot as soon as possible, meaning that the locks of ignorance that darken the reason should be shorn so that the reason (which has its seat in the head), stripped of hair, that is, wickedness, may the better retrace its course to repentance.[3]

This is bad exegesis, of course; but the question is not only exegetical. It is doubtful whether even the ethics are valid when

---

[1] To this topic we shall return in part III.

[2] In Irenaeus it is, however, directed to the individual and to an individual context which makes it necessary to reverse the New Testament's use of typology. For since Marcion accepts, at least theoretically, the revelation in Jesus, the argument aims to convince him of the validity of the same kind of revelation in the Old Testament history.   [3] *Paidagogos*, 1. 2. 5.

shorn from the head of *their* consecration, that is (to interpret the allegory), separated altogether from their original context in the old or new covenant. Judaism (which we too easily call 'legalistic') never wholly forgot this; still less did St Paul or the other New Testament writers forget it. But Bultmann's bleak picture of later Christianity, though perhaps somewhat over-pessimistic, points a contrast between the first and (say) the early third centuries which, as most scholars would allow, does to some extent correspond with the facts. 'The believer', he writes, 'stands under the imperative, but the imperative no longer (as in the New Testament) stands in the dialectic relation to the indicative, *where to stand under the imperative means at the same time to stand under grace.*'[1]

In contrast to this later development therefore we may compare with the passage from Clement's *Paidagogos*, a Rabbinic Midrash which keeps to the ethical tradition of the Old Testament:

It says in Lev. 11. 45, 'For I am the Lord your God who brought you up out of the land of Egypt to be your God: ye shall, therefore, be holy, for I am holy.' That means, I brought you out of Egypt on the condition that you should receive the yoke of the commandments: he who acknowledges the yoke of the commandments acknowledges that I have brought Israel out of Egypt, and he who denies (or rejects the obligation of) the yoke of the commandments, denies that I brought Israel out of Egypt. (Sifra 57 *b*)

Needless to say, this passage is a simplification of the issue and perhaps an oversimplification. It is impossible to say whether the reception of 'the yoke of the commandments' here is, in Bultmann's phrase, the 'self-evident fruit of the gift of salvation'[2] or only the deliberate acceptance of a condition for the sake of the life upon which one depends. Yet it is clear that obedience is here related to history in a way quite consistent with the Old Testament's ethico-historical relation, and that it is related to past history in faith and dependence rather than to a future salvation which depends upon it. It is one's *present* existence in the chosen nation which depends on obedience,

---

[1] *History and Eschatology*, p. 50 (my italics). For a similar view cf. the accounts of 'moral behaviour' in the apostolic and sub-apostolic ages on pp. 65 f. and 110 in J. G. Davies, *The Early Christian Church*.

[2] *History and Eschatology, loc. cit.*

even as the possibility of obedience depends upon the grace which created this present existence. This is the dialectic which the apparent simplification only conceals, not denies.

That the same dialectic is behind the New Testament's ethics may be inferred from what was said on the subject of the existentiality of the tension between present and future. In I Peter the same verse is quoted as in the Midrash, and the same fundamental argument applied, except that the new gospel replaces the old.

You must therefore be like men stripped for action, perfectly self-controlled. Fix your hopes on the gift of grace which is to be yours when Jesus Christ is revealed...The One who called you is holy; like him, be holy in all your behaviour, because Scripture says, 'You shall be holy, for I am holy.'

If you say 'our Father' to the One who judges every man impartially on the record of his deeds, you must stand in awe of him while you live out your time on earth. Well you know that it was not perishable stuff, like gold or silver, that bought your freedom from the folly of your traditional ways. The price was paid in precious blood, as it were of a lamb without spot or blemish—the blood of Christ.   (I Pet. 1. 13–19)

The argument stands, scarcely changed: your freedom was bought, you are redeemed—*therefore* be perfectly self-controlled and stand in awe of him who redeemed you. Or as Paul puts it, you have been given the Spirit (i.e. you *are* thus) therefore walk by the Spirit (i.e. *be* thus) (Gal. 5. 25); according to Col. 2. 6, you have received Christ, so you should 'walk in him'.[1] There is a characteristic tension here between an obedience which is the natural fruit of salvation and an obedience which is commanded—and only attained, therefore, by the continual surrender of the will. However firm the conviction of the New Testament authors that Christ suffered vicariously 'for the sins of many', they declare too the need to imitate that suffering by taking up one's own cross. The New Testament's ethics are so rooted in the gospel 'history of salvation' that they not only take God's prior action in that history for their motive; they also enjoin the rehearsal of Christ's way to the cross, and the conforming of the mind to his (e.g. I Pet. 4. 1; Eph. 4. 21–4). In a word, the New Testament writers teach, as Jesus did,

---

[1] Cf. W. D. Davies, *The Setting of the Sermon on the Mount*, pp. 342–5.

discipleship, following. Like the sacraments of baptism and the Lord's Supper, therefore (and, for that matter, like the Old Testament *Torah* and festivals) ethics are so conditioned here as to be themselves a recital of history and a manifestation of the Lord's life and death 'till he come'.

But indeed the same intricacy of connection between ethics, theology and the history of salvation exists, as C. H. Dodd says, in every New Testament letter and gospel, even in some ways controlling their structure. 'The ethical materials', he writes, 'in gospels and epistles alike have a general similarity of form and content, but in the epistles they are related to theological doctrine' which has its basis (as Dodd goes on to show) in the narrative of events; 'while in the gospels they are related to a narrative' which 'as all recent criticism agrees, is coloured throughout by a religious, if not a theological, valuation...The ethical teaching of the New Testament is embedded in a context which consists of a report of historical facts and an explanation of their religious significance, and this fact gives to Christian Ethics (their) peculiar character.'[1]

It is likely, in view of these statements, that the New Testament's use of typology will express the same kind of *formal* relation between history and commands as the Old Testament exhibited. And indeed typology of that kind which we called 'subfulfilment' in the Old Testament's law and liturgy is already suggested in the typical linguistic structures we have just quoted from St Paul. A subfulfilment, also, clearly, is involved in the New Testament's conceptions of the *imitatio Christi*, the believer's 'incorporation', and the 'dying and rising' of the Christian with Christ. Discussion of the fuller implications of these concepts must be postponed. Three things, however, vindicate our calling them 'typology'. First, both 'type' and 'subfulfilment' depend upon the action of God and its consistency; then, the 'subfulfilment' depends on the 'type' (God's act in Christ) as its own cause and grounds; and, finally, both 'type' and 'anti-type' are firmly set within history.[2]

---

[1] *Gospel and Law*, pp. 6–8. See also A. N. Wilder, *Early Christian Rhetoric*, esp. pp. 63–78.

[2] This means, of course, that it is freely admitted that only when the commands are obeyed may the word 'typology' be properly used of them, and then rather of the 'obeyer' than of the commands. So long as an idea remains an abstraction it is misleading to call it 'historical', but as soon as someone commits himself to it and

But Christ not as 'type' of the Church but as 'anti-type' of the Old Testament history will from now on be our main concern in this chapter, and 'subfulfilment' only as an aspect of that. Already from what we have said in the last few paragraphs there is some presumptive evidence that 'typology' in this form and usage will be more than a matter of dogma ('*quid credas*'); and indeed—in intention at least—for the New Testament writers it is always at least an aid in apologetics, and sometimes, as we shall argue, still more an aid to the Church's *kerygma*.

Yet whether misled by a static and abstract idea of typology or whether considering that the weapon is blunted now and so of no more than historical interest, to this aspect of its New Testament use few theologians, even among its defenders, have testified. They remark on its patterning use in the gospels (e.g. Matthew's Pentateuch and Luke's Hexateuch), which need imply no more than an aesthetic justification. They notice the numerical symbolism (loaves and fishes, forty days, twelve disciples, seventy missionaries) which, though it is 'typological' in the sense that these numbers do have their Old Testament parallels, has, surely, no *inherent* significance.[1] Finally, when typology is seen as possessing a theological import, there is a tendency to conceive its import statically not dynamically. Thus 'import' becomes for Daniélou 'the deposit of revelation' of which typology is 'part and parcel'; and, for the *Dictionnaire de Théologie Catholique*, typology shows that

Dieu, en effet, a préordonné certains événements de l'histoire juive, le renvoi d'Agar et d'Ismaël, Gal. 4. 30–1; le passage de la mer Rouge, I Cor. 10. 1; certaines institutions, les victimes et les cérémonies du culte juif, Heb. 9. 9; les jours de fête, Col. 2. 16–17; certains personnages, Adam, Rom. 5. 14; Melchisédech, Heb. 7 etc., à représenter, en outre de leur réalité historique, des événements, institutions ou personnages futurs de la nouvelle alliance.

lets it control his decisions it has flesh and blood for the moment and is history in the only sense which concerns us—the biblical sense: it is part of the action of man, of the reaction of man to events outside him, or, in the case of commandments, of the reaction of man to God in the existential encounter with him in his act or its word.

[1] In this context I may quote from the 'blurb' on the dust-jacket of Dr Farrer's *Matthew and Mark*: 'Not (as their critics allege) believing that Christ patterned his life on a series of numbered acts or days, the typologists merely hold that the Evangelists used a numerical symbolism of their own to pattern their exposition.' One may hold that, but to hold 'merely' that, is to hold something not worth holding. Nor does Farrer himself, of course, hold 'merely that'.

With regard to the last of these statements—which is not a view strictly peculiar to Roman Catholics—I can only say that I cannot myself see the rationale of typology in these terms: for 'what', as Bultmann asks of a similar treatment, 'would be the point of such a proceeding on the part of God?'[1] With regard to the others, I believe that if they contain a version of the truth it is at any rate a greatly abbreviated one. While these views are current it is no wonder if many assume that there is an impassable gulf between typology (whether in the New Testament or elsewhere) and the existentialist and kerygmatic hermeneutics of Ernst Fuchs and Bultmann who insist that a really 'historical' understanding is irreconcilable with the kind of 'historical interest' to which we referred a moment ago, and cannot be 'objective' (as nineteenth-century historiographers often hoped) but involves a response or reaction, in other words a 'commitment' towards or away from the proclaimed word of God, the *kerygma*.[2]

But this gulf, if it exists, is not necessarily, and ought not to be, impassable. The New Testament's use of typology reveals its structure and its existential bearing the more clearly as the insights of the existentialist hermeneutics are applied—this we have already indicated, with regard to the present and future, and it will turn out to be true, also, of the relation between the past and the present, between the Old and the New Testament —and the structure thus revealed cannot easily be dispensed with, along with the three-storey universe, as 'myth' or 'first-century thought-form'. For without typology the apostles' *kerygma* loses its chief testimonial—its consistency with the Old Testament words and actions of God—and its chief explanation —the Christology of the New Testament.

These two aspects together focus the problem of the use and necessity of typology. For the New Testament's witness is a witness to Christ and the meaning of Christ; that is to say, it bears witness to a Christology. But just as 'Christ' (Messiah) is not a term that can be understood apart from an historical

---

[1] 'Prophecy and Fulfilment', *Essays, Philosophical and Theological*, p. 187.
[2] See Bultmann's essay on 'The Problem of Hermeneutics', *Essays, Philosophical and Theological*, pp. 234–61; and 'Is Exegesis without Presuppositions Possible?', *Existence and Faith*, pp. 289–96. Among E. Fuchs's numerous contributions to the topic his book *Hermeneutik* is the chief and should be consulted for its account (pp. 192–201) of typology.

function, so, in the New Testament, as Cullmann and others have repeatedly stressed, Christology in general is no edifice of speculation about substance and natures; but rather an interpreted history whose subject is Christ's mission and work in the providence of God. For example, it is the unity of his mission with God's purpose, by obedience, which validates his 'Sonship', and this unity, this obedience, is apprehensible only when we see how, in history, he fulfils the 'ways of the Lord'.[1] And in general this is the case with Christology in the New Testament: although the presence of Hellenistic influence is not negligible, it is true to say that the work and person of Christ are explained for much the most part in Old Testament terms and in what are in the last resort typological terms.[2] So that if, as seems to have happened in the times of the Fathers, there is no understanding of the existential direction of Old Testament language, on the one hand, and of its understanding of history, on the other, there is a danger of missing also the existential conception of Christ in the New Testament proclamation. Then the conception of Christ the New Israel loses its point,[3] and Christ as God seems an intrusion without rhyme or reason.

We may illustrate this from the form of the *kerygma* itself. The *kerygma* is the proclamation of a history. But if the bare events were its only constituents it would hold no one's interest. There is therefore also an interpretation of the significance of the events, which proclaims that in them God has acted to redeem mankind. But if only a statement of faith of this kind were added, who would believe it to be anything but the

---

[1] To recognize this needs an act of faith, just as did the truth of the Old Testament interpretation of history. Here as there the historicity of 'interpretations' —i.e. as 'acts of God'—rather than that of 'outward events' is the object of faith.

[2] Cf. W. Pannenberg, 'Heilsgeschehen und Geschichte', *KD*, v (1959), pp. 225 f.; also J. L. McKenzie, 'The Significance of the Old Testament for Christian Faith in Roman Catholicism', *The Old Testament and Christian Faith*, ed. B. W. Anderson, pp. 107–12.

[3] As early as the second century we find that apologetic is content on this point to show only how Christ is by the prophets 'symbolically called Israel'. See, for example, Justin, *Dialogue*, chh. 36, 75, 100, 123, 125, 126. How little even this aspect of the identification interested the Fathers may be judged from the fact that these passages are the only evidence offered by Rendell Harris for the suggestion that the postulated *Testimony Book* contained a section proving that Jesus is Israel: cf. *Testimonies*, i, 126–8.

blatantest blasphemy and presumption?[1] So an argument in favour of the interpretation is also added and evidence brought. This states that these things happened 'according to the Scriptures' and 'in fulfilment of Scripture'.

We should note, however, that this is evidence of a particular kind, which does not pretend, nor could claim, to be logically conclusive. It does not set out to *prove* that God was in Christ reconciling the world to himself. This cannot be proved to the hearer, but, as Bultmann is always and rightly asserting, must be affirmed by the hearer's own existential decision, by a faith which is prepared, on the strength of the testimony alone and without any security, still and nevertheless to meet the demand which this interpreted history in the *kerygma* makes upon those whom it questions: the demand, 'Repent, and be converted!' Objective certainty is ruled out by the nature of the case. But the argument from Scripture is still evidence of a kind, and we may see what kind if we have recourse to Bultmann's own hermeneutical category of 'pre-understanding' (*Vorverständnis*),[2] i.e. that which the hearer understands already about the general subject which the preaching or text is concerned with, and his understanding of his own relation to the subject.[3] In this instance, to adapt something Bultmann says, 'the understanding of reports about events as the activity of God presupposes a pre-understanding of what an activity of God *can* mean'.[4] The assumption upon which the 'according to the Scriptures' of the apostolic preaching is based—and here we

---

[1] Bultmann's refusal to look behind the *kerygma* for its support in the history of Jesus (above all in the resurrection) flies in the face—as it seems to me, needlessly—of apostolic practice. W. Pannenberg's criticisms of his position here ('Kerygma und Geschichte', in *Studien zur Theologie des alttestamentlichen Überlieferungen, Festschrift*, pp. 129–40) are apposite too to the subject in hand, the argument from Scripture: see esp. *art. cit.* p. 132. A. Richardson has also some valuable arguments on this subject, both in his essay, 'Is the Old Testament the Propaedeutic to Christian Faith?' (*The Old Testament and Christian Faith*, ed. B. W. Anderson, pp. 36–48), and in his book, *History, Sacred and Profane*, ch. 6 (pp. 184–212).

[2] See the essays cited above, p. 95, 'The Problem of Hermeneutics'; and 'Is Exegesis without Presuppositions possible?'.

[3] Compare, besides the essays of Bultmann mentioned in the previous note, H. Thielicke's 'Reflections on Bultmann's Hermeneutic', *ExpT*, LXVII (Feb. 1956), pp. 155 f. Cf. also K. Frör, *Biblische Hermeneutik*, pp. 34–44, esp. p. 40, and the defence of Bultmann's account of *Vorverständnis* as applied to the Old Testament in C. Michalson, 'Bultmann against Marcion', *The Old Testament and Christian Faith*, ed. B. W. Anderson, pp. 49–63.

[4] Cf. 'The Problem of Hermeneutics', *Essays*, p. 257.

97

part company from Bultmann—is that it is in the Scriptures that this pre-understanding may be found: the Scriptures, i.e. the Old Testament, show what is meant by God's acting. To the Jew, therefore, whose relation to this understanding is immediate, the argument may run in some such way as this: if you believe that God acted in such a way in the past, see how here he has done so more thoroughly. To the Gentile, on the other hand, whose relation to this understanding can only be that of one who allows the hypothetical possibility of God's so acting, then the argument runs: if you believe that God might act in such a way, see how in Jesus he has so acted. And to both, Jew and Gentile, the *kerygma* says: if you believe that God *has* acted here, in Jesus, then repent, and be converted.[1]

Again, to look at the problem of 'proof' from another angle, it is plain that typology in the Old Testament is not employed as an exegetical method, concerned with old text or, primarily, even with old event. Instead, its employment is all for the sake of the new, the present situation, the present or coming event the announcement of which it helps to articulate. The emphasis in Old Testament typology all falls on that. The typological presentation of a prophetic message exists for the sake of the new happening, the prophesied event, that that happening or event may be heard rightly, understood, taken seriously.

And this, surely, is the case with the New Testament, at least usually.[2] Typology does not exist there for the sake of interpreting the past—though the past is, incidentally, *re*interpreted, as historians always tend to reinterpret it, in the light of the present.[3] Rather, it is the past's meaning 'for us', its relevance

---

[1] Bultmann himself provides a formula which would apply to this use of typology, when he speaks of the 'indirect' (*vermittelt*) Word of God— 'words which help to make' God's direct Word, embodied in Jesus, 'understandable, by bringing man into the situation in which he can understand it' ('The Significance of the Old Testament for the Christian Faith', *The Old Testament and Christian Faith*, ed. B. W. Anderson, pp. 35 f.). But it is doubtful how far Bultmann himself sees New Testament *typology* in this light (despite his correct remarks in *loc. cit.* on I Cor. 10), and it is likely that he would make the mistake of including it in his strictures on scriptural proof. Cf. also the essay, 'Ursprung und Sinn der Typologie als Hermeneutischer Method', *TLZ* (1950), col. 204–10.

[2] Cf. S. Amsler, *L'Ancien Testament dans l'Église*, pp. 93 ff.: 'Les auteurs du Nouveau Testament sont d'abord des témoins du Christ et non des exégètes de l'Ancien Testament. Toute leur attention est concentrée sur l'événement historique de Jésus auquel ils rendent témoignage' (p. 93).

[3] See A. Richardson, *History, Sacred and Profane*, pp. 221 f., quoted on p. 3 above.

'for us' (cf. I Cor. 9. 10; 10. 6, 11; Rom. 4. 23 f.). This is not to deny that the exegesis of the Old Testament which we find in the New appears sometimes to have concerned itself very much with the old text, sometimes straining it out of all recognition in order to prove that the Christian message was prophesied even in detail.[1] This is what appears to be happening in Acts 17, where Paul, at Thessalonica, is reported as 'quoting texts of Scripture which he expounded and applied to show that the Messiah had to suffer and rise from the dead' (17. 2 f.); and at Beroea, his next port of call, we read that the Jews 'studied the Scriptures every day to see whether it was as (he) said' (17. 11; cf. 28. 23–5). There is no means of telling, in the case of some of these stories, how aptly the Scriptures were used. But at Thessalonica the argument can hardly have been typological. The treatment of the Old Testament which it would seem to imply is that which we find in Acts 2 (25–32; cf. 13. 32–9): the witness of the text to Christ depends on a misunderstanding.[2] But typology is a way of regarding history rather than texts, and if the textual treatment (exegesis) is erroneous it is not always possible, on *that* account, to dismiss the historical treatment too. For example, as Amsler has remarked *à propos* of Hebrews, although early Christian hermeneutics sometimes

---

[1] It is worth remarking in this connection that C. F. D. Moule (*The Birth of the New Testament*, pp. 62–7) and S. L. Edgar ('Respect for Context in Quotations from the Old Testament', *SNTS Bull.* IX, 1962, 55–62) have pointed out that Jesus himself seems to have used the Old Testament with a regard for its original meaning and setting that is unmatched by the writers of the New Testament.

[2] For the treatment of the exegesis of the Old Testament in the New Testament we must refer the reader especially to the work of C. H. Dodd, *According to the Scriptures*; S. Amsler, *op. cit.*; E. E. Ellis, *Paul's Use of the Old Testament*; C. F. D. Moule, *The Birth of the New Testament*, pp. 53–85; and B. Lindars, *New Testament Apologetic*. It is important to regard, too, the contemporary exegetical practices revealed in Rabbinic, Qumranic and Hellenistic writings. For the first, see especially J. Bonsirven, 'Exégèse Allégorique chez les Rabbis Tannaites', *RechSR*, XXIII (1933), 513–41, XXIV (1934), 35–46; *Le Judaisme Palestinienne au Temps de Jesus-Christ*, I, ch. 5; *Exégèse Rabbinique et Exégèse Paulinienne*; H. L. Strack and P. Billerbeck, *Kommentar zum Neuen Testament aus Talmud und Midrash*, III, 391–9 (on I Cor. 9. 8–10). For Qumranic exegesis, see especially F. F. Bruce, *Biblical Exegesis in the Qumran Texts*; J. A. Fitzmyer, 'The Use of Explicit Old Testament Quotations in the Qumran Literature and in the New Testament', *SNTS*, VII (1961), 297–333. For Hellenistic allegorical exegesis, see especially J. Pépin, *Mythe et Allégorie*; R. M. Grant, *The Letter and the Spirit*, pp. 1–30. See also the excellent comparative account of these three fields by R. P. C. Hanson, *Allegory and Event*, chh. 1 and 2.

found its task eased by exegetical procedures which were currently practised and respected, still the hermeneutics of Hebrews ultimately does not depend on them;[1] and we might adapt this statement to the subject of typology within and beyond the Epistle. When we seek to evaluate typology, the exegetical procedures which a particular passage may involve are much less relevant than the hermeneutical aims which lie behind the exegesis. The procedures only help us to evaluate that passage, not to evaluate typology. But the aims behind the procedures, and the idea of hermeneutics which these aims reveal, lead us often more or less directly back to the author's (or speaker's) interpretation of history. And again and again we shall find in this inquiry that it is an interpretation to which typology may do, and even has often done, justice.

Therefore if, as is clearly the case with most of the New Testament's references, citations and reminiscences of Scripture, some form of argument is involved, it is upon the form of this argument, and the implicit understanding of history, that we should concentrate, rather than upon the understanding or mis-understanding of the Old Testament text which the understanding of history has called to aid its expression. Clearly, no form of argument, whatever the included presentation of the Old Testament may pretend, can reach to the point of proving the *kerygma's* claim about Jesus; and if the exegesis should purport to do this it would be taking a short cut that simply does not exist, and simply should not.[2] But in fact the New Testament generally does recognize the limits of the argument from Scripture; and in using typology in the course of such an argument, as we shall show in the following four sections, the New Testament develops the argument to those limits and not beyond them. The typological argument from Scripture shows again and again that its basic concern is with historical consistency, the consistency between the 'new' events of the gospel and the divine acts in the past which are received as fundamental to her own existence by Israel. It is an argument which leads not to the formula, Q.E.D., but to the question mark: 'Can these new things be, as their consistency with the former things seems to make feasible, also, like them, divine acts?' It is an argument which we can find developed at varying levels of

---

[1] Cf. S. Amsler, *op. cit.* p. 26.   [2] Cf. *ibid.* pp. 96 f.

explicitness in literary and narrative complexes in the New Testament, and also, as we shall argue in dealing with the term 'Son of Man', more or less 'undeveloped', implicit, in complexes which are bound together only by common themes or common phrases. It is an argument which, though we would not expect to find it developed at length in the authentic *logia* of Jesus—who characteristically asserts divine activity to be breaking in in his time while leaving his own part in it to be inferred by his hearers—still appears to accord with his practice. And since all this talk of the 'scope' of typology, and the 'point' of its argument, may otherwise leave the impression that it is a very sophistic philosophy, and not, for all its declarations, direct and simple enough to really concern, existentially, the farmers, the fishers, the townsfolk, to whom Jesus addressed himself, we may conclude this chapter suitably by pointing to the narrative in Luke 11. 14–23 (= Matt. 12. 22–30; cf. Mark 3, 22–7), which, simply and tellingly enough, presupposes the idea of typology working on a quite subconscious level, as a natural movement of feeling and of the mind in the search for significant analogy.

There are those, we are told, who think Jesus exorcises by Beelzebub's power. Jesus turns to them and in a series of pointed, even epigrammatic, phrases faces them with the question they raised—'Do you recognize such action as God's, or the devil's?' But his hearers are not left helpless, to guess at the answer. Jesus seems to have had no (Bultmannian) inhibition to prevent him from declaring at least that the work he accomplishes would be incongruous work for the devil (Luke 11. 18). And surely the positive argument is implicit: 'It is, on the other hand, congruous for God, as a moment's reflection (and it must be, in the last analysis, typological reflection) would convince you!' Once this congruity is perceived, something more, an identity, or equation, becomes feasible. And then: 'If by the finger of God *I* cast out devils, then be sure that the kingdom of God has (already) come upon you!' (Luke 11. 20). It is a brief passage, and it is not hard to follow, but it is in the realm of typology; for here both the past (by implication) and the eschatological action of God are focused on, and applied to, the present occasion in a way which demands our decision. Acceptance of Jesus' message, as of the apostles' *kerygma*, brings one inevitably under the imperative: 'Repent, and believe in the gospel' (Mark 1. 15).

In the four chapters which follow and which could have been headed collectively 'Christus Recapitulator', I shall study the typological argument from Scripture as it emerges from certain suggestive thematic and (in the case of Matt. 1–4) literary complexes, in the gospel tradition.

CHAPTER 7

JESUS-ISRAEL (i): THE WAY OF JESUS

'CHRISTIANITY arose within Judaism and was first offered to Jews by Jews as the true Judaism, not as replacing but as fulfilling the faith of their fathers.'[1] This faith, whether expressed in law, discourse, prediction, or historiography, amounted above all to a confession that God worked in and through history, that in history certain 'mighty acts' were more or less directly ascribable to him, and that man's existence stood totally in dependence upon God and the activity of God.

So that if Jesus offered himself or was to be offered to Jews as the fulfilment of this history he must show himself or be shown as doing something essentially comparable and related to the decisive works of God in the Old Testament.[2] It is not only a matter of fulfilling the promises made to Abraham, Moses and all the prophets, though that too Paul claimed that Jesus had done: 'He is the Yes pronounced upon God's promises, every one of them' (II Cor. 1. 20). It is also a matter of showing that, despite the apparent unlikeliness, the obscure rabbi who set about preaching in Galilee and continued upon his way up to Jerusalem to be hanged as a criminal, did this, as he claimed, in fulfilment of a requirement already laid down in the Scriptures: 'The Son of Man is going the way appointed for him in the Scriptures' (Mark 14. 21).[3]

Now without denying that this kind of statement, which occurs fairly frequently in the Gospels, is still, as it was to Jesus' contemporaries, enigmatic, and apparently deliberately so, I believe that we can in the light of biblical scholarship make several points about its significance with some certainty. First,

[1] M. Burrows, *More Light on the Dead Sea Scrolls*, p. 46.
[2] Cf. A. A. van Ruler, *Die Christliche Kirche und das Alte Testament* (1955), p. 70 (cited by W. Pannenberg, 'Heilsgeschehen und Geschichte', *KD*, 1959, p. 225): 'Mit der Messianität Jesu steht und fällt, christlich gesprochen, alles. Und über diese Messianität kann nur entschieden werden, indem die Frage aufgeworfen und beantwortet wird, ob Jesus wirklich die Werke Gottes tut. Was aber die Werke Gottes sind, dass lässt sich nur an Hand des Alten Testaments feststellen.'
[3] See, on this subject, C. K. Barrett, 'The Bible in the New Testament Period' (*The Church's Use of the Bible*, ed. D. E. Nineham), pp. 9–16.

that the metaphor of the 'way' probably goes back to Jesus himself,[1] and is in any case a primary category for the explanation and understanding of Jesus' earthly mission and work. Secondly, that (despite popular impressions) the form of this 'way' is appointed not only in the predictions of the Old Testament and in the expectations of later Judaism, but also, and mainly, in something less specific and more fundamental to the Old Testament message, namely, the Old Testament's general understanding of Israel's election and calling. And thirdly, that when we (and Jesus and the New Testament writers) apply the idea of 'fulfilment' to this concept of an appointed way and locate this fulfilment in Jesus' mission we are making a claim that is incomprehensible except in terms of typology, namely, that Jesus 'recapitulates'—i.e. repeats and fulfils—the historical existence of Israel.

The first of these points may be substantiated only sketchily here. For a fuller treatment I must refer once again to the work of E. J. Tinsley,[2] upon whose discussion I here mainly depend. To begin with, the fact that the Christian religion was first known as 'the Way' (Acts 9. 2; 16. 17; 18. 25; etc.) already suggests a high degree of probability that the term goes back, almost as a *terminus technicus*, to the teaching of Jesus, who was himself, as John saw, 'the Way' (John 14. 6). The same image and significance is present in the phrase 'follow me'. By thus personifying 'the Way' in the person of Jesus the early Christians mean not only that he 'teaches the way of God' (Mark 11. 14, where the way of God is the law, as the continuation makes plain) but primarily that it is through him that one may have access to God (cf. again John 14. 6, especially 'no one comes to the Father except by me'; also Heb. 10. 20). Yet the pre-condition for Jesus to 'be the Way' must be that he himself 'goes on the way'. The image which Luke develops at length in his long central narrative of the journey to Jerusalem (Luke 9. 51–19. 44)—a journey which is determined, not only by Jesus (9. 51), but also by Scripture (18. 31; 13. 33)—has a

---

[1] The Greek text of Mark 14. 21, has ὑπάγει, 'going', without using ὁδός (way). The directional image still seems to be implied, though Fr B. Lindars considers that Mark uses the word as equivalent to παραδίδοται, 'is delivered up', which he requires for its more specialized sense, 'is betrayed', later in the sentence (*New Testament Apologetic*, p. 81). The 'way' image is in any case frequent enough.

[2] *The Imitation of God in Christ*, pp. 67–72.

secure place too in Matthew and Mark, where once again it is accompanied by the notes of compulsion and foreordination (e.g. Mark 10. 32 ff.; 14. 21; Matt. 16. 21).

It will be noticed that several of these instances (e.g. Mark 10. 33; 14. 21) are associated with the term 'Son of Man' and with suffering and death. The extent to which these ideas are themselves typological will be discussed later; in the meantime we must note that, while the Passion is conceived as the end of Jesus' mission, the mission begins with the narratives of baptism and temptation, and these narratives, too, are linked with the idea of a 'way'. The beginning of Mark is a case in point, where the prophecies in Mal. 3. 1 and Isa. 40. 3, both of which refer to the preparation of a way, are brought together to explain the coming of John the Baptist. The inference is clear: John is to prepare the way, but Jesus will walk in it. Although in a certain sense verses 2–3 suggest the fulfilment of prophecy they still offer a prophecy whose fulfilment at that stage had not come about, they still look forward to an event of fulfilment proper. It is only with verse 15, in the preaching of Jesus, that this time-shift is said to have happened: 'The time is fulfilled, and the Kingdom of God has drawn near.'[1] Thus 'the way of the Lord' is initiated, and it is initiated, significantly, with Jesus' baptism and the temptation 'in the wilderness'.

We have noticed the frequent parallelism in the Old Testament between *derek* (way) and *torah* (law). Obedience to the commandments meant 'following after' God who had led Israel on the way through the wilderness. 'In the Book of Deuteronomy there is a continual oscillation between *derek* meaning the actual historical way which Israel has traversed from Red Sea to Promised Land, and *derek* meaning the "way of life" to which the people are consequently summoned... The image of the "Way" is never detached from the historical journey once taken.'[2] Much nearer New Testament times the same alternation between the two contexts of *derek* is to be

---

[1] See J. M. Robinson, *The Problem of History in Mark*, pp. 23 f. esp. p. 24: 'For even though we must understand ἤγγικεν (*v.* 15) to mean "has drawn near" rather than "has come", it still refers to something having taken place: the times have shifted, the kingdom is now near because it has moved from a vague distance to a near position, a shift which has already taken place.' Compare with this treatment of the Markan Prologue that of U. Mauser, *Christ in the Wilderness*, pp. 77–102.   [2] Tinsley, *op. cit.* pp. 34 f.

found in the 'Dead Sea Scrolls'. The Qumran community, indeed, made the synthesis closer even than it was in the orthodox *cultus*. They thought of their mission and existence as 'the perfect way' which they traversed in the wilderness to 'prepare the way of the Lord' (Isa. 40. 3). The verse from Isaiah is quoted in the *Manual of Discipline* (8. 12–14) and applied to their own situation both as explaining their presence in the desert and as implying the duty of studying the law. 'When the (Covenanters) first established themselves in the Wilderness of Judaea, they predicted a forty years' period for their stay, showing that they conceived this time as parallel to the Desert Sojourn of the Hebrews.'[1] Thus the Jewish recital of history becomes in this sect more literally mimetic than in Judaism generally. But at the same time it is clear that they conceived this mimesis as the outward and visible sign of something essentially spiritual and ethical: they intended 'to repeat the experience of their forefathers...while overcoming the trials through which that generation had failed to come successfully'.[2] So that the self-understanding at Qumran was essentially typological, an 'applied typology' whose fulfilment was ethical, or at least involved ethics, and of which the sect's external conformity to the 'accidents' of historical circumstances was merely a sign. They claimed that their ethical imitation of the 'way of the Lord' would fulfil Israel's call, show them to be the true Israel—'the righteous remnant', indeed—and serve to atone for the sins of the nation at large.

That the same kind of principle has been at work in the Gospels, and, in particular, in these stories of the temptation of Jesus, need not surprise us therefore. There are the same overtly repetitive configurations of place (a wilderness) and period (forty days for forty years). There is the same awareness that these things themselves are symbolic of less 'accidental' matters, the repeating of Israel's experience and the perfecting of Israel's response to the call of God, on the one hand, and the temptations of Satan, on the other. And there is the same sense that this obedience makes the obedient figure the true Israel,

[1] J. T. Milik, *Ten Years of Discovery in the Wilderness of Judaea*, pp. 115 f. So central was this parallel that Milik justly refers to their 'mystique of the desert' or 'desert ideology'.

[2] Milik, *loc. cit.*

whose 'remnant' is now concentrated in one individual, who may atone by his work for the sins of the people.

The attributing to Jesus of a personal repetition of historic events is therefore not in itself unique. Nor, indeed, is the idea of this repetition, the perfecting of the nation's response to temptation by a man or sect on behalf of the nation, unique either. What is unique is Jesus' perfect fulfilment of this aim, the achievement of perfect response to the moral demand on the people which the original Exodus-complex implied and had ever since symbolized. In the Qumran literature, the note of actual, present, fulfilment is absent.[1] The Covenanters were impressed with the call but they knew that for all their attempts to respond they were sinful. But the Gospels present Jesus as himself perfectly obedient. He goes through the same temptations as Israel—as the answers, drawn from Deut. 6–8, in Matthew and Luke, are probably intended to suggest—but he, unlike all others, truly perfects man's or Israel's response to them and so treads the 'way' which the Old Testament, the Covenanters, and all 'until John' only 'prophesied' (Luke 16. 16; cf. parallel in Matt. 11. 12 f.).[2]

Therefore if, as is asserted by J. M. Robinson, the fact that Mark 1. 2–3 'offers a prophecy, and verse 15 speaks of the time having been fulfilled' means that we are 'to look in the intervening narrative (vv. 4–13) for an event of fulfilment', then we can locate this event in the 'initial victory over Satan' in the forty days' fast[3] which Mark records and which Matthew, at least, interprets as the perfection of Israel's elected existence in the sole person of Jesus.[4] In him the wilderness-people has at last stopped its 'murmurings'. It is because of this event that the Evangelists can say that the time-shift has happened and

[1] See J. A. Fitzmeyer, 'The Use of Explicit Old Testament Quotations in the Qumran Literature and in the New Testament', *SNTS Bull.* VII (1961), 297–333.

[2] I cannot refrain here from quoting Brevard Childs's statement of a similar position: 'The ultimate criterion for determining the new reality (i.e. the fulfilment of Israel's election) does not lie within the Old Testament. In Jesus Christ *the* new reality has appeared as the self-authenticating "New Israel". As the truly obedient man Jesus is the new existence in its fullest and most concrete form...Not just in his teachings or in particular actions, but in the total existence of the Jew, Jesus Christ, the entire Old Testament receives its proper perspective. It is fulfilled in its obedience, but judged in its disobedience' (*Myth and Reality in the Old Testament*, p. 104).

[3] J. M. Robinson, *op. cit.* pp. 28–32.

[4] See below, Jesus-Israel (iii).

that history is now in process of being fulfilled;[1] and, conversely, it is because they now see in Jesus the fulfilment of Israel's existence that they explain so much of his mission in terms drawn from Israel's history.

But before we elaborate this by examining further examples of the Jesus-Israel typology we should take stock of some of the inferences which may already justly be drawn. First, the idea of God's action which is essential to all proper typology. God's action in this case is his call to Israel which provokes a decision and therefore implies a temptation. It is as old as the wilderness-journey and yet, because God is steadfast, always contemporaneous. Here it is made specific: Jesus, like the Israel of Moses, is led *by the Spirit* into the wilderness (Matt. 4. 1; Exod. 13. 18).

But biblical history includes not only the actions of God but the actions and reactions of man. If the initiative is always God's and God consistently takes it, the decision is always man's, who reacts towards or away from God's implicit call. Within any occurrence which brings man face to face with divine self-revelation—within God's act or its proclamation—his reaction (in either form of it) still implies repetition; man repeats his forefathers' rejection or repeats their surrender to God. Therefore my second point is that if typology really exists as an expression for the relation between acts of God, it must also involve a relation between acts of man in response to the old and new acts of God. So, in Jesus' response to a call like Israel's he repeats Israel's commitment, and perfects it.

Thirdly, we should note that it is the repetition of this response, the victory over Satan, the refusal to be tempted from his 'way', that makes the temptation narrative typological. The repetitiveness of the setting here, like the symbolic configuration of numbers at other points in the Gospels, may or may not be 'historical' but in either case points to the real, and really historical, parallel between the actions which they help to interpret—between, on the one hand, the actions of Jesus, which they 'surround', and, on the other, the actions of Israelite history, which once they surrounded and henceforth (at least in Israel) recall.

---

[1] We must note that not 'all is fulfilled' until the Passion and Resurrection (Matt. 5. 18 may have meant no more than this, in Jesus' mouth, and certainly John 19. 28, 30 interprets the idea of all being fulfilled as applying to this time).

Finally, we should, I think, notice how the concept of 'history' with which we have worked makes sense in a special way of the idea of history's fulfilment. For places and times and people cannot in themselves be fulfilled by other places, times, people;[1] but an emphasis on 'actions' and 'responses' already leads to a region of thought where the idea of 'fulfilment' repeatedly shows itself relevant. For free, responsible actions have a purpose: purposes point to fulfilment and can be fulfilled. 'Response' and 'reaction', in turn, besides being 'actions' themselves, also suggest something else, an obedience to some prompting, the fulfilling of a demand. Clearly, 'demand', 'prompting', 'purpose', will often belong together on the side of the agent who takes the initiative in this dialectic; the fulfilment of the demand and the prompting in that case also involve the fulfilment of the purpose behind the demand and prompting. And in this case, so long as there is only imperfect response, the purpose, prompting, and demand

[1] This is to mistake, as the Fathers sometimes in their typological interpretations mistook, the 'accidents' of typology (i.e. 'things') for its essence (i.e. 'actions'). The error is evidenced throughout the patristic tradition, where time and again it is assumed that because such and such a person is (perhaps traditionally) 'typical' of Christ then the details surrounding that person, or all the events of his life, that are recorded in scripture, are 'typical' too. But this is in such total contradiction to a basic, perhaps even the basic, principle of typology (the principle, once again, that it is primarily events, and not persons or places or things, which are potentially typological, the *res gesta* first, and the *res* or *persona* only in relation to that deed) that however unexceptionable certain typological passages may seem we are led to conclude that they are unexceptionable only fortuitously. This is where H. de Lubac's account of medieval exegesis finally fails to convince as a defence of the empirical practice (*Exégèse Médiévale*, I, *passim*, cf. esp. pp. 457-66). The contradiction in question is most strikingly exemplified in the case which (digressing for a moment in Book III of the *Moralia in Iob*) Gregory I considers; how it often happens that a circumstance 'per historiam virtus est, per significationem culpa; sicut aliquando res gesta, in facto causa damnationis est, in scripto autem prophetia virtutis' (III. xviii). From the example he takes, that of Uriah and David, it is evident how this paradoxical situation has come about. That David prefigures the Redeemer is a typological *datum*; that he does so only in so far as he is a king, and one who recognizes his responsibility before God, is forgotten. The verbs, actions, now only correspond secondarily, and in a case like the present one, in which they *reverse* their significance, they correspond at all only by allegory's aid. In any case the result is the emphatic formula, 'sic gesta damnat ut haec mystice gerenda persuadeat'.

The same explanation of the incident in question is to be found in Augustine, and the same false presupposition at the basis of it: 'The names occurring in the narrative show what it prefigures. "David" means "strong of hand" or "desirable"; and who can be stronger than the Lion of the tribe of Judah, who has conquered the world, or more desirable...etc.' (*Contra Faustum*, XXII, 87).

are together only imperfectly fulfilled. We have only to see these points in terms of historical existence and they show their significance in relation to the Bible.

For according to the Old Testament it is the purpose of God that a new kind of historical existence should come into being. God 'prompts' or promotes this existence by historical action on Israel. He demands (and the Law gives expression to this demand) that Israel should live this existence, that each Israelite should surrender himself to what God has prompted, should ratify the history in the response, should 'fulfil' it. For, in the confession of faith, all Israel's history, in the last resort all human history, and even the Creation, has gone into the making of Israel's and the Israelites' opportunity for new existence.[1] *Tua res agitur*!

But the other side of the same historical condition and conditionality exists in empirical fact so long as Israel's response is only imperfect. God's act and demand and purpose are only imperfectly fulfilled, 'subfulfilled' within the Old Testament and within Israel's history before Christ. This, at all events, is the case as it is seen by Christian belief. But also, so long as the demand upon Israel exists and so long as the promoting activity of God is not broken off or undone, Israel's present existence in subfulfilment still points to a time which God's act and word promise, a time of future, perfect fulfilment, in which her existence in election will be (wholly) existent in empirical fact. At that time, the law, the promoting and prompting of Israel by God, and God's purpose revealed by past action, will together come to fulfilment along with the prophecies in which this existence is promised.[2] Behind the typology of the New

[1] 'Presumptuous as it may sound', writes von Rad, 'Creation is part of the aetiology (and soteriology) of Israel' (*Old Testament Theology*, I, 138).

[2] In this convergence of prophecy, purpose, demand, and historical 'promotion', upon the one goal of an existential fulfilment, one might find the (or at any rate 'an') explanation of a kind of coherence which scholars have felt to exist between different meanings of single words in the semantic field of 'fulfilment'. (See, on πληροῦν and its compounds, especially C. F. D. Moule, '"Fulness" and "Fill" in the New Testament', *SJT*, IV, 1951, 79–86, and the same author's article 'Fulfil' in *Interpreter's Dictionary of the Bible*; and cf. G. Delling, 'πληρόω', *TWNT*, VI, 285–96; and on the various Aramaic words see especially T. W. Manson on '*kayyēm*' ('*kiyyēm*'), 'The Argument from Prophecy', *JTS*, XLVI, 1945, 129; cf. M. Black, *An Aramaic Approach to the Gospels and Acts*, 2nd edn. 1954, pp. 165–72). The fulfilment of Scripture, which Jesus' words in Matt. 5. 17 amplify to incorporate both the Law and the prophets (see Strack-Billerbeck, *Kommentar*, I, *in loc.*; C. F. D. Moule,

Testament lies the claim (not the proof) that Jesus uniquely fulfilled the existence of Israel and, thereby, the imperatives and
the indicatives of law and election. Thus Israel's history has
reached its fulfilment: 'the time is fulfilled' (Mark 1. 15). This
claim was made by Jesus, and—whether certain of the settings
and datings and numberings, such as we find in the wilderness
narratives, are 'myth', and invented by the early Church, or
'prophetic symbolism' on the part of Jesus—in the Gospels the
claim comes pointedly to our minds for its confirmation. This
is 'applied', or perhaps 'kerygmatic' typology, and the 'myth'
or 'prophetic symbolism' serves only to drive it home.

The point of the wilderness imagery is not lost upon the
author of the Epistle to the Hebrews when (Heb. 3–4) he re-
adopts it, exhorting his readers, who 'share in Christ' (3. 14),
to apply this typology radically to their lives, not hardening
their hearts, like the 'murmuring' Israel, but like Christ keeping their original confidence firm to the end. Nor does St Paul
hesitate to give these Old Testament events a similar application: 'all these things happened to them symbolically (τυπικῶς),
and were recorded for our benefit as a warning. For upon us
the fulfilment of the ages has come' (I Cor. 10. 11).

'"Fulness" and "Fill" in the New Testament', p. 83) may be, more often than at
first sight appears, intended to mean the fulfilment by Jesus of texts which, before
they came into service (on account of his having fulfilled them) as 'testimonies',
existed for him as imperatives, laid upon Israel by her history and upon him as her
representative. This is, in my view, a real and significant possibility. Yet so far as
I am aware it has never been properly explored. In the next section, particularly, I
shall try to indicate its relevance, but the main task must be left to the professors
of form-criticism.

CHAPTER 8

JESUS-ISRAEL (ii): THE 'SUFFERING SERVANT' AND 'SON OF MAN'

THE New Testament contains a number of passages where some sort of typological link is made between Jesus and individual figures in the Old Testament. For example, there are parallels between Jesus and Moses (notably, in the Matthean 'sermon on the mount') and between Jesus and Jonah (Matt. 12. 38–41; Luke 11. 29–32; in both of which Jonah is taken as an historical person) which present Jesus as respectively the Law-giver and the 'sign'-giver who comes to demand repentance. Similarly there are parallels between Jesus and Elijah, Melchizedek, David—to the Christian writers he is the apotheosis of Prophet, Priest and King.[1] Notable in all these cases is the fact that it is from the point of view of vocation, and action in response to vocation, that the parallels are established.[2] This is not concealed even in the parallel with Melchizedek, where the author of Hebrews has filled out his argument by making use of a rather dubious etymological link and some forced analogies, for the writer never loses sight of the main point of his proof-text, the supreme High-priesthood of both 'type' and 'anti-type': 'Thou art a priest for ever, in the succession of Melchizedek' (Ps. 110. 4).[3] We will pause here only to point out that all these vocations, though symbolized by the named individuals who in Old Testament times most completely em-

---

[1] D. Daube, *The New Testament and Rabbinic Judaism*, pp. 3–26, points also to parallels in the New Testament between Jesus and Saul, Joseph and Samuel.

[2] This is only true of the reference to Jonah if we ignore Matt. 12. 40: for this verse directs the attention away from the preaching of Jonah ('vocation') and focuses instead upon his miraculous entombment in the sea-monster's belly. That this is an interpolation I find it hard not to believe, notwithstanding the existence of one or two pointers to the contrary (see O. Cullmann, *Christology of the New Testament*, pp. 62–3). Our point, however, is perfectly valid of the Jonah-logion as it stands in Luke.

[3] S. Amsler, *L'Ancien Testament dans l'Église*, p. 22, presents Hebrews' treatment of this figure, from Gen. 14. 17–20, very clearly. It is a resemblance, not identity, and valid only on certain points (king and priest, king of justice and peace, without beginning or end). It is a case of 'explicit' typology.

bodied them, are to some extent the vocations of the whole nation (Exod. 19. 6; Num. 11. 29; Isa. 61. 6; and see Tinsley, *op. cit.* pp. 37 f., 43 f., 61 f.), and are therefore perfectly capable of being discussed within the typological category of 'Jesus-Israel' with which we are at present concerned. This is also the case with those more controversial 'figures', or rather 'offices', of the 'Suffering Servant' (or better, the 'Servant of God') and the 'Son of Man'. We must consider these at greater length.

It cannot be said that they are generally considered to be typological; and that there are the elements of a paradox in calling them so is undeniable. We have here a case which entirely reverses that envisaged in the previous chapter, where the Old Testament events were so clear and specific that the 'accidents' of their setting, by being repeated and perhaps in some cases constructed round their Gospel fulfilment, were sufficient to call up their meaning in their *heilsgeschichtlich* context. Here it is the history of the fulfilment that is specific, whereas it is not at once clear whether the 'figures', now purportedly 'fulfilled', were ever before historical. There is so little historical detail, indeed, in the Old Testament passages, and so much in the New, that it becomes a real danger that the interpreter will read back into the former details and meanings which only the latter properly contains.[1] Nevertheless I believe that the Old Testament passages in question (chiefly: the Servant Songs, Isa. 42. 1–4; 49. 1–6; 50. 4–9; 52. 13–53. 12; and the visions of the Son of Man in Daniel, especially 7. 13) are, on the one hand, to some extent and in some way historical—being concerned, that is, with the interpreting not of the abstraction, 'history', but of the specific history of the Israel of their own times; and that they are, on the other hand, at the same time (perhaps in virtue of this historical reference) to some extent and in some way both predictive and prescriptive of the future 'Israel of God'. In support of this claim we must summarize and evaluate a great deal of critical discussion.

The Servant of God in Deutero-Isaiah has by and large been

---

[1] Cullmann does this when in his *Christology of the New Testament* he speaks of the '*voluntary atoning suffering*' of the Servant (pp. 58, 70; italics mine). Morna Hooker, in *Jesus and the Servant*, p. 46, makes the point: 'Deutero-Isaiah nowhere says that his "Servant" is a willing sufferer', etc. Her reading depends in part on a rejection of the traditional interpretations of Isa. 53. 12 and 50. 6 f. and her note on this point should be consulted.

interpreted in three different ways. There are those who relate the figure to an individual, either historical (perhaps the author, or Moses, or Jehoiachin) or to come (i.e. most often, the Messiah). Then there are those who relate him to Israel (either as a whole, or 'ideally', or as a pious remnant). Finally there are those who relate him, by means of some such idea as that of 'corporate personality', to Israel at large and some or any pious representative of Israel. The Messianic interpretation is not our present concern. Of the other so-called 'historical individual' theories I shall only say that it does not seem to me probable that except perhaps for one or two details of his portrait the prophet had any particular person in mind. The facts which might seem to suggest it are elusive. For example, 'it is argued that the strength of these...theories lies in the fact that the character and fortunes of the Servant are so vividly drawn that we can only think of a portrait from life'.[1] But, as North goes on to say, 'on that principle we should have to say that every convincing character in drama or fiction is taken from actual life'.[2] As for the particular elements which have struck various writers as suggestive of events in particular persons' lives, it would be strange if a figure of such stature and resonance should not show parallels of some kind with known persons in any age. The element of truth in these speculations is only that which the idea of 'corporate personality' already contains: as, according to Zimmerli, it is with the phrase 'Servant of God' in the Old Testament at large, that 'the individual can become the servant of Yahweh only in so far as he is a member of Israel',[3] so it is likely to be with it here.

The evidence for the 'collective interpretation' is stronger. To begin with, both in the whole book of 'Deutero-Isaiah' (i.e. chh. 40–55) and at specific points in the course of the 'Songs' themselves, we meet the phrase 'my Servant, Israel'. It is possible that a gloss has been introduced in the text of the sole instance of the phrase in the Songs themselves (49. 3), this certainly having happened in the Septuagint version of the first song (which there reads (42. 1) 'Jacob my Servant... Israel my chosen'). But in 49. 3 this can by no means be

[1] C. R. North, *The Suffering Servant in Deutero-Isaiah* (2nd edn. 1956), p. 199.
[2] *Ibid.*
[3] W. Zimmerli, in *The Servant of God* by Zimmerli and Jeremias, p. 15.

assumed.[1] That the received reading is the *lectio difficilior*, since in the same song the Servant is spoken of as having a mission *to* Israel, might argue only that the scribe (who believed as later Judaism in general believed that the Servant was Israel) deemed a gloss all the more necessary, but we shall see that the particular paradox which the reading involves is of a piece with the nature of the whole. Meanwhile we must take it as evidence of a sort in favour of the collective interpretation.

Further evidence, and much stronger, is provided by Morna Hooker:

Almost all that was predicated of Israel outside the Songs is attributed to the Servant within them. The Servant, like Israel, is the chosen one of Yahweh, and his mission, like hers, is to bring glory to him; this will be accomplished by the Return from Exile, and by bringing other nations to acknowledge Yahweh. The Servant has been taught by Yahweh through suffering, but this suffering is now at an end, because Yahweh will vindicate him...Even more distressing than the...pain, however, was the Servant's humiliation before others, who have treated him with the same contempt which was shown to Israel by her neighbours. All, however, will be more than made up by the coming exaltation: then the Servant will be rewarded by seeing the increase of his family, now accounted righteous because of his sufferings.[2]

It would seem incredible that these parallels come about merely by chance, and some form of the collective theory must be an essential part of the truth. But it is not necessarily the whole truth. For we may agree that the Servant is an image of Israel without denying the possibility of his having individual existence as well—not, indeed, outside Israel, but as a pious member of Israel. Indeed, on the same principle as that involved in the making of Israel's determinative history 'contemporaneous' in liturgy and law it devolves upon each member to make the sufferings of the nation his own, to realize his own, in the nation's, helplessness and dependence on Yahweh: for this is to ratify his existence in the elected people of God.

Of course there is a paradox here. 'Election' is apparently

---

[1] Cf. H. H. Rowley, 'The Servant of the Lord in the light of three decades of recent criticism' (*The Servant of the Lord and other essays on the Old Testament*), pp. 8 f. and 29 n.

[2] *Jesus and the Servant*, p. 29 (for references to Deutero-Isaiah see the notes on p. 169), and cf. Rowley, *op. cit.* pp. 49 f.

one thing—self-evidently an act of grace, or good fortune (however uncertain, *un*-self-evident, the divine agency in it)—but suffering and exile are another. Neither the hand of God nor the gracious effect are self-evident here. But to just this concern the prophet says, 'Nevertheless! All that has happened is by Yahweh's hand, and for good'. Through these events God lays a great task on the nation, and each member must strive to fulfil it. The individual, like the nation, is to accept suffering, knowing that it is God's word, but not God's last word, that good will come of it, and salvation, because Yahweh is gracious, and the Lord of all history.

In so far, therefore, as any description of the state of Israel standing in history before God (even in exile) as God's true servant, must imply a command to 'do likewise', the collective interpretation of the Songs cannot stand quite alone and unmodified. In positing and developing the picture of an Israel acting in and reacting towards its present situation in Babylon in perfect harmony with and acceptance of its religious vocation, the prophet necessarily (and with C. R. North I would say 'consciously') adumbrates the picture of a man who does so act and react in the face of tribulation.

Miss Hooker, however, denies this by implication when, although she has said that 'the Servant is Israel and the prophet and the Messiah, so that although one concept may be primary' (she thinks, as I do, the collective one), 'we cannot deny the presence of others',[1] she goes on to say of the last Song that 'it is difficult to see how he could have had in mind any one single individual in this chapter...It is certainly unlikely that he saw himself or any past or present figure in quite the light in which the chapter in question sees the Servant.'[2] This is probably true as it stands, so long as the argument is applied to the past and present exclusively. But we may quite fairly point out that it would be difficult, equally, for the prophet to have seen Israel 'past or present' (as Miss Hooker's argument suggests) in quite that light. C. R. North, indeed, has made the point for us:

The prophet can hardly have been blind to the inadequacy of his own people to be the perfect Servant of Yahweh. Nor was he. This is quite clear from what he says about them, even if we regard as

[1] *Op. cit.* p. 44. [2] *Ibid.* p. 47.

later insertions those passages in the book which depict them in the darkest colours. After all, no nation, no religious community ever has acted, or perhaps ever can act, as the Servant does in the last Song; and the prophet was realist enough to know it. Cyrus failed. Israel failed.[1]

So far as the collective interpretation of this Song is concerned the most we can say is that the prophet hoped Israel would approximately conform with his picture.

But with regard to the future, that is, to the consummation of history, the position is different. To that time this prophet looks forward as confidently as the others, and he expects, and demands, of the future Israel a more than approximate conformity. There can be no final fulfilment of God's plan if Israel does not wholly fulfil its part in it. So, at least, in the previous chapter, we have argued of the work of Deutero-Isaiah apart from the Songs,[2] and if, as Miss Hooker believes, these latter are not simply separable from the rest of the book, on her own terms it should be so here. But, as it is, the logic of Miss Hooker's position *vis-à-vis* the Servant's identity leads her to deny not only the presence of an expectation of an ideal individual 'Servant' in the time of fulfilment, but also to deny that Songs' reference to the time of fulfilment itself is in any way separate from the return from the exile. To this argument we oppose ours. The prophetic foreshortening of history, whereby the 'figure' in the foreground merges with the 'fulfilment' behind it, is we believe quite sufficiently attested of the future as of the past in this prophet as in others.[3] And with regard to the Servant poems already H. S. Nyberg[4] has stressed that here too there is a fluidity of time, past, present and future. Moreover, in addition to this 'fluidity' and to the other fluidity involved in the concept of corporate personality, there is reason to postulate a third, a fluidity between indicative and imperative. Far from incurring the suspicion of expediency, this third fluidity ought to support and explain the nature of the two others. We have found it to be fundamental to Old Testament theology in general, where the indicative and the imperative are related

---

[1] North, *The Suffering Servant in Deutero-Isaiah*, p. 217.
[2] See above, pp. 77–9.   [3] See above, p. 78.
[4] In an article, 'Smärtornas man', *Svensk Exegetisk Årsbok*, VII (1942), 5–82, known to me only through summaries by Rowley, *op. cit.* p. 42, and North, *SJT*, III (1950), 366 ff., and *The Suffering Servant in Deutero-Isaiah*, pp. 220 ff.

organically inasmuch as the statement of God's action implies a command or a challenge to those who are acted upon: to be what God's action makes of them. Applied here, this would show the figure of servant to be a picture and a demand—on the one hand, a description of Israel as 'servant' which is realized 'more' or 'less' (fluidity of person and group) from time to time (fluidity of time) and as such is 'indicative'; and on the other, a divine command to Israel and Israelite, of any time, to be Yahweh's wholly committed servant in the way which history and Yahweh's word through the prophet lays upon them, even in suffering.

If this is accepted it follows that Israel in the empirical present has positive elements which, despite her imperfection, point to the nation's perfection as possible in, and in any case as required categorically by, the eschatological future of God's providence. Miss Hooker's belief that the prophet sees the sufferings of the Israel of his own time as undergone vicariously for the sins of the Gentiles, needs to be supplemented with another, which holds that the prophet looked to a future, more perfect, atonement to be brought about by God through Israel. And from this it is no great step to conceive of a man, the ultimate contraction of the 'remnant of Israel', suffering, of necessity as an Israelite standing before God as Israel, for the sins of his nation and others, precisely 'as a (sacrificial) lamb, that is led to the slaughter' (Isa. 53. 7).

We may certainly conclude, then, that the image of the Servant has an original, direct reference to history and to the history of which the prophet himself was a witness: Israel suffering in Babylon but expecting her triumphant return. But it does not stop there. The fourth Song in particular seems to require a more fluid interpretation: implicitly it points to the future and suggests the possibility that the ideal Servant of the prophet's hope might be, after all, an individual, without ceasing to represent Israel.[1] If we are to make sense of the

---

[1] Compare the view of H. H. Rowley: 'In general I believe the author was personifying Israel, but in the fourth poem that personification is carried to a point where it is hard to escape the feeling that he really thought of an individual, so supremely the Servant of Yahweh that within the Servant community he stood out as its representative and leader' (*Israel's Mission to the World*, p. 13). For Rowley's fuller discussion of his view, with which mine almost completely agrees, see his *Servant of the Lord*, esp. pp. 49–57.

evidence which has been presented we can only say of both the image and the history, that already they are conceived by the prophet as typological. This conclusion is roughly the same as North reaches. What he does not go on to say, however, is that if here at their inception in Deutero-Isaiah they are, implicitly, typological, then the appropriation of the image by or for Jesus is at least consistent with the claim that he not only is the image's fulfilment but the fulfilment of the history behind the image too—in other words, that by his fulfilling of the image Jesus has fulfilled typologically the foreshadowing history of Israel in exile.[1]

Daniel's Son of Man (7. 13) is less controversial. It is now generally regarded as a symbol of Israel, exalted and vindicated after the collapse of the four great empires (symbolized by the four beasts of *vv.* 3–7).[2] So much is made plain by the pseudo-nymous writer himself in the latter part of the chapter. Some scholars have been led by the fact that the exaltation of the Son of Man here is so evidently the aftermath of a period of intense tribulation to take a further step and say that this figure derives from the Isaianic Servant of God. F. F. Bruce, for example, believes this: 'there is', he says, 'good reason to hold that Daniel's visions are in part dependent on the Servant Songs of Isaiah, and (more particularly) that Daniel's "one like a son of man" was from the first intended to be identical with the Isaianic Servant'.[3] This puts the case too positively, for the evidence is not strong; but the fact remains incontro-

---

[1] The question of the interpretation of the Servant Songs in later Judaism has been the subject of much discussion. Briefly, it would appear to be established that at about the time of Christ the Songs were not read as entities separate from the rest of the book of Isaiah, the exception being the last Song, which was interpreted Messianically, the suffering of this Messiah being, however (possibly in reaction to Christianity), muted or wholly ignored. For a fuller discussion we must refer above all to those of Jeremias (*The Servant of God*, pp. 43–78) and Cullmann (*Christology of the New Testament*, pp. 52–60).

[2] Compare, for example, H. H. Rowley, *The Relevance of Apocalyptic*, pp. 29–33, and T. W. Manson, *Studies in the Gospels and Epistles*, pp. 125–7.

[3] *Biblical Exegesis in the Qumran Texts*, p. 65. The case is argued by other scholars; see C. F. D. Moule, 'From Defendant to Judge—and Deliverer', *SNTS Bull.* III (1952), 40 ff.; M. Black, 'Servant of the Lord and Son of Man', *SJT*, VI (1953), 1 ff. Important support for this theory, and for the likelihood of Jesus' linking the two 'offices' is adduced from the Qumran documents, several passages of which seem to necessitate the conclusion that the Sect viewed themselves as embodying this link, as a community.

vertible that the two figures are more or less compatible.[1] The Servant of the last Song is 'to be vindicated' (Isa. 52. 13; 53. 12), the mighty of the earth will then be astonished by the unheard-of prosperity of one hitherto despised (Isa. 52. 14–15). And behind the more conventional phraseology of Daniel (i.e. the 'dominion' and 'kingdom' which are to be taken away from the mighty and bestowed upon Israel) one can sense the same feeling: the nations will be overawed by what they see coming to pass by God's act; though they 'think to change the times and the law...(their) dominion shall be (altogether) taken away' (Dan. 7. 25–6) and given to 'the people of the saints of the Most High' whom they believed to be quite 'worn out' (Dan. 7. 27, 25).

Now for our purposes there is no need to postulate more than this similarity. For it is enough to have shown that it is certainly Israel that the Old Testament views in this light. The two cases of Dan. 7 and Isa. 53 corroborate one another in this, quite apart from the question of influence. And therefore if Jesus at all fulfils these prophecies it is as Israel that he must do so. It only remains to establish, first, that the New Testament claims that Jesus did fulfil these prophecies; secondly, that though later editing in the gospels may have misunderstood the mode of the prophecies' fulfilment, Jesus at least saw himself (or some very primitive moulder of the tradition saw him) as fulfilling them primarily as the representative of Israel; and then, finally, it remains for us to see in what way this claim presents itself to our judgement. For all these objectives the main field of inquiry may be the 'Son of Man' sayings within the Synoptic Gospels.

First, that the term, 'Son of Man', goes back to Jesus himself seems sufficiently clear, above all from the fact that outside these sayings it is extremely rare. But it is also clear that the complexity of the term's use in these sayings defies any one, univocal, sense by which to interpret them. Sometimes it refers, as in Daniel, explicitly to a future vindication; sometimes, as is implicit in Daniel, it refers to the necessity (or actuality) of present tribulation; sometimes it refers to the present without regard to whether or not it involves suffering; and in some of these latter cases it is possible that the phrase means, as the Aramaic of the original, *bar-nasha*, certainly does, no more than

---

[1] Compare, recently, N. Perrin, *The Kingdom of God in the Teaching of Jesus*, pp. 99 f.

'man' in a quite general sense: this could be the case with Mark 2. 27–8; Matt. 8. 20 (less probably) and Matt. 12. 31–2.[1] The authenticity of the 'suffering' usage[2] is contested by Bultmann, who argues from the fact that there are no instances of this in Q that it is secondary in character, comprising *vaticinia ex eventu* which have been invented by Mark.[3] The other 'present' uses are acceptable for Bultmann on the grounds that they represent the simple Aramaic *bar-nasha*, and the 'future' usage is genuinely Jesus' but refers to another figure, whom he expected to come as Messiah. The title 'Son of Man' was in this case never used by Jesus as a self-designation. Against this we may put the assertion of E. Schweizer, which is certainly true of the 'present' uses of the term as we have them: 'In most places the word is plainly used in an individual sense. There is no place where a collective interpretation is necessary.'[4] And with regard to the 'future' use, R. H. Fuller's point is at once subtle and fair:

That there is a distinction between (Jesus and the glorified Son of Man) is shown by Mark 8. 38, cf. Matt. 19. 28. But that there is also an organic connection between them is also shown by the same texts. For it is a man's attitude to Jesus in his proclamation and activity in his earthly life...which determines a man's status before the glorified Son of Man...Moreover, while Jesus frequently exhorts his followers to wait for the coming of the Son of Man he never includes himself among those who are to wait. He stands as it were on the same side as the glorified Son of Man over against his disciples...Jesus suffers [Fuller concludes] as the Son of Man designate.[5]

Now it is the merit of Fuller's analysis, as it is of the differing ones of T. W. Manson, Cullmann and Schweizer, that it

---

[1] See the discussion of these instances in O. Cullmann, *The Christology of the New Testament*, pp. 152–4.

[2] We shall make use of the categories used by Fuller in *The Mission and Achievement of Jesus*, pp. 96–7.

[3] *Theology of the New Testament*, I, 30–2. But cf. N. Perrin, *The Kingdom of God in the Teaching of Jesus*, p. 105: 'The Passion sayings are obviously out of place in a collection which, no doubt deliberately, excluded the Passion, and it can occasion no surprise therefore that they are not to be found in Q'. Perrin's whole discussion of the Son of Man sayings is valuable (*ibid.* pp. 90–129) as a means of orientating oneself to the recent arguments.

[4] *Lordship and Discipleship*, p. 44.

[5] *The Mission and Achievement of Jesus*, pp. 102–3.

attempts to do justice to all three categories of 'Son of Man' sayings which have been distinguished (i.e. 'present', 'suffering' and 'future' usages of the phrase), by treating them as in some sense a unity. It is a merit because there can be no doubt that although the task is difficult, since, as we have seen, both the meaning of the phrase and its object of reference are obscure, the feeling remains with us as we read the Gospels that the phrase as Jesus used it in fact was a 'unity'. The diversity and frequency of the phrase and its contexts in the Gospels and its uncommon occurrence outside them alike suggest that it was the occasion of some bemusement in the early Church and that nevertheless it was regarded as peculiarly applicable to Jesus: to fit these facts no better hypothesis can be constructed than that which says that Jesus had himself used it as a self-designation but in ways whose apparent multiplicity then and later produced much perplexity. In this case, it is at least possible that the mode of its 'unity' already contained the seeds of perplexity, that the sayings had, in Jesus' mouth, an ambiguous scope, a scope which left it in doubt as to who was the object of reference, whether Jesus or some future Messiah, whether 'man', or Israel, or the disciples.[1] The form of some of the sayings suggests that this is the truth. We will take instances that are agreed to be crucial.

For example, the sayings which speak of the Son of Man proceeding as was written of him in the scriptures,[2] or which speak of

---

[1] 'We must reckon with the possibility that Jesus always used "Son of Man" in a deliberately ambiguous sense' (Cullmann, *The Christology of the New Testament*, p. 154). Undoubtedly Jesus used it in a special sense of himself, but it should be noted that there is no doubt whatever that he was aware that it applied in Daniel to the whole 'people of God' as the saying in Luke 12. 32 indicates. This would fit in with S. L. Edgar's conclusion that 'the Old Testament passages quoted by Jesus were used with a respect for the original context that is unmatched by other New Testament writers' ('Respect for Context in Quotations from the Old Testament', *SNTS Bull.* IX, 62).

[2] Though by no means all of the sayings which refer to the Son of Man can of course be taken as authentic, there is no reason why we should *a priori* reject all those which refer to scripture for authentication, as H. E. Tödt thinks, *Der Menschensohn in der synoptischen Überlieferung* (cited from N. Perrin, *op. cit.* pp. 109–11). Jesus' 'sovereign authority' is not impaired by the kind of authentication that is involved—which is more an aid to the interpretation of his mission than a genuine 'authentication' of it, and sets his actions in the historical context proper to them, the time of fulfilment to which the Old Testament looks forward, the time when the Kingdom of God enters history and human experience. Whatever doubts may attach to the historicity of the story in Luke 4. 16–21 ('Today this text has been

him in terms drawn from passages of scripture, may be intended by Jesus to indicate not merely the fulfilment of prediction, and prediction of which he is the object,[1] but also the fulfilment of prescription, of which he is only one object in so far as the demand of the passage rests on the whole nation of Israel and yet also the sole object in so far as the demand is fulfilled wholly only by him. In this case the primary sense of the sayings would remain, 'I go as it is written of the one who comes to fulfil the Scriptures', but behind this meaning would lie the implication, 'should not you have gone in this way also? For this was written of Israel'.[2]

In this connection we may refer once again to the work of R. H. Fuller. He maintains of the five prophecies of the Passion in Mark[3] that within their detailed predictions of the circumstances surrounding the Passion—which are most likely secondary in character—lie genuine *verba Christi* which are couched in more general terms and between them 'form a clear description of the Suffering Servant of Isaiah 53'.[4] The conflated sayings as he presents them run as follows:

(The Son of Man) must suffer many things, and be rejected and set at nought, and delivered up into the hands of men and they shall kill him. (For he came) not to be ministered unto, but to minister (=be the servant of Yahweh), and to give his life a ransom for many.

fulfilled in your hearing'), there is every indication that the story from Q where Jesus replies to the doubts of John the Baptist by an indirect citation of eschatological prophecy (Isa. 35. 5; 61. 1) is genuine and a true mirror of his practice (Luke 7. 22 ff.; Matt. 11. 4 ff.). His mission, and God's action through it, fulfils what was prophesied. *Now* is the time of decision.

[1] As they are taken by Matthew (who stresses God as the fulfilling agent: see 8. 17; 12. 17; 13. 35 in the light of such texts as Matt. 1. 22; 2. 15, 17; 27. 9; etc.) and Luke (who sees Jesus as deliberately fulfilling prophecies which apply to the 'Son of Man' regarded as signifying the Messiah: see Luke 18. 31; 22. 37 in the light of 24. 25 ff. and 44 ff.). Cf. S. Amsler, *Ancient Testament dans l'Église*, pp. 77–85.

[2] It is worth noting the similarity between this idea of fulfilment and the one attributed to the author of the Fourth Gospel by R. Morgan, 'Fulfilment in the Fourth Gospel, the Old Testament Foundations', *Interpretation* (1957), pp. 155–65: 'Fulfilment as pictured in the Fourth Gospel is not the mechanical external thing which many people conceive it to be. It is not that Jesus deliberately acted to vindicate some literal prediction of a prophet. *It is rather fulfilment by recapitulation.* Jesus accepts Israel's vocation as Servant, and in his life, death and resurrection fulfils this destiny, and thus consummates the purpose of God for Israel.'

[3] Mark 8. 31; 9. 12, 31; 10. 33–4, 45.

[4] *The Mission and Achievement of Jesus*, pp. 55–7.

As it stands this is clearly intended to refer quite simply to Jesus. So Fuller takes it, and deduces that Jesus interpreted his death in the light of Isaiah 53.[1] All this is quite arguably so. But it is not quite the whole of the picture as the Markan contexts, even as they stand, make plain.

The first saying, Mark 8. 31, is followed immediately by certain sayings which apply to the people the same demand as that contained in the prophecy of Jesus' Passion: 'Anyone who wishes to be a follower of mine must leave self behind; he must take up his cross, and come with me' (Mark 8. 34). And Mark notes of this saying that it was spoken to 'the people, as well as his disciples'—a fact whose significance the usual translation of ἀκολουθείτω μοι as 'follow me' tends to disguise. Jesus is speaking to Israel as his contemporaries; they are under the same demand as he himself, and they are called to discipleship *alongside* him and not only behind him.[2] Mark 10. 45, similarly, with its reference to the 'servanthood' of the Son of Man, is indissolubly connected with verses 43–4: 'whoever wants to be great[3] must be your servant, and whoever wants to be first must be the willing slave of all' (cf. Mark 9. 35). It is hard to assess with any certainty on what principle the prediction of suffering in Mark 10. 33–4 is linked up with the verses which follow: James and John at all events have it here in their minds that Jesus is to be exalted as 'Son of Man' and ask that they may in some measure share his glory; but as the Son of Man's glory requires that first he must suffer, so is it with their own: 'Can you drink the cup that I drink, or be baptized with the baptism I am baptized with?' (Mark 10. 38). Mark 9. 31–5 has precisely the same dialectical catenation: Jesus' suffering, the idea of exaltation in the minds of the disciples, and their master's insistence that they, like him, must first be 'the servant of all'.

This leaves only the saying in Mark 9. 12 f. The prediction of the suffering and contempt which the Son of Man must undergo seems at first sight out of place in the context of the disciples' question about the return of Elijah, and some scholars think it misplaced here. But we should take it as it

---

[1] *The Mission and Achievement of Jesus*, pp. 58–9.

[2] Compare, here, T. W. Manson, *The Teaching of Jesus*, pp. 231–4.

[3] μέγας γενέσθαι here, as the context in verse 42 makes plain, is to be equated with 'be exalted'. Cf. Dan. 7. 14, 27.

stands. According to these verses, it is not only the Son of Man, but Elijah, who is spoken of in the scriptures as to endure great sufferings:

How is it that the scriptures say of the Son of Man that he is to endure great sufferings and to be treated with contempt? I tell you, Elijah has already come and they have worked their will upon him, as the Scriptures say of him.

That verse 12 is genuine is made probable by the indefiniteness of the passion-prediction.[1] And it would seem to be very unlikely that the early Church should connect such a prediction with the prophecy of the return of Elijah if they were not already joined, and presumably by Jesus. It is hard to determine, however, whether the reference to the new Elijah which Jesus sees in the prophecies of the Son of Man means that Jesus, not John (as Matthew takes it, cf. Matt. 17. 13), is the expected 'Elijah *redivivus*', or whether the prophecies refer both to Jesus and John the Baptist, and are interpreted by Jesus as meaning that John has to some extent already fulfilled the Son of Man prophecies which Jesus will wholly fulfil. The latter alternative, which has the slight advantage of fitting the Markan *Sitz im Leben Jesu*, is possibly only if Jesus apprehends a fluidity in the prophecies' precise reference, a fluidity between the returning Elijah and the Son of Man which is difficult to account for except by suggesting that Jesus takes the latter's mission to be an imperative laid not upon him only but upon all men, an imperative which has been in fact most nearly fulfilled by Elijah (as symbol of the suffering prophet) and John the Baptist, but remaining for Jesus himself to fulfil absolutely. The other explanation, however, since it requires that as Elijah *redivivus* the Son of Man must have already undergone suffering and rejection, will not fit into any *Sitz im Leben Jesu* except that of a Resurrection-appearance. The transfiguration prefigures the Resurrection, of course, but that does not justify the use of the past tense in verse 13. In any case, by placing the narrative here it would seem that St Mark, like St Matthew, understood the reference to be to the Baptist. If he was wrong, and the

---

[1] Now generally accepted. Cf. Jeremias, in *The Servant of God*, p. 90, n. 406. Of verse 12 W. Manson has written that 'it has the rugged and irreducible form of an original oracle' (*Jesus the Messiah*, p. 129).

reference is to Jesus himself, who has after all been revealed on the mount of transfiguration as the one who sums up and consummates the mission of Moses and Elijah, then the saying is easily to be understood as implying that Jesus, like the original Elijah, and like the Servant of God in Deutero-Isaiah,[1] has suffered rejection. In this latter case, it is at least notable that the Son of Man reference still includes the original Elijah and hence all the prophets who, like Elijah, were rejected, and that it may perhaps also include the whole people of Israel of whom it was demanded by Isa. 53 that they should all accept suffering as their glory's precondition. And on the other hand, if the former case is the true one, then as Lindars says, 'the scope of the scripture is made to include John the Baptist as well as Jesus himself, which means that it is being viewed simply as the appointed way of salvation in the pre-Messianic'—i.e. 'non-Messianic'—'sense'.[2] The choice between these alternatives cannot be made with certainty.

An argument similar to that used in the case of the other Passion-predictions applies to the saying in Matt. 8. 20 (parallel in Luke 9. 58): 'The Son of Man has nowhere to lay his head.' This constitutes, as Fuller says, 'a *figurative* expression for rejection',[3] and the context makes it quite plain that Jesus' way of life is to be that of his disciples. What is spoken of the true Israel as Son of Man and has been taken by Jesus as applying to him as representative of the true Israel is to be appropriated also by others.[4]

There is thus an ambiguity about the 'suffering' uses which, since it is creative and at the same time (in view of the Old Testament origins of the ideas involved) also legitimate, is

---

[1] There is no prophecy of the returning Elijah's rejection or suffering in the Old Testament, or, so far as is known, in Jewish tradition. The original Elijah, however, was rejected (cf. I Kings 19. 10, etc.) and it may be to this that Jesus refers. But the main Old Testament passage is still, I think, likely to be Isa. 53: cf. Lindars, *New Testament Apologetic*, p. 81.

[2] *Ibid.* Cf. also A. Farrer, 'Typology', *ExpT*, LXVII (May 1956), p. 231.

[3] *Op. cit.* p. 105.

[4] Cf. T. W. Manson, *Studies in the Gospels and Epistles*, p. 143: 'We should be prepared to find that "a" corporate entity is embodied *par excellence* in Jesus himself in such a way that his followers, who together with him constitute the "Son of Man" as a group, may be thought of as extensions of his personality... And I think that all the authentic instances of the use of the term "Son of Man" should be interpreted along these lines.'

likely to be deliberate.[1] Jesus is Israel's representative, but he fulfils the vocation of Israel without making it any the less the vocation of Israel still. What is truly indicative only of him is imperative for all others if they would be God's own people. Therefore the notes of compulsion and fore-ordination which in one way appear to be taken as purely prophetic of the mission of Jesus, in another way tend to rebound as demands made on the people and on his disciples: 'The Son of Man must suffer.' And we are bound to ask in this connection whether it was not in part to further this aim that Jesus used a phrase to designate his mission which was most commonly used to mean 'man'. If the people are blind to the 'Son of Man's' work in the book of Daniel and even quite unaware of its peculiar aptness to Jesus, an aptness which is validated, as Fuller points out, above all by his accepting a life of humility and suffering,[2] yet they may still see the term as it were without capital letters, merely as *bar-nasha*, 'man', and therefore as spoken about themselves as men and members of Israel, called to live in the same way as Jesus. It seems probable that Jesus courted this ambiguity, and if the disciples understood the phrase rightly of him the people were not wholly wrong in understanding it of themselves. For the truth lay on both sides, and to maintain one side exclusively is to limit it. The vocation of Jesus is still the vocation of Israel.

We must just add a word, though, with regard to the more important uses of the term 'Son of Man' which have not so far been dealt with. The unity of the 'future' usages, and of those 'present' usages which refer not to duties but privileges, with

[1] These conclusions, I am aware, run counter to the main stream of modern 'Son of Man' interpretation. Yet I am strongly of the opinion that once the typological thought-form is appreciated they will appear not only defensible but, so to speak, aggressive. Two faults in the 'main stream' (Tödt, Vielhauer, Miss Hooker, etc.) are particularly revealed: its failure to appreciate the claims of the conversational locus of the most probably authentic sayings, and its failure to take sufficiently seriously the probability of Jesus using the term with deliberate ambiguity. These faults seem to me to disqualify the more sceptical treatments of these *logia*, at least *pro tem.*; and if typology renders both locus and ambiguity (as I have argued) intelligible, there is a case here to be answered.

[2] 'Jesus...knows that he was sent to fulfil the mission of Israel...(He does not) *claim* to be the Son of Man. He speaks of himself as Son of Man with a certain detachment and reserve, for it speaks to him not of a claim to be asserted, but of a life to be lived, a life of humility and self-oblation even unto death, and, solely on the grounds of that..., of his ultimate vindication by the Father' (Fuller, *op. cit.* p. 108).

the 'suffering' usages has been shown by several scholars as intelligible of Jesus. But is it intelligible of Israel, and of the disciples? The question has been partly answered already by Jesus' words which we quoted not long ago.[1] He does not deny that they will enter into the Son of Man's glory—Luke 12. 32, indeed, expressly affirms that they will, and it is worthy of note that the phrase used by Jesus looks at least very like a reference to Dan. 7—but he makes it plain that they must first accept for themselves the way of life of a servant. Nor does he deny, explicitly at any rate, that his privileges while on earth (Mark 2. 10, 28) might apply to others besides him (according to Matt. 9. 8 the people gladly seized upon Jesus' words about the Son of Man's right to forgive sins as applying to them: they were 'sons of men'); but, again, obviously they can apply only conditionally, for as the fulfilment of the Servant's vocation is, as Jesus teaches, the necessary precondition for the Son of Man's glory, so the privileges of the Son of Man are only for his true disciples; the duties are all men's; all men are called to be his disciples.

To sum up; I believe we have now sufficiently proved that Jesus' use of the term 'Son of Man' and of the concept 'Servant of God' are, like the term and the concept themselves, typological, and that Jesus' realization of his uniqueness in fulfilling the demands which are made on the nation by Yahweh coexists with the knowledge that he is fulfilling something which has already, if imperfectly, happened within Israel's history— in particular, in the exile, and, behind that, in the bondage in Egypt. Therefore the New Testament claims that he represents and fulfils the existence of Israel, and we may take it that it was in these terms that Jesus preferred to interpret his Messiahship. But we may note, too, that another concept and term lies in the background, one which we have already discussed, the idea of the 'way', which is the way of Israel as well as of Jesus, and which is linked with the call to follow and implies, as we now see more fully, that to suffer as a Servant is still a duty to men who are not Messiahs. Thus the disciples must all be baptized with the same baptism as he (Mark 10. 38), which is suffering and death, so as to 'fill up'—we might say, in our terms, 'subfulfil'—the sufferings of Jesus (Col. 1. 24; and com-

[1] Mark 10. 43–5. See above p. 124.

pare also the summons to fortitude in I Pet. 2. 18–24 which again recalls Jesus as Servant of God in the terms of Isa. 53, and adds, by way of comment, that it was done for our example). This is, once again, an 'applied' and existential typology: it claims not only our decision, with regard to its truth, but over and above that our imitation. We must participate in the existence which it presents.[1]

---

[1] Since this book went to press an important new book on *The Foundations of New Testament Christology* by R. H. Fuller, revises, sometimes quite radically, some of the views set forth in *The Mission and Achievement of Jesus*. I regret that this recent book appeared too late for me to consider it in the present chapter, and must here refer the reader to Fuller's chapter v ('The Historical Jesus: His Self-Understanding') in particular.

CHAPTER 9

JESUS-ISRAEL (iii): MATTHEW 1–4

THE Exodus-typology which is at the heart of the temptation narratives is prominent in all four Gospels, and, indeed, in all the New Testament.[1] This fact, by itself, is a mark of some kind of continuity between the two Testaments for we have observed that, in the Old Testament, the complex of events which we focus in the term 'Exodus' had achieved a dominant position in the self-understanding of Israel.

Yet even those aspects of the mission and achievement of Jesus which could be expressed typologically could not be explained entirely in terms of one period, and in the prophets, too, though the Exodus period is pre-eminent, the whole 'way' of Israel cannot be described, or foreseen, or urged upon the people, without reference to at least three other periods: the period of the Babylonian exile, the Davidic kingdom, and the age of the patriarchs—above all, the covenant with Abraham. The apparent absence of any great interest, in the New Testament, in the first of these, the exile and return from Babylon, may, as we have seen, be no more than apparent, and is in any case easily accounted for by the extent to which, even in the exilic prophets, Deutero-Isaiah and Ezekiel, this period was merged in the national consciousness with the earlier period of slavery which it seemed in some ways to repeat.

With regard to the other two periods, though Paul also makes use of an Abraham typology, not only with reference to the Church (Rom. 4; Gal. 3) but also with reference to Christ (Gal. 3. 16) by virtue of whose unique sonship of Abraham the Church has become the new Israel (Gal. 3. 26–9), yet they are particularly of interest to Matthew; and to conclude my discussion of Jesus-Israel typology in the New Testament I shall argue that his use of these themes—taking the first four chapters of his Gospel as illustration—is more typological than has been

[1] This has been generally recognized. See W. D. Davies, *The Setting of the Sermon on the Mount*, pp. 349–52, and the literature cited there—to which we should add: J. Marsh, *The Fulness of Time*; U. Mauser, *Christ in the Wilderness*; and T. F. Glasson, *Moses in the Fourth Gospel*.

generally thought, and, moreover, that his use of the Old Testament is not so naïve as it is commonly held to be.[1]

The curious form of chapter 1, verse 1 is most noteworthy: 'A table of the descent of Jesus Christ, son of David, son of Abraham.' David and Abraham are introduced too abruptly for their presence to be accidental. The verse, of course, highlights their presence in the genealogy and may therefore be simply intended to give a kind of *kudos* to Jesus' ancestry. It certainly does that. But it does it in a particular way, and in connection with a particular claim: that Jesus is the Messiah, *Christos*.[2] The Messiah must be 'of Israel': Jesus is of Abraham's seed (cf., again, Gal. 3. 16, where the argument is very similar). The Messiah must be of David's family: Jesus is.

As regards the genealogy itself, it is interesting that Matthew underlines these three periods (*v.* 17): 'Thus there were fourteen generations in all from Abraham to David, fourteen from David until the deportation to Babylon, and fourteen from the deportation until the Messiah.'[3]

---

[1] Daniélou speaks of Matthean typology as the search for correspondences between the events of the Old Testament and the biographical details of Jesus' life, as distinct from the Johannine 'theological' and 'sacramental' typology (*Theology*, LVII, March 1954. The same view is expressed also in his *Origen* and *From Shadows to Reality*: e.g. *Origen*, p. 161, *Shadows*, pp. 287 f.; K. J. Woollcombe criticizes this position in *Essays on Typology*, p. 68). One feels a distinction between John and Matthew in their use of typology, but I do not think Matthew is any less 'theological'. For a later view of Daniélou's, however, which goes to the other extreme, see n. 5 to page 134 below. Against that too one can only urge caution. It is undeniable that Matthew misunderstood certain Old Testament texts (cf. S. V. McCasland, 'Matthew twists the Scriptures', *JBL*, LXXX, 1961, 143–8), and though I do not see why this should necessarily also make him a bad theologian it does not inspire confidence. Nevertheless, the more intently one focuses upon the gospel of Matthew as a theological work in its own right (as two recent publications, Bornkamm, Barth, Held, *Tradition and Interpretation in Matthew*, and W. D. Davies, *The Setting of the Sermon on the Mount*, strongly confirm), the more respectable it appears.

[2] This claim cannot, of course, be proved. There is no question (*pace* Bultmann, 'Prophecy and Fulfilment', *Essays*, p. 186) of trying to remove the 'scandal' of the gospel here or elsewhere. The fact that Jesus 'fulfils' is part of the content of the *kerygma*, not a mistaken attempt to provide it with dubious corroboration. The decision remains with the one who hears the message and recognizes it, or does not, as 'gospel', i.e. good news. What the Christian apologist, and Matthew as Christian apologist, must do is to remind the hearer of those things in the received Jewish religion by comparison with which the desired recognition is possible, and to show that there is no contradiction.

[3] See K. Stendahl, 'Quis et unde? An analysis of Matthew 1–2', *BZNW*, XXVI (1960), *Jeremias Festschrift*, 100 f.

The threefold assertion of 1. 1 is, surely deliberately, recalled by three biblical quotations which are introduced in the same order. All three are read as Messianic prophecies. In 1. 23 he refers to the prophecy, 'the virgin will conceive and bear a son, and he shall be called Emmanuel' (Isa. 7. 14). This is taken to be a clear prediction of the birth of the Messiah. Next, in 2. 6 he refers to the prophecy 'Bethlehem in the land of Judah...out of you shall come a leader to be the shepherd of my people Israel'—a quotation which, composed as it is of II Sam. 5. 2, as well as Mic. 5. 2, necessarily implies a typology, and not just the fulfilment of a prediction.[1] Jesus, it is claimed, is the new David. And in 2. 15 the verse from Hosea, 'I called my son out of Egypt' (Hos. 11. 1), which refers in its Old Testament context to Israel ('When Israel was a child, I loved him, and out of Egypt have I called my son') is now taken as applying as literally to Christ as to ancient Israel, so that thus his membership of that people is ratified 'in the letter' as it will be 'in the spirit'.[2] Both these latter prophecies are typological, and provide circumstantial evidence to support the twin contentions that Jesus fulfils David's kingship of Israel and that he fulfils Israel's vocation as the people chosen by God.

All this indicates the feasibility of the claim 'Jesus is Christ', but though Matthew has shown that it is a special and even a unique feasibility which supports this claim, the claim remains, at this stage, precisely a 'feasible' one and no more than that. According to the flesh, as it were, the Christian contentions about Jesus' person are strong ones; but they stand in need of a vindication which is spiritual, of being justified by the action of Jesus.[3] Just this point is implied by the ministry of John the

[1] Cf. W. D. Davies, op. cit. p. 77.

[2] As A. Richardson has said (Introduction to the Theology of the New Testament, p. 150), 'Matthew's quotation of Hos. 11. 1 contains profound theological truth, whatever we may think of the historicity of the Flight into Egypt. A new Israel is called out of "Egypt" in order that a new and better covenant may be made, and one which will not be invalidated by inability on the human side to fulfil the essential condition of obedience.' I should only add, as regards 'historicity', that a certain amount of historicity attaches in any case to the fulfilment of the exodus history in Jesus by the very fact that each Israelite made that history his own in liturgy, ritual, and indeed to some extent in life in general. This is, in that case, a 'subfulfilment' only, but 'historical' none the less, especially, we would claim, in Jesus' case.

[3] The same kind of argument may lie behind Paul's formula in Rom. 1. 3–4, RSV, '...his Son, who was descended from David according to the flesh and

Baptist, with which the narrative immediately proceeds. The very fact of John's baptizing Jews casts a very serious doubt upon the sufficiency of claims to special religious privileges that were based only upon the flesh. Previously only proselytes to Judaism would undergo Baptism, as a mark of their entering into membership of Israel. Jews had never been baptized: 'no-one', says William Barclay, 'had ever conceived that a Jew should need Baptism'.[1] By preaching their need for it now, John had, in effect, 'excommunicated the whole nation'.[2]

In view of Matthew's interest in the descent of Jesus from Abraham, then, the preaching of John the Baptist in Matt. 3. 8–10, with its radical calling into question of all claims based on birth and descent, must bring us back to the question of what is meant by true sonship of Abraham with a new emphasis.[3] 'Do not presume to say to yourselves, "We have Abraham for our father". I tell you that God can make children of Abraham out of those stones.' True sonship depends on behaviour, and in that the whole nation has failed. Therefore John preaches repentance, a repentance which is urgent because 'the King-dom of Heaven is upon you' (3. 2).

Is there no true son of Abraham, then? The question is forced upon us by the account of John's preaching, and with a finely dramatic effectiveness (3. 13) Jesus is modestly but im-mediately reintroduced in the narrative. Jesus alone is a true son of Abraham; he is in no need (v. 14) of baptism, although (v. 15) he will undergo it 'to conform...with all that God requires' (lit. 'to fulfil all righteousness').

Matthew's claim, then, is that Jesus is perfect and that he alone perfectly fulfils the vocation of Israel. Nor is it merely an implication of this that Jesus represents, or is identified with, Israel. For the words which are spoken from heaven, as Jesus

designated Son of God according to the Spirit of holiness by his resurrection from the dead'. In this instance, however, the intermediate stage is left out, but it need hardly be said that Jesus was, for Paul too, designated 'true son of Abraham' or true Israel by his life and work.

[1] *The Mind of Jesus*, p. 30.

[2] A. Plummer, *An Exegetical Commentary on the Gospel according to St Matthew* (London, 1909).

[3] Again we cannot fail to notice the agreement of this argument with that of Paul (Rom. 9. 6, etc.). The relation between Paul and Matthew to which C. H. Dodd draws attention (*New Testament Essays*, pp. 53–66) makes our interpretation explicable.

comes out from the river (*v.* 17), makes this point sufficiently plain. Where Mark and Luke have the form 'Thou art', Matthew, as if addressing the reader directly, has '*This is* my Son'. That the phrase 'Son of God' in its application to Jesus develops in this Gospel (as in others) a special meaning cannot be denied, but to a Jew, brought up on the Old Testament, the phrase means primarily 'Israel'.[1] Indeed, as Miss Hooker points out, all three of the keywords in this speech (υἱός, 'son'; ἀγαπητός, 'beloved'; εὐδόκησα, 'I was well pleased') which have been traced—she considers, 'somewhat dubiously'—to Isa. 42. 1 (the first 'Servant Song') 'together form a concept which in the Old Testament is applied only to Israel'.[2]

As Israel, therefore, in the next section (Matt. 4), Jesus enters a period of temptation like that in the wilderness of Sinai.[3] He perfects what was previously imperfect in Israel's response, and in this respect thereby fulfils Israel's history.[4] For the first time man acts in perfect harmony with the will of God and thereby initiates God's reign, the 'kingly rule'—which Jesus now (Matt. 4. 17) preaches.[5]

[1] A brief summary of the evidence on this point is in A. Richardson's *Introduction to the Theology of the New Testament*, pp. 148–9.

[2] *Jesus and the Servant*, p. 73. It is strange that Miss Hooker fails to consider the possibility, even, that therefore Jesus is being presented *as* Israel. Perhaps she does not think it relevant to her subject.

[3] Perhaps the Exodus typology which is employed here may be traced in the baptism too. St Paul (I Cor. 10. 1–2) appears to presuppose a connection between Baptism and the crossing of the Red Sea, and W. L. Knox argues that this connection was involved in the Jewish proselyte-baptisms (*St Paul and the Church of the Gentiles*, p. 97). The most detailed examination recently of the typological implications of these early chapters of Matthew is W. D. Davies, *op. cit.* pp. 25–93: 'New Exodus and New Moses.' Davies concludes, with regard to the baptism of Jesus, that the motif of a New Moses is not present either explicitly or implicitly, but that there *may* be an implicit identification here of Jesus with the New Israel, undergoing a baptism corresponding to that of the first Exodus (p. 44). With regard to the temptation, the same conclusion is reached, but more positively: in the Matthean version, 'Jesus does re-enact the experience of the "Son of God", the Old Israel' (pp. 47 f.). And similarly, for the Prologue (Matt. 1–2), Davies concludes that the New Moses motif is at the most 'one strand in a pattern which equally, if not more, emphasized the Christ as a new creation, the Messianic King, who represents Israel and is Emmanuel' (p. 92).

[4] See Jesus-Israel (i), above.

[5] It remains for us to make some reference to the feasibility of a much more critical and sceptical view of St Matthew's use of the Old Testament than that expressed here. Such a view is taken by B. Lindars in his *New Testament Apologetic* (see esp. pp. 259–65). Fr Lindars says, however, that his argument does not necessarily invalidate 'the claim that there is a theological purpose in these opening

chapters of Matthew. It is still tenable that his collection of infancy traditions is intended to imply that the history of Israel ("God's son", Hos. 11. 1) is gathered up into the history of Jesus' (*op. cit.* p. 261). Daniélou, however, goes too far when he says that 'it would be childish to suppose that Matthew's application of Osee's prophecy... to the flight of Jesus to Egypt and his return, had this detail of the life of Christ as its essential object. It suffices to re-read it in its full context to see that its object is the Fatherhood of God towards Israel, and that its meaning is to show us in Jesus the true Israel. Matthew added it to the episode of the flight to Egypt because of the reference to Egypt, but it could just as well have been added to some other episode' (*Christ and Us*, p. 73). For however much in sympathy we may find ourselves with Daniélou's aim it is surely not childish but, on the contrary, only fair to point out that if this is the case Matthew is asking to be misunderstood precisely because he places his quotation here: it would have been less ambiguous had he in fact 'added (it) to some other episode'. But still, without wishing to behave too cavalierly towards the critical problems of Gospel-interpretation, we may point out that even if Matthew has no such theological purpose as that we have outlined, and if, therefore, our exegesis of chh. 1–4 is wrong, it still remains true that the use of Old Testament history and scripture which our argument has involved is, in an age even 'of historical science'—*pace* Bultmann—a valid way of presenting the content of the Christian *kerygma* by means of typology: 'Christ the fulfilment of Scripture' is presented as the object of faith.

CHAPTER 10

JESUS-YAHWEH

THE history of Jesus embodies the fulfilled vocation of Israel. The New Testament claims that it also embodies the fulfilled action of Yahweh. We shall discuss this second facet of Jesus' work, the typology 'Jesus-Yahweh' (using 'Yahweh' to mean God as revealed and spoken of in the Old Testament, rather than God as Holy Trinity in Christian faith) in this chapter. First, however, there are two factors which may ease the transition from the Jesus-Israel typology we have been considering.

For it is remarkable—if twenty centuries have not dulled the marking and remarking senses—that Jesus in one ministry should fulfil, or even be claimed as fulfilling, both sides of the historical dialogue between God and man. He fulfils Israel's vocation, and it presumably follows from this, from the Old Testament standpoint, that he also fulfils man's proper response to God. But the claim that he also fulfils Yahweh's revealing, calling, redeeming, judging and in a sense creating activity— all Yahweh's man-ward work—by no means, even from the same standpoint, does follow. How, we wonder, can these two activities co-exist in one?

The paradox is the paradox of what is called the Incarnation. It is also called the 'mystery' of the Incarnation. In what follows I do no more than draw attention to two considerations which do nothing to solve that 'mystery', but which may show how the union of God's action with man's in one man's can, *qua* mystery, be conceived.

Biblical typology, let us recall first, is an analogy between actions. If we speak of men or even of things as 'types', we do so legitimately only in so far as we think of them as acting or as involved in an action. Moreover, the particular actions between which analogies are traced are those between God and the world and especially between God and man: that is, the actions which are seen as particularly constitutive of *Heilsgeschichte*.

This being so, when we speak of Jesus as recapitulating or

fulfilling the historical existence of Israel we mean that he responds to God's action, and to history, in the way in which Israel should have responded if she had been more true to the Covenant. The prophets believed that God was present in history, and that historical circumstances were always controlled by him in such a way that Israel might do his will in the midst of them, might act according to his word. The New Testament carries the same conviction. The present time is for Jesus of the highest importance, because he believes God has invested it with crucial, with critical significance, and therefore has laid upon him a burden of immediate responsibility. All that he does, therefore, may be seen as response to God's action. He is 'led by the Spirit' into the wilderness (Mark 1. 12). The period of his ministry is seen by him as 'the acceptable time' (Luke 4. 19, 21), and each stage of it has its own special task: 'Today and tomorrow I shall be casting out devils and working cures; on the third day I reach my goal' (Luke 13. 32). It is only a difference of degree between this and the Fourth Gospel's specialized use of ὥρα, 'hour', as the hour of Jesus' death and glorification: at bottom, it marks the same sense of his crucial need to respond to the time which God sends him: 'Now my soul is in turmoil, and what am I to say? Father, save me from this hour. But it was for this that I came to this hour' (John 12. 27). Time is laden with crisis. God is acting in the present time. Jesus perfectly responds. And so doing, in his life as in his teaching, he mediates God's will directly to others. By the very fact that he responds to God in this way he makes time all the more critical for others, if only because he is for them a part of their God-given circumstance, and a uniquely momentous part.[1] He is the 'sign of Jonah' to his contemporaries, even without regard to the question of his 'divine nature'; he mediates God's will to them; the Jews, given this 'sign' by his mission, are faced, like the Ninevites, with the issues of life and death (Luke 11. 29–32).

Similarly, as Cullmann points out,[2] 'upon the basis of the

---

[1] Cf. W. D. Davies, *The Setting of the Sermon on the Mount*, p. 386: 'It seems clear from *Q* that...the Church had preserved a tradition of the ethical teaching of Jesus which it regarded as in itself part of the crisis wrought in his coming. To put it yet more forcibly, this teaching itself helped to constitute that crisis.'

[2] *Christ and Time*, p. 42. Few words are strictly technical terms in the New Testament and it is quite clear, as James Barr has shown (*Biblical Words for Time*, pp.

deed of Christ... there also exists in... the... Christian Church a divine *kairos* for the believer', and he quotes, 'The *kairos* has come for judgment to begin at the house of God' (I Pet. 4. 17) and the demands in Colossians and Ephesians (Col. 4. 5; Eph. 5. 16) to 'redeem' the *kairos*. We can see from these quotations that it is not a very great step—and certainly not incompatible with the humanity of Jesus—to go on to: 'Everyone who acknowledges me before men, the Son of Man will acknowledge before the angels of God' (Luke 12. 8) for already the claim is that Jesus is God's *will* incarnate.

The second factor which is worth recalling here is that Israel's obedience to the Torah was already seen as an 'imitation' of God.[1] The commandment, 'You shall be holy, for I the Lord your God am holy' (Lev. 19. 2), was expanded in others where the specific moral attributes of God as revealed in his treatment of Israel are commanded as proper to Israel too.[2] Israel must follow the way of God. It is of course not the same thing to say 'you must be merciful because God is merciful' (as e.g. Deut. 10. 18 f.; Mic. 6. 8), as to say 'because you behave like God you are God'. But if, as a man, Jesus fulfils the Torah (Matt. 3. 15; cf. 5. 17) and thereby 'imitates' God, then his actions will have at any rate nothing inconsistent with the claim that he is God or fulfils God's work. His life may not prove this claim—it is not, by the nature of things, susceptible to proof—but it may make it feasible.

It is worth noting here, by the way, that Jesus as the New Law[3]—a typological motif in the New Testament which we have no space to discuss in detail—is an idea which follows quite logically from what we have been saying about the 'imitation of God'.[4] His response to God's call, is of such a kind

47–81) that Cullmann is wrong to treat *kairos* as if it were one. In the present quotations it means, as in much modern theology, 'the decisively opportune time'.

[1] See above, ch. 3; and, for a fuller treatment, Tinsley, *op. cit.* pp. 35–49.

[2] See Isidore Epstein, *Judaism*, pp. 28 ff.

[3] W. D. Davies, *Torah in the Messianic Age*, pp. 91–4, and *Paul and Rabbinic Judaism*, pp. 147 ff. provides a useful discussion of this.

[4] It is worth noting here that though the Old Testament parallelism between *derek* and *torah* has been, so to speak, swamped in the New Testament by that between ὁδός (way) and Jesus, it still lies in the contextual background, being implicit, for instance, in Mark 12. 14 where Jesus is asked 'is it lawful...?' because he teaches 'the way of God'. This, of course, provides a strong reason—if any is needed—for accepting the authenticity of the pericope in which it occurs in something at least very like its present form.

that it gives new definiteness to the old Law which it fulfils.[1] He focuses godly behaviour in a way that transcends the Law of Moses. By living the Torah he 'personalizes' it and translates it more directly into the sphere of life. His imitation of God is itself, therefore, a new 'sign-post' to those who see him or come after him. That is why he can say 'follow me' with unheard-of comprehensiveness.[2] That is why the Law becomes in the Gospels not merely 'graphic' (written), like the old Law, but 'biographic'. It is because of this that the New Testament as a whole urges upon us the 'imitation of Christ' as something not distinct from, but giving new clarity to, the Old Testament's imitation of God.[3]

(This is a point which will be of the greatest importance when we ask, as in pp. 172–8, 254 f.[4] below, to what extent the 'moral' sense of medieval exegesis is, or can be, typological.)

But it would be a mistake to conclude from the motifs of *imitatio patrum* and *imitatio Dei* in the New Testament's presentation of Jesus, that his ministry up to the Passion was solely a 'subfulfilment' of the old Israel's vocation, even if we take this to be perfected uniquely here. It is not as if there were two wholly separate temporal stages, the 'old' Israel's fulfilment simply preceding the eschatological act which creates the Church as 'new Israel'. The fulfilling of the old Israel's vocation does not, in the mission of Jesus, *simply* or *only* precede God's eschatological act, even in the sense (true in itself) that this fulfilling is a necessary precondition for the new act's realization. Such a picture is unsatisfactory because it ignores, and cannot do justice to, the motif of the *presence* of God's kingdom in the sayings of Jesus. God's kingdom—which is of course to be understood as something brought about by God's action, and not as

[1] Compare, for Matthew's special emphasis on this, G. Bornkamm on 'the better righteousness' (Bornkamm, Barth, Held, *Tradition and Interpretation in Matthew*, pp. 24–32). See also with regard to Jesus' fulfilment of the Law of Moses, M. Black, *An Aramaic Approach to the Gospels and Acts*, pp. 168–70 (on Luke 22. 16).

[2] Cf. Bornkamm, *op. cit.* p. 29: (For Matthew) 'Fulfilment of the commandments and perfection can no more be realised anywhere except in "following" Jesus.' Similarly, W. D. Davies, *The Setting of the Sermon on the Mount*, pp. 94–9.

[3] Cf. *ibid.* p. 95: 'Coincident with the demands expressed in the words of Jesus is another demand, which is not another, that the disciple should be conformed to the person whose are the words. The demand for *imitatio Dei*, expressed in (Matt.) 5. 48, becomes that for *imitatio Christi*.'

[4] Cf. also pp. 199–206, 246–8, below.

a natural growth[1]—is, in his ministry, *being* established. It is probable that we should not regard it as *wholly* established here, to the same extent as it is established in the events, subsequent to the ministry, out of which the Church was born—the Resurrection and the gift of the Spirit.[2] But in Jesus' ministry the kingdom's gifts pre-exist; its powers are available to him already. As well, therefore, as 'recapitulating' Israel's past, Jesus is in some sense living the life of the future.

Structurally, this relates to the concept of the 'remnant' in the book of Isaiah, and we need only recall our account of this concept to see how the structure relates to typology. In Isaiah and Deutero-Isaiah, the word of God's future act, as we have seen,[3] demands from the remnant to whom it is addressed an active and prior conformity to and participation in the expected future situation. This demand, and the offer, too, which goes with it, of a present enjoyment of the benefits of that future, is similar to and exists alongside its reverse, the demand for participation in and enjoyment of the continuing benefits of Yahweh's past 'mighty acts' in the Exodus and elsewhere. Typological subfulfilment of the future here co-exists with the typological subfulfilment of the past. It is not difficult to see how, *mutatis mutandis*, this may apply to the ministry of Jesus, and clearly it is a factor to be taken into account in connection with the Jesus-Israel typology at least—to which, inasmuch as in both Gospel and prophet it has to do with response to the action of God, it directly relates. Jesus, as Israel or man in Israel, responds, and calls others to respond, by preparing for God's future reign, and by living the life of the Kingdom.

But this structure has to do, also, with the typology of the action of God to which the typology of human response is after all only the reflex. In that context, the dialectic changes subtly, but, once changed, it helps to advance the present account of Jesus-Yahweh typology considerably. It provides, first, a corrective to any suggestion that New Testament typology of this general category presents the deeds of Jesus' ministry only or primarily as corresponding to God's saving acts *in the past*. And

[1] Cf. N. Perrin, *The Kingdom of God in the Teaching of Jesus*, pp. 13–56 and *passim*.
[2] Cf. A. Richardson, *An Introduction to the Theology of the New Testament*, pp. 62–4.
[3] See ch. 5, above, esp. pp. 74–7.

this corrective is necessary. For if that suggestion were true it would lead ultimately, I suspect, to somewhat embarrassing conclusions. The obvious and initial corollary, admittedly, seems harmless enough. There would only be room for legitimate speech about God's *new*, his eschatological, action in Jesus in connection with the climactic events subsequent to—but perhaps also including—the Crucifixion. The deeds of Jesus in his ministry might be related, by this account, never so firmly (by the principle of the *imitatio Dei* for example) to God's past 'mighty acts'; but of the actual fulfilling, by God, of his action on Israel, of the coming of the 'new age', of the transforming of the people's existence, the ministry (and the Jesus-Yahweh typology associated with it) would have nothing to say. Certainly, with the climactic events of Passion and Resurrection, the position would alter. The conditions could then be said to have changed; God could be said to have acted in a new way, and a new Redemption could be said to have taken place. But when dealing with these events, we must note, the Jesus-Yahweh typology in the New Testament concerns itself, as in the circumstances it would naturally do, only with the action of God upon Jesus and *thence* through him—with actions, in other words, of which Jesus is object rather than subject, with actions (that is to say) which may be classified technically as 'Jesus-Yahweh typology' only inasmuch as this is a category which is concerned with Jesus' 'history', not simply his 'actions', i.e. with the whole complex of happenings which make up the 'Christ-event', and not simply with the *gesta Christi*. 'As God raised Joseph to be a ruler in Egypt, so he has raised up Jesus, to rule over all' (cf. Acts 7. 9 f.).

But this, Christologically, is insufficient; not only from the point of view of Church dogma, but, in the last resort, exegetically. Clearly there are Christological implications in this typology even were it to be so confined, but these implications still *directly* relate only to the inquiry what God has done to Jesus and through him; and only indirectly and one-sidedly to the inquiry what or who Jesus was. For if the typology which concerns Jesus as acted upon, rather than acting, reveals him as, in the Church's teaching, 'perfect man', 'fulfilled Israel', and 'saving remnant', it leaves almost untouched the fact of his being, in that same teaching, also the 'Word' and 'Wisdom' of God (John 1. 14; I Cor. 1. 24), the 'power of God' (I Cor. 1. 24), the 'Lord' (ubiquitously), the 'first and the last' (Rev. 1. 17; cf. 1. 8), and the one in whom the Godhead dwells 'bodily' (Col. 2. 9). What the Church claims by these divine titles may or may not be regarded as self-authenticating. But unless they have some support in what Jesus himself *does* they are in such radical discontinuity with the Christological implications which we are allowed to draw from the ministry that they must appear hard to account for.

And in fact, as we shall shortly see, the early Church recognized this. The most sceptical reader would allow that the Fourth Gospel, at least, presents the Christology, 'what Jesus *does* is what God does', and presents it already in connection with the ministry of Jesus. And I believe that it is possible to show that, less overtly no doubt, and perhaps with a different emphasis, but still challengingly, Jesus' own discourse and actions as recoverable through the Synoptic tradition also imply that conclusion: what Jesus does is what God does, not only in the sense of the 'imitation' of God, which looks to the past for analogy, but also in the sense of an 'anticipating', by which Jesus looks to the future and *actively* embodies the future action of God.

Nevertheless, the typology which sees in the Resurrection of Jesus and in the gift of the Spirit the culmination of God's past 'mighty acts' upon Israel is among the most primitive of Christian typological arguments, and it would be as wrong to ignore it as to make light of it. To this category belong the 'key-correspondences' (Creation–New Creation; Exodus–Redemption; etc.) which as R. A. Markus says, 'form the accepted background of New Testament thought'.[1] Certain of the sermons in Acts reveal the fundamental structure of the argument. God, says Paul in the sermon of Acts 13, who with a high arm led our fathers out of Egypt (*v.* 17), and gave them the land taken from the Canaanites for their inheritance (*v.* 19), has now raised Jesus from the dead (*v.* 30) and, withdrawing the gospel of salvation from those who, though of Abraham's stock, did not recognize him (cf. *vv.* 26 f.), has given it even to the Gentiles (cf. *vv.* 46 f.). Stephen, similarly, chooses those parts of

[1] 'Presuppositions of the Typological Approach to Scripture', *CQR*, CLVIII (1957), 446 f.

the Joseph saga which most obviously parallel the history of Jesus in order that his hearers may infer that as God rescued Joseph from his brothers and made him chief administrator of Egypt and all the royal household (Acts 7. 9 f.), so also it is he who raised Jesus from the dead and made him (like Moses also, *v.* 35) ruler and liberator. This is typology in the generally accepted and basic sense: God is the agent, and because he is steadfast and his acts accord with his nature his acts correspond, too, with one another. This typology, except as it stands already in the age of 'fulfilment', corresponds to the typological prophecy of the Old Testament, and it corresponds simply. We pass over it quickly because it is at present a well-known phenomenon and a well-worked field.

So we return to the questions earlier raised. Is Jesus, at any stage in the transmission of the gospel traditions, presented as *himself* the agent of divine action in the period preceding the Crucifixion? Does such agency involve God's future, or only the past? And what of the Christological implications where we do find an implicit typology of this kind, or these kinds?

Clearly, we should not expect much typology of the kind which presents an analogy between specific acts of God in the past and specific actions of Jesus. It is the *kind* of work, rather than a specific action or number of actions, which distinguishes itself to faith as the action of God. But a few such analogies there are. There is, for example, Luke 9. 31, in which the author has adapted the basic Exodus–Redemption typology in such a way as to make Jesus the agent of the 'Exodus' which he is to accomplish at Jerusalem. And L. S. Thornton points also to a parallel between the wording of Mark 3. 1–5 and the Septuagint version of Exod. 4. 4 (in which 'stretch forth thy hand' is said by Yahweh to Moses as here by Jesus to the man with the withered hand), and 4. 7 (in which the phrase 'the hand was restored' is applied to Moses' leprous hand as here to the hand of the man in the Gospel). If the recurrence of these two phrases signals, in the mind of St Mark, a typological correspondence—and it seems to me rather doubtful—then its significance is not, as B. Lindars assumes,[1] that Jesus acts as the new Moses, but that he acts as God.

But more commonly it is Jesus' general conformity to God's

---

[1] 'The Image of Moses in the Synoptic Gospels', *Theology*, LVIII (1955), 132 f.

character, his assumption of God's powers and prerogatives, which meets us in the Gospels. The stilling of the storm, in Mark 4. 35–41 and parallels, is a case in point. This too has been invoked as an instance of Moses-typology. But as W. D. Davies has pointed out, 'the motif of the stilling of the sea frequently occurs in the Old Testament in connexion with the figure of Yahweh, not with that of Moses'. And he goes on, 'it is probably over against this tradition that we are to understand the description of the sea, the terror of the disciples, and the action of Jesus'.[1] Here our hands find a little more purchase than in the typologies quoted in the last paragraph. For Davies's careful work on the whole section into which Matthew incorporates this story (Matt. 8. 1–9. 34) leads to the conclusion that it is intended to express, in terms reminiscent of the creative activity of God, the infinite resources of power which are available to Jesus in his ministry.[2] And that this intention is not peculiar to Matthew is likely from the very fact of the numerousness of the miracle-stories, and from their diffusion. Wherever they are told they carry, not the implication that Jesus is God, to be sure, but the implication that he has access to God and may call upon his power. And for anyone who does not rule out the possibility of any of these stories being authentic they provide evidence for a Christology that is already implied, as Fuchs says,[3] by Jesus' conduct.

But we must not take such stories as proving more than they do. None of them may be taken as representing in itself the culmination of God's action, and even together they are never taken, either by Jesus or by the Evangelists, as representing more than the near-approach of such a culmination. The miraculous feeding in the wilderness was at least at certain stages in its transmission intended to recall God's action in feeding Israel with manna from heaven. But the grace of God which once preserved Israel is not fulfilled, does not culminate, with this new event. Rather, this is another foreshadowing. So, clearly, John interprets it. The miracle is a 'sign' (John 6. 14) of God's action, and the action it signifies is more thoroughgoing and has still, with Jesus' own self-giving, to arrive at its

---

[1] *The Setting of the Sermon on the Mount*, pp. 88 f.
[2] Cf. *ibid.* pp. 86–92.
[3] *Zur Frage nach dem historischen Jesus*, p. 185, n. 36.

culmination: 'I tell you this: the truth is, not that Moses gave you bread from heaven, but that my Father gives you the real bread from heaven. The bread that God gives comes down from heaven and gives life to the world...I am the bread of life' (John 6. 32–5). It is more than likely that even in the Synoptics these meals are intended as 'types' and 'figures' of the Church's sacraments, of the community's sharing in the benefits brought about by the sacrifice of Christ. We must reckon it a probability that the miracle-stories in general are at least as prefigurative as reminiscent, and that in the context of the ministry of Jesus the mighty acts on which they are founded were intended and taken to represent much more the drawing-close of the kingdom of God, or its incipience, than its ultimate climax.

Much more significant Christologically, however, than the miracles are the prerogatives which Jesus assumes, the confidence and authority with which he declares God's will (not as the scribes, Mark 1. 22, 27, but, indeed, not as the prophets either!), his daring to act in God's place as he forgives (cf. Mark 2. 1–12: 'Who but God can forgive sins?'), and draws near to, sinners who would otherwise have to flee from God.[1] This behaviour may, like the miracles, foreshadow the future. *But it also presupposes equal terms with the future which it foreshadows*, in a way which the miracles alone by no means necessarily do.

Once again the Fourth Gospel's interpretation of Jesus' mission may throw light on both the Christology implicit in such conduct and the bearing of such conduct on the typology 'Jesus-Yahweh'. The activity in question is the healing of infirmities on the Sabbath. In John 5. 16 Jesus is challenged with Sabbath-breaking. The reply is, 'My Father has never yet ceased his work, and I am working too' (*v*. 17). In the background of the story lies the concept of the Jewish Sabbath as an *imitatio Dei* (the explanation given for the custom in Exod. 20. 11), and at first sight one implication in the Jews' question seems to be: 'If God ceased work on the seventh day why do you not do as the law requires and imitate him?' In this case Jesus' reply would contradict the theological point—viz. that God ceased work—rather than the ethical principle of the *imitatio Dei*, and we might paraphrase his reply as, 'God never ceased,

[1] Thus E. Fuchs, *op. cit.* pp. 154–6.

and I imitate him in that'. But the contradiction in theology may not be as radical as it seems, for Lightfoot refers to the Jewish belief that God did not *altogether* cease work on the seventh day, but continued his work of mercy and judgement.[1] In that case, the incident would have to be read somewhat differently, so that after as it were affirming Jewish theology on this point, Jesus' claim is that, far from falling short of the law's requirements in the following of God's ways, he follows him in fact more closely than the law-abiding Jew. No wonder, then, that the closeness of this claimed connection (like a son who imitates his father), now (*v*. 18) leads the Jews to charge him with blasphemously claiming to be equal with God. And instead of refuting the charge, according to the present narrative Jesus commits himself more deeply still: 'What the Father does, the Son does' (*v*. 19); and he expands upon his claim to unity of action with the Father by supplementing the backward glance to creation which was involved in the argument over the Sabbath with a reference forward to God's eschatological work, the work of judgement and of the raising of the dead, which is, in Jewish thought, exclusively the work of God (*vv*. 20–30).

This pericope cannot, of course, be taken as evidence for the claims made by the historical Jesus. But it may, still, radically expose the claims which better authenticated stories and sayings in the Synoptics imply. In the Synoptics, too, as Fuchs says, Jesus 'dares to act in God's place';[2] and the scandalized reaction of pious Jews shows that his daring was recognized. Jesus' conduct in his ministry implies more than a 'subfulfilment', however ideal, of God's past actions; it implies more than what was regarded as a legitimate *imitatio Dei*. The sense people have of Jesus' unconditioned authority, power, and prerogative, is the sense that he embodies God's own power and prerogative, the sense that there is something of 'ultimate' fulfilment here. In other words, Jesus mediates the sense of God's eschatological kingdom, and binds it, by his action as by his sayings, implicitly with his own person. The relation of Jesus' deeds to God's eschatological action is so close that the least we can say is that his deeds intimately associate *him* with that action already in his human life. And the bearing of all this on typology is

---

[1] R. H. Lightfoot, *Commentary on St John's Gospel, in loc.*
[2] *Op. cit.* p. 156.

precisely that which the passage from John makes so clear, that it is typology that bears on all this, and ultimately carries (or may carry) the weight of expressing it. When what the parables and sayings of Jesus predicate of God's future dealings is activated in the present in Jesus' conduct (as, for example, the eschatological table-fellowship with sinners, Luke 14. 15–24, cf. Luke 19. 1–10 and Mark 2. 15), we are faced with a situation which we may properly express dialectically thus: Jesus' present is being presented (and by himself) as realizing typologically the future of God. This situation takes us beyond anything which we find in the Old Testament, even in the Isaianic and Deutero-Isaianic commands to 'live up to' the future and represent it to others, and in treating New Testament typology it is a necessary complement, even if so briefly indicated, to my account of Jesus-Israel typology.

CHAPTER II

SUMMARIES

A. CHRIST AND HISTORY

Of the two major theses I have set out to justify in connection with biblical typology, one has to do with its existentiality, its 'application', the other with the nature of its 'fulfilment' as 'history' and 'event', and with the Christian claim that in fact the event of fulfilment has happened in the history of Christ. The first of these will be reviewed in the light of the biblical evidence in the next section (B). In this section I shall sum up the relevance of the biblical evidence, and in particular of the discussion (in the four preceding chapters) of Christ as 'recapitulator', to the second of these two theses, which was expressed at the beginning by characterizing biblical typology as the science, or more commonly the partial presentation, of history's relations to the event which 'fulfils' it, and Christian typology as concerning the relations of history to its fulfilment in Christ. Two points, however, remain to be made. They have been implied, if not stated, so that I may be brief.

The first is that there exists alongside the typology of salvation and salvation history a typology of rejection, of judgement and condemnation. This is explained easily enough on the dialectical level: man in Israel exists in relation to the action of God either as he is called to exist, as 'elected' in the Old Testament sense, fulfilling the covenant, living the 'new existence' of man under grace, or as he may live if, relying on his natural powers, he refuses the call of God's saving action and lives on the merely natural plane, being thus 'judged' and 'un-made' on the plane of election.[1] Therefore, if Christ as Israel fulfils Israel's vocation in salvation-history, the resistance of those who reject him and God's action in him may be said to fulfil[2] its own

---

[1] See above, p. 19, etc.

[2] For this use of 'fulfil' in connection with rejection, wickedness, rebellion, see C. F. D. Moule, '"Fulness" and "Fill" in the New Testament', *SJT*, IV (1951), 86; and cf. Matt. 23. 32; I Thess. 2. 16.

148

'type' in Old Testament history—the resistance of Israel to Moses and the prophets.[1]

This, too, is part of the empirical use of typology in the New Testament. It lies behind Christ's terrible irony in Luke 13. 33; 'I must be on my way. . .because it is unthinkable for a prophet to meet his death anywhere but in Jerusalem.' In a more developed form it lies also behind the parable of the land-owner who let out his vineyard (Mark 12. 1–12), and behind the passage in 'Q': 'you acknowledge that you are the sons of the men who killed the prophets. Go on then—finish off what your fathers began!. . .Believe me, this generation will bear the guilt of it all' (Matt. 23. 26–9; Luke 11. 47–51). We may also compare, from among the sayings of Jesus in 'Q', his exclamation upon the unbelieving cities on the shores of Galilee:

Alas for you, Chorazin! Alas for you, Bethsaida! If the mighty works that were performed in you had been performed in Tyre and Sidon, they would long ago have repented in sackcloth and ashes. But it will be more bearable for Tyre and Sidon in the judgment than for you. And you, Capernaum, will you be exalted to the skies? No, brought down to the depths! It will be more bearable, I tell you, for Sodom in that day than for you.   (Luke 10. 13–15, 12; Matt. 11. 21–4)

Finally, we point to the same motif, even more developed but equally pointed and telling, in the defence of Stephen (Acts 7). The speech has its positive aspect, providing an account of the origins of Israel which subterraneously, beneath its story of the faith of the heroes, preaches Christ in his 'types'.[2] It is done, as C. F. D. Moule says, 'in such a way as to indicate that every advance involved the rejection of the traditional and the static; and that at every point the Holy Spirit is the Spirit of advance, of movement, of the refusal to be static; so that the heroes of Israel are all people of gigantic faith, exchanging the

---

[1] F. Hesse's position in his essay 'Zur Frage der Wertung und der Geltung alttestamentlicher Texte' (*PAH*, pp. 266–94) differs from mine and is in several respects unacceptable to me. But in two or three pages (282–6) he treats this particular (and generally neglected point) with exemplary clarity, remarking that to some degree the 'line of obduracy' (*Verstockungslinie*) involves even the heroes, prophets, writers of the Old Testament, because (as we should say, cf. pp. 19 n. 2, and 59, above) even the existence of these participates in the equivocal nature of all existence in Israel—or humanity.

[2] See R. P. C. Hanson, 'Studies in Texts, Acts VI, 13 f.', *Theology*, L (1947), 142–5.

known for the unknown, abandoning the security of the familiar in blind obedience to the call of God'.[1] But the speech's critical side is even more emphatic, telling how Joseph was betrayed by the patriarchs, and Moses rejected with the words 'who made you ruler and judge?' though he was commissioned ruler and liberator by God himself, before reaching the climax of its indignant crescendo: 'Was there ever a prophet whom your fathers did not persecute? They killed those who foretold the coming of the Righteous One; and now you have betrayed and murdered him—you, who received the Law as God's angels gave it to you, and yet have not kept it' (Acts 7. 9, 35, 51–3).

Not all types, therefore, have the single figure of Christ as their centre and fulfilment; but, as a history, Christ's life, death, and resurrection, fulfils them all. They are all types—we are thinking at the moment of the Old Testament alone—by virtue of their relation to a revelation that is fulfilled in him. Thus the doctrinal subject-matter of Christian typology, at least in so far as the relations between the two Testaments are concerned, is as we defined it: history's relations to its fulfilment in Christ. For, positively or negatively, the history of Israel's response to God comes to a head in the compass of the story of Christ.

But before, on biblical grounds, we can justify this thesis of all, and not only Israel's, history, a second point has to be made. It emerges from the same narrative concerning Stephen that we have just been considering. When Stephen had said his say and was stoned, he died—or is reported as dying—with words closely parallel to the words of the crucified Jesus: 'Lord, do not hold this sin against them' (Acts 7. 60; cf. Luke 23. 34). And similarly, later in Acts, the author, remembering how he had used Christ's compulsion to get to Jerusalem more or less as a formal device to foreshadow and lead up to the Passion, now repeats the device for Paul's journey, the journey which led to his arrest: 'He was eager to be in Jerusalem' (Acts 20. 16). This latter parallel, indeed, is worked out rather closely. With the notes of impulsion and determination that sound in this journey of Paul's in Acts 20. 16, 22 and 21. 12–15 we may compare those in Luke 9. 51; 13. 22 and 32 f.; 18. 31; 19. 28. In Acts 20. 28 f., Paul gives the same warning and in the same

[1] C. F. D. Moule, *The Birth of the New Testament*, p. 75.

language as Christ had given at a similar stage in his mission, according to Luke 10. 3; and in each case, four verses later, the traveller speaks of the way the preacher should gain his livelihood. Finally, in Acts 21. 11 we hear that a prophet named Agabus came, took Paul's belt, bound his own hands and feet with it, and said, 'These are the words of the Holy Spirit: Thus will the Jews in Jerusalem bind the man to whom this belt belongs, and hand him over to the Gentiles.' Luke 18. 31 f. is the parallel: 'All that was written by the prophets will come true for the Son of Man. He will be handed over to the Gentiles...'

One of the interesting things about the Acts passage is the glimpse it gives of an early Church 'prophet'. It is worth remembering that prophets held an important place in the Early Church, second to the apostles themselves,[1] and it has been suggested that their main function was not so much 'to foretell the future...as to lead the congregation into a deeper understanding of the mystery of Christ through inspired exegesis of the Old Testament Scriptures'.[2] In this view, the Epistle to the Hebrews is an example of Christian prophecy. But though there is no necessary reason why the functions of foretelling, exegesis, and (I Cor. 14. 24) edification, should not be separate functions even when performed by one person, one may wonder whether the combination of functions may not have been closer, whether in fact the 'prophets' may not have been, so to speak, the specialists in typology. Be that as it may, Agabus here behaves in the Old Testament tradition of prophecy, even to the extent of making a symbolic action, a piece of 'prophetic symbolism'; and, although when all that can be has been explained an element of mystery ('the words of the Holy Spirit'—cf. 'Thus says the Lord') remains, we should notice that, just as the narratives in Stephen's speech must have warned him of his own fate, so here Paul's fate is foreseeable by remembering Christ's: the prediction of Agabus, like most of those in the prophetic books of the Old Testament, may well be based in part on hindsight and be typological.

But one implication of this passage and of several others in

---

[1] See particularly I Cor. 14. 1–6, 22–33; and cf. A. Richardson, *An Introduction to the Theology of the New Testament*, p. 335.

[2] S. Neill, *The Interpretation of the New Testament 1861–1961*, p. 185.

Acts[1] is of much greater significance. We move in a realm where typology, at least the typology of salvation, is still relevant after Christ although fulfilled in him. It is evident that, for Luke, Paul's 'passion', like his master's, begins in Jerusalem, and that, though the apostle's martyrdom is more protracted, the events which will bring it on are henceforward in train. The Pauline theology of living 'in Christ' and dying 'in him'—'to share his sufferings, in growing conformity with him, if only I may arrive at the resurrection of the dead' (Phil. 3. 11; cf. II Cor. 4. 10 f.) —has its counterpart here in his life.

In the last resort therefore, as we have already implied in the introductory chapter (6) of this part as well as in treating the theme 'Jesus-Israel',[2] typology stays with us even in the new dispensation, in the Church's and the believer's commitment to the 'imitation of Christ'. There is no call to repeat the reasons for insisting that the 'ethical conformity', or 'subfulfilment', is part and parcel of the subject of typology; for it is in any case now clear from Acts that the New Testament—Luke at least— compels us to consider it so. The presentation of the fate of Stephen and of Paul's way to Jerusalem is typological in the way that frequently the gospel narratives themselves are: the narration of one event is designed to recall the circumstances surrounding another. This, by the way, is the kind of typology, also, which we find in Dante's *Divina Commedia*; nothing in the New Testament is nearer to its typological method than these echoing narratives, and the historical or biographical recapitulations or subfulfilments to which they witness. Yet it may be worth stressing once more that this *presentation* of typology is *in itself* without any significance, that it does not imply (still less advocate!) either a literalistic imitation of Israel's and/or Christ's earthly journey or a static and complacent conformism to past ways. It is rather that the typological presentation signals a life which grows out of a spiritual conformity to Christ and which participates in the new existence which God opens up.

---

[1] On this subject, compare M. D. Goulder, *Type and History in Acts*, which came out, I regret to say, too late for me to make proper use of it in the text. Here I can only say that though it is doctrinaire and extreme—e.g. in its insistence upon 'cycles' and 'patterns'—and though there is much with which one may disagree, yet it is an important book and a useful one. After it no one, I think, can ignore the formative place of typology in Luke's writings.

[2] See above, pp. 91–3, 111, 127–9.

It signals a life that is in this way the fruit of redemption, an ethical existence, 'righteousness', which is given from heaven (according to Eph. 2. 8) through faith, and whose only form is the form Christ gave it. 'Can you drink the cup that I drink, or be baptized with the baptism I am baptized with?' (Mark 10. 38) is the question which this typology answers on behalf of its subject; 'Anyone who wishes to be a follower of mine must leave self behind; he must take up his cross and come with me' (Mark 8. 34) is the demand which it presents its subject as now fulfilling. The Bible's peculiar dialectic of imperative and indicative is still here. The existence 'given' by God is still existence in a history which is always in detail unrepetitive, unprecedented, and demanding, an existence from which—as Stephen's speech and Hebrews strongly remind us—terror of the future may still tempt us to draw back, unless faith fixes upon the God who is steadfast even—as Christ's resurrection 'means to' the Christian—in death. In a word, this typology signals a way of life, and of waking life, not a way of sleeping (cf. I Thess. 5. 5 f.); and it is a way of life which is both the gift and the demand of Christ who is Law and Gospel.

Existentially then, as well as formally, this typology of sub-fulfilment resembles the Old Testament's. It may be worth remarking that it resembles the Old Testament's also in being capable of being eschatologically as well as historically orientated, or rather, since Christian existence as well as God's act in Christ is characterized in the New Testament, as the Bultmann school properly stresses, by being already itself eschatological, this typology's subject-matter, 'Christian existence', is orientated to the future as well as the past 'fulfilment'. Christians, according to Phil. 3. 20, are citizens of heaven. Between the 'already' and the 'not yet', the marks of both past and future, of Christ's history and their own 'eschatology', should begin to be traced in their lives. And, conversely, this typology of subfulfilment in the new dispensation, which has its own future 'fulfilment' at the last day, may be said to involve, also, a typology of rejection, of judgement. Neutrality is not possible in encountering God's word in Christ. Refusing the call of Christ's life and death, which still meets him in the witnessing Church, man rejects too the power of Christ's resurrection. Out of harmony with Christ he repeats the Jewish disharmony and shares their fate in the judgement. (We confine ourselves to New Testament conceptions, regardless, at least for the present, of the question of the meaning of the 'myth', if myth it is; suffice it to say that I believe it has some meaning, and that Part III may, I hope, help it to be clarified.) His 'future' is known by their past, typologically and prophetically.

The orientation of existence in the new dispensation towards the future is not, however, in the New Testament worked out in typological narrative,[1] though the phraseology of the New Testament, as we saw above,[2] and, indeed, its theology, strongly authenticate such a development. This is another reason why I believe that the *Divine Comedy* has something useful to add to our study; and it will be best to postpone further discussion of this issue until the next part.

Enough, now, has been said concerning the two points which still needed to be established—the relation to Christ of the New Testament's typology of judgement, obduracy, or rejection, and the relation to his own life and history of the life and history which follow him—for us to return to our thesis and generalize it. Christian typology, we may now confirm, presents, fundamentally, the relations of all history, and not Israel's only, to its fulfilment in Christ. Positively or negatively, the history of all men's response to God, and of God's dealings with men, comes to its fulfilment in the compass of Christ's history. C. F. D. Moule notes, and our study confirms, that when Luther affirmed as the principle of scriptural interpretation the summing up of all things in Christ (Eph. 1. 10), he was affirming also the practice of the primitive Church.[3] But it is plain too that for the primitive Church this principle is also that by which to interpret history. If gloss is required, the dictum of C. K. Barrett, with its eminently right, precise brackets, provides it. 'That which has been fulfilled has been fulfilled in him (or at least in relation to him); that which is yet to be fulfilled will be fulfilled in him (or at least in relation to him).'[4]

---

[1] In the Old Testament, interestingly enough, the books of Chronicles provide an example of a similar process, depicting the history of the Davidic kingdom, in I Chronicles especially, in deliberately idealized lineaments in order to foreshadow the eschatological kingdom of God or the Davidic Messiah: thus, W. F. Stinespring, 'Eschatology in Chronicles', *JBL*, LXXX (1961), 209-19.

[2] See p. 87.   [3] *The Birth of the New Testament*, p. 71.

[4] *The Church's Use of the Bible*, ed. D. E. Nineham, p. 9.

It is in John that this whole conception of fulfilment comes to its clearest expression in the New Testament. N. A. Dahl, who properly characterizes the fourth Gospel's conception of history as 'Christocentric', is right to say that John does not write as a theologian of *Heilsgeschichte*, if this means seeing as *Heilsgeschichte* only a series of redemptive acts of God in history.[1] For rather, according to John, the whole of history is implicit in the story of Christ, the 'world's' hostility to God being focused in the hostility of the Jews to Jesus, and God's love for the world, and his victory, in the mission of Jesus to Israel, and his resurrection.[2] But clearly, this is a conception which, in principle at least, relates all history to the divine act which for John is climactic, and it does not, because the one act is climactic, at all tend to deny the reality, or, for their time, the validity, of the others. Indeed, if the direct encounter between God and the world which takes place in the mission of Jesus truly focuses history and provides a criterion for God's judgement, this direct encounter must have its mediating witnesses in the past as well as the future. For John, the history of Israel provides such a witness, comparable in kind, if not quality, to the continuing witness of the Church.[3]

The history, and not just the isolated predictions—this view of 'witness' is obligated by John's faith in the Christ-event as ultimate criterion for God's judgement upon the world. But it is a view of prophecy which in fact finds other support than the

---

[1] 'The Johannine Church and History', *Current Issues in New Testament Interpretation*, ed. W. Klassen and G. F. Snyder, p. 140.

[2] *Art. cit.* p. 129.

[3] Compare again N. A. Dahl, *art. cit.* pp. 130–6. Note particularly, however, the probability, to which Dahl does not do justice, that, as the wording of John 5. 46 ('It was about me that (Moses) wrote') suggests, it is the whole corpus of Torah and not just isolated prophecies, which we are to understand by the phrase 'testimony of the Scriptures' (John 5. 39). Support for this view may be found in the extent (variously assessible, admittedly) to which a statement like John 5. 17 ('My Father never yet ceased his work, and I am working too') logically conditions the meaning of verses 39 and 45 f. The works from which, according to contemporary Jewish belief (cf. R. H. Lightfoot's commentary on John, *in loc.*), God has never rested, even on the Sabbath, were his works of mercy and judgement—that is, works such as the Old Testament records, and such as Jesus now continues to perform (John 5. 16). The implication here, surely, is that Jesus is truly the Son of God—i.e. though much more than this merely (cf. above, pp. 145 f.), his Father's perfect 'imitator'; but it also confirms the point we are making, and which Dahl seems inclined to deny: viz. that the past history of salvation does indeed reveal the workings of God's judgement and salvation, and that it points forward to Christ *because* it does reveal them.

logical. It is confirmed by the nature of 'prophecy' in the Old Testament, which simply is not to be dissociated from the history which gave rise to it. Our study of the Old Testament endorses the view of prophecy which, by so far as I can see a rather daring substitution of the later Heidegger's concept of *Lichtungsgeschichte* for the theory's original Hegelian concomitants,[1] James M. Robinson has recently adopted from J. C. R. (not 'Von') Hofmann:

Truth is more basically an 'unveiling' (*a-lētheia*) than a correlation of objects to a subject's patterns of thought. Hence the history of thought is itself only a reflection of the history of the subject-matter unveiling itself. The task in studying the history of thought is thus to move through the thoughts themselves to the subject matter from which the thoughts arose and to which they refer.

Similarly, according to the view of Hofmann (who first introduced the term *Heilsgeschichte*), 'the prophecy is not the saying of the prophet; rather the prophecy is the history whose inherent prophecy the prophet merely expresses in language'.[2]

And again, that not only the conception of prophecy implied by John's gospel, but also the basic conception of history as being judged according to its relation to a climactic event, is biblical, and not only Johannine, can be shown from our study of the Old Testament, even though the climactic event is not yet there found where John finds it, in Christ. For the same critical relation between history and the 'pivotal' acts of God is the theme of the Old Testament too. The act of God in the Exodus is a norm by which to evaluate and guide other times, other situations, other events. Deuteronomy, with its blessings and cursings, is a fairly elementary expression of the working of this conception, and beside the application of the Exodus-motif in the prophets and in the historical books of the Old Testa-

[1] Though I have not seen Hofmann's book (*Weissagung und Erfüllung*, 2 vols. 1841–4), from the account which Bultmann gives of it in his essay of the same name (*Essays*, pp. 188–91) I suspect that his theory is altered by its new philosophical context more radically than Robinson suggests. At the same time, if it is to be made to agree with the biblical evidence presented in chapter 1 (i.e. with the way in which history does in fact stand behind prophecy in the Old Testament), some such alteration as Robinson's treatment implies, and especially the freeing of the theory from Hegelianism, is both legitimate and necessary.

[2] J. M. Robinson, 'The Historicality of Biblical Language', *The Old Testament and Christian Faith*, ed. B. W. Anderson, p. 153.

ment (cf., for example, I Sam. 10. 17 ff.; 12. 6–12; I Kings
8. 16–21), the festivals themselves, by their witness to the past
Heilsgeschichte, play a part in bringing subsequent generations
into a critical encounter with the God of the Exodus.[1] The
more 'pivotal' the event which faith sees as an act of God is
conceived to be, the more regulative and critical for the rest of
history it is. And since, even in the Old Testament, a 'fulfilment' is anticipated which, even judged by the Exodus
criterion, eclipses the Exodus, consummating what the Exodus
revealed of the purpose of God (cf. Isa. 43. 18 f.),[2] the New
Testament is perfectly consistent with the general intention of
the Old when, finding this 'fulfilment' in Christ, it presents the
whole of history as now to be judged according to its relation
to him or his witnesses. Such an event, an event which would
ultimately discriminate between the faithful people of God and
those who reject him, the Old Testament itself looks forward
to. And such an event, according to the New Testament and the
Church, has come about in Christ, by God's acting. The event
of Christ, by this witness, is the *absolute* existential norm to
which the Old Testament looked forward.[3]

Therefore if, as Bultmann suggests, 'Christ the Crucified and
Risen One comes before us in the Word of the proclaimed
message and nowhere else',[4] it is equally true that we know
ourselves only in the encounter with him in that Word, as it is
more or less directly presented to us. And if typology (however
undeveloped and unrecognized as such it may be) is the fundamental means by which the indirect, pre-understood, word,
gained from our historical experience and beliefs, is brought to
assist our decision when faced with the direct Word in Christ,
the direct Word in Christ is also the judge of all those beliefs
and experiences which we summon to judge him. In other
words, it is the judge of all our typologies. If an act of God can
mean nothing to us unless it has some analogy in our experience, the analogy is only valid if it teaches that God's acting
transcends our experience, and makes all things new. Typology
in both Testaments does not exist to inhibit God's speaking any
word but a word from a past grown rigid; it is used instead to
allow the right hearing of a word which concerns the present

---

[1] See esp. ch. 3 above. [2] See esp. ch. 5 above.
[3] Cf. the Introduction, p. 5. [4] *Kerygma and Myth*, ed. R. H. Fuller, i, 41.

and is new. It was thus that the call at the Exodus must have struck home to Israel, compared with the ancient 'archetypes'. But when the act of God at the Exodus lost its precarious dependence on faith and became, or seemed to become, their possession, which nothing could shake or alter, and so itself only an 'archetype', a 'security', preventing the hearing of God's new word and the seeing of his new act, it was thus, in turn, that the word of a future was spoken, which would correspond to the past but transcend it. This is how genuine typology works in the Bible always. We have just seen it in Stephen's speech. And it is particularly clear already in Isa. 43. 16–21, which could serve as a touchstone. The memory of the Exodus is called up, not only, in *vv.* 16 and 17, to be dismissed by verse 18 ('remember not the former things') but that the new act of God (*vv.* 19–21) may be recognized for what it is, an event brought about by the same God, furthering the same ends by so much that henceforth the Exodus will be eclipsed in Israel's experience of her history, 'unconsidered'. It is with typology's need and ability to do justice to the transforming character of God's action that our next section, fundamentally, is concerned.

B. APPLIED TYPOLOGY

OUR purpose has been, and is, not primarily that of defending a system of typological exegesis, but to contribute towards the understanding of the Bible's own use of typology in its writing and speaking. Within that broad aim a narrower aim is enclosed: to clarify the claim which the New Testament's use of typology seems to involve, that Christ is the fulfilment of history. But though this is a claim which typology has (or so I have argued) a special aptitude for expressing, it is not a claim which may, by this means or any other, be proved. Typology's province extends to making intelligible, not to demonstrating, a claim which would otherwise be unintelligible, and unable, therefore, legitimately, to require a decision, even by faith, as to its truth.

But although the function of 'making intelligible' is in this case a vital and critical one, it is not the end of typology's purpose in the Bible. For the decision about the claim's truth, by this means invited, involves, from the nature of the claim, also assent to the claims *of* that truth on the individual to whom it is presented and who may, now, give to it his assent.

If this is really the case, then the intellectual claim of typology is nothing without the existential claim, and demand, which accompany it. The proposition 'Jesus Christ is history's fulfilment, to which all history is related in as much as in him it finds its norm, its perfector and judge', is not a proposition to which one can assent without affirming also 'Christ is my perfector and my judge'. We may believe that it is valid to make the claim, in some such form as this, almost abstractly, as a dogmatic statement; but it exists as genuinely true, as Bultmann said of all statements of 'God acting', only as confession and as self-surrender, here and now.[1]

This means already, when we draw out its consequences, that all 'genuine' typology is 'applied'. This is true, we have argued, even of Old Testament typology. The prophet speaks there of a future in-breaking of Yahweh; essentially this message can no more be proved as true than can the kergymatic claim that the prophesied event has come about; in its nakedness as 'brute assertion' it is unlikely to receive assent *in vacuo*. To receive assent, even to be intelligible, it must either be delivered in a context in which it is already related to the hearer's pre-understanding of God's acts, or it must itself contain an element (which there is no reason why we should not call 'apologetic') which will so relate it. Thus, in fact, the prophecies of Yahweh's future acts are always—even when the prophet does not offer an 'apologetic' by typology—spoken in a situation whose world of faith contains this religious pre-understanding. It is judged according to, and in turn judges, the quality of the pre-understanding of the hearer. The message of the coming act of God is, then, a question to the present about the present's whole relation to God's action, past and future. For according to the hearer's understanding of the situation he will not only choose to believe or disbelieve the prophet; according to his understanding, also, he will act. Typology in this case can be seen as an encouragement to acting rightly in relation to God's acts by assisting the hearer to hear rightly the message of God's act (or his new act). It is 'applied' because it is a means of producing an existential confrontation between man and the action of God.

---

[1] See above, pp. 29–32.

TYPOLOGY IN THE NEW TESTAMENT

But we have argued also that typology is 'applied' in another, though not separated, sense. It is applied, that is to say, not only *to* the hearer and his existential understanding, but *in* the actual response of the hearer to God's acts. The hearer's right response means that there is initiated a self-conforming with the act of God, a subfulfilment. In its simplest terms this is what exists in the Old Testament concept of an imitation or following of God, but the eschatological message of the prophets deepens the conception by setting the object of the new conformity also in the future: it is now God's eschatological act, known only in the word of prophecy, to which the remnant must conform their existence. In the New Testament, the central concept of the imitation of Christ itself contains both the idea of eschatological self-alignment and the idea of an alignment with the past.[1] For God's future is contained already in Christ's history and the individual's relation to the one involves him in the same relation to the other. He who follows Christ the servant is already sharing in the eschatological kingdom of God. He who rejects Christ rejects also the life which is promised and present in Christ.

But the conforming of the self with Christ is also anthropologically a self-*trans*forming, a move from one existence to another, from one conformity to another. In the Old Testament, again, we have found a similar pattern of thought: Israel 'migrates' by God's mighty act from natural existence to existence in election. For St Paul the decisive change has occurred not with Moses but with Christ: natural existence (typified by Adam) under the rule of sin and doomed to death was altered by the Law only in so far as the Law increased law-breaking (Rom. 5. 20); but the Christian has now at length a new existence in the life of Christ, the realm of grace (Rom. 5. 12–21). The 'applied typology' of the human individual's incorporation 'in Adam' is thus set as an antithesis to the alternative 'applied typology' of incorporation 'in Christ'. A choice confronts man now which was not there before, between two kinds of existence. But there is more than an antithesis here, in the passage from Romans. The total incorporation of all men in Adam means that there is a certain continuity, identity, between man in Adam and man in Christ, that no

---

[1] Of this again, the next part will have something to add.

one is free from Adam's death (cf. I Cor. 15. 21 f.).[1] This is a typology essentially concerned with change in existential situation rather than with the absolute antithesis between the two existences. Hence St Paul can say, with Adam still in mind perhaps, 'the man we once were has been crucified with Christ' (Rom. 6. 6), while the man we are now shares in his resurrection (Rom. 6. 5). The typological 'subfulfilment' thus has its true place in baptism (cf. Rom. 6. 3 f.) and, derivatively, in repentance, in which Christ and Adam meet in such a way that henceforth, or again, the one becomes our future and the other recedes into our past. St Paul's exhortation (Rom. 12. 2) expresses the individual's change of life, as this change is in process of fulfilment, in terms which epitomize the typological structure of conversion: 'Do not be conformed to this world, but be transformed by the renewal of your mind.'

It remains for us only to indicate, briefly, the contrast between our view of typology's 'application' in the Bible, and certain other views of Biblical typology. For it is here that our various criticisms of these approaches culminate.

We point first to the devaluation of history and the 'historic' which the allegorical exegesis of the patristic tradition implied. It was impossible, in Christianity, that this devaluation should

---

[1] I should make it plain here that the relation between Christ and Adam in the passage under discussion does not seem to me 'typological'—not, at all events, if St Paul is envisaging their relation only as antithesis: and it remains essentially 'only antithetical' even if one were to stress the analogy between their circumstances, and that between their representative natures, for these factors are merely the grounds upon which the antithesis is possible. E. Fuchs, therefore, rightly says that E. Auerbach's definition of typology as, 'the interpretation of one worldly (*innerweltlich*) event through another', so that 'the first signifies the second, the second fulfils the first' ('Figura', ET, *Scenes from the Drama of European Literature*, p. 58), 'trifft für Paulus an unsrer Stelle schon nicht mehr ganz zu' (E. Fuchs, *Hermeneutik*, p. 193). What we discuss here is not the relation between Christ and Adam, but those between Adam and man, and between Christ and Christian; and thence the relation of the change Adam-to-Christ to the change man-in-Adam to man-in-Christ. These relations are all properly called 'typological' in that they involve a 'subfulfilment' of man's response *vis-à-vis* God's act of creating him in his own image. Needless to say, however, a certain degree of antithesis exists even in relations which do include 'fulfilment', and are properly called 'typological' on that account. We would not, for example, call Christ's fulfilment of Israel's history 'typology' if there were nothing in that history which positively prefigured that 'fulfilment'; nor would we if the history of Israel contained no conflicting or contrasting side: for in that case there would be no need for a fulfilment (cf. W. Eichrodt, 'Ist die typologische Exegese sachgemässe Exegese?', reprinted from *VT*, Suppl., IV, 1957, in *PAH*, esp. pp. 206 f.).

take such extreme form as that which was current in the mythopoeic religions. The historical nature of the revelation in Christ did not go unregarded, and the Augustinian doctrine of the six ages attempts, at least, to do justice to the element of 'newness' and change by which even the Old Testament acts of God have in the last analysis an eschatological character. But the connection between this 'historic' character of the divine activity and typology was very imperfectly realized in exegesis, and it would be hard to deny that the allegorical methods deriving from Philo and Hellenism carry, even among the Christians, a tendency to transpire in propositions of stable and general truth which may be quite unconnected with revelation. For the allegorical method in exegesis represents fundamentally a desire to sophisticate a mythological view of life about which one has become self-conscious, a wish to make a revered and traditional myth or *cultus* respectable intellectually; and as such, therefore, when the Christians or Philo apply it to a history whose very historicity is of the utmost significance, it tends by its very nature to conflict with and even to dissipate this significance, to bring about a 'devaluation of history'.

Another point of contrast may be related to this. If, in the Bible, the act of God alters the conditions of existence and demands 'newness of life' in response to such alteration, then the word of God in the Bible, the word *of* that act in whatever form it comes to us, must come both as gospel and challenge, as eschatological news and existential vocation. Therefore its truth cannot be received in passivity like that which is rationalized and presupposed by the Platonic doctrine of 'recollection'. The response it demands is '*metanoia*', 'repentance', a 'change of mind'; and it means that a new self-understanding has been brought into being by a new understanding of God and his action on history.

Now with regard to the Christian's 'conversion' this change is, and has always been, acknowledged as a *sine qua non*. But I wonder whether the ramifications of the principle as it applies to the need for continual repentance on the part of the Christian, are not put in danger by the patristic practice of moving directly from the 'historical' to the 'moral' sense of an Old Testament text. This may seem enigmatic. In any case, de Lubac considers that the practice is explained sufficiently by the familiarity of the *sensus allegoricus* to the people for whom these expositions were intended. But this explanation—even where it is true— still reflects a change of emphasis in the conception of the point of typology, a change which has taken place since New Testament times. Typology is no longer so intimately linked with the *kerygma*; instead of an openness to the *kerygma* with its call to repentance and a new life in respect of the historical and historic occurrence which has taken place, a call which is still new and relevant after 'conversion', which still comes to us from the questioning God, the change intimates an acceptance of dogmatic facts which, once known (and no doubt still remembered), now lose something of their relevance existentially.[1]

We are led back finally, then, to the separation of 'senses' to which we referred in an earlier chapter.[2] The apparent objectivity of the facts *quae credas*, their frequent dissociation from the *quid agas* of the *sensus moralis*, this again seems to us to signify a blunting of the sense of the Christian's perpetually equivocal life-relation to and dependence on the past acts of God, his perpetual need of that relationship's reaffirmation and ratification in the spirit.

Our study, therefore, points to three faults in particular in the patristic exegetical tradition, the faults of allegorizing, of detraction from the eschatological character of the history upon which God has acted, and a dissociation of the acts of God from the demanded actions of men. But these faults are not peculiar to these writers, nor to this tradition. Is the eschatological character of history always detectable in the modern defence of typology, and are the causes of its absence more distinguished than those to which we have attributed it in the earlier period? We cannot often charge these modern writers with allegorizing. But the 'separation of senses' has its own modern dress, a 'typology without application', a 'pattern' without an imperative. And the devaluation of history has its modern dress too, so long as it is possible for writers to talk of 'the pattern of God's revelation' in 'the sacred era', the period of the Exodus from Egypt, and of the pattern's recapitulation in the other 'sacred era', that of our Lord's Incarnation.[3] That the whole tenor of

---

[1] See above, pp. 88–91.   [2] *Ibid.*
[3] The phrases are from W. J. Phythian-Adams, *op. cit.* pp. 9, 13, 17.

the two Testaments is quite different from either thought-form and thought-formulation, the Fathers' or that of the modern defenders of typology, we have tried to show in this essay. And agreement with this view comes from an unlikely quarter, at any rate at first sight, from Friedrich Baumgärtel who believes typology now to be an anachronism. Since, clearly, there can be no question here of special pleading, we record his remarks as of particular value:

Die heutigen Typologeten begnügen sich mit dem Aufzeigen von Entsprechungen, ihre Typen sind blosse Vorausschattung Christi... Ihrer Aufzeigung von Typen fehlt der Verkündigungscharakter, der der Herausarbeitung des Typologischen im Neues Testament eignet.[1]

And Baumgärtel says elsewhere:

Es geht nicht an, unbegrenzt typologische Entsprechungen zu konstatieren. Neutestamentlich ist das jedenfalls nicht. Stets hat das Neues Testament bei der Feststellung einer typologischen Entsprechung eine kerygmatische Intention: Vergegenwärtigung von Zorn und von Gnade Gottes. Das Neue Testament typologisiert durchaus innerhalb dieser Grenze...Das parakalein ist einbeschlossen im Typus: für uns geschrieben, uns zur Warnung, uns zum Trost.[2]

The difference of accent when one returns to the New Testament after reading the modern accounts of typology is striking. All history, not just an era, is sacred once God acts within it. Our own time as well as the past is made critical once these acts have happened. For this reason the Israelite learned in the Passover ritual to identify himself with his ancestors in their experience: '(This is what) the Lord did for *me* when *I* came up out of Egypt' (Exod. 13. 8).[3] And it is thus that these things to us also happened, 'as examples (τυπικῶς) to *us*, upon whom the ends of the ages have come' (I Cor. 10. 11).

[1] 'Das alttestamentliche Geschehen als "heilsgeschichtliches" Geschehen', *Geschichte und Altes Testament* (A. Alt Festschrift), p. 27. Cf. also Baumgärtel's *Verheissung*, p. 79 f.
[2] 'Das hermeneutische Problem des Alten Testaments', *TLZ* (1954), col. 204 n., and 204 = *PAH*, p. 123 n. and 123.
[3] Cf. Pesach 116 *b* (Babylonian Talmud, Soncino ed., pp. 595 ff.).

PART III

TYPOLOGY IN THE 'DIVINE COMEDY'

CHAPTER 12

INTRODUCTORY

THE statements from Baumgärtel which we have just quoted are applicable to the *Commedia* too, 'für uns geschrieben, uns zur Warnung, uns zum Trost'. It is the whole of my aim in this final part to show how the *Commedia*'s typology is 'applied' to that purpose of warning and comfort. I hope that by treating the subject here in the context of biblical typology, light will be cast back upon the Bible's use of typology, whose potential is here developed in a direction literally 'extraordinary' without involving fundamental change in its rationale. And I hope too to be able to show that the *Comedy* gains no less from this concatenation—or rather, that its criticism gains. For in the perspective which the Bible's use of typology gives us, we can go a great way towards overcoming the idea which amounts almost to a fixation in Dante criticism, that the 'allegorical meaning' (and the extent to which this is co-terminous with 'typological meaning' will be discussed later) is a subject for special study, something apart even, in the view of many critics, from the interpretation of the *Comedy*'s 'thought'.

The *Divine Comedy* is a poem about conversion.[1] It is, no doubt, incidentally about much else. But that is its main subject: becoming a Christian. The poem being directed (in current parlance, one might say 'geared') to the conversion of the world, or society, or his readers, its author works out his purpose as best he can and as, perhaps, he best can, by narrating his own. It is this enterprise which makes his poem significant in the history and theory of typology. It is this theme, in its working out through typology, which relates the *Comedy*, suggestively, to the Bible.

For we have seen, in the previous chapters, how, by its very

---

[1] Cf. H. Ostlender, 'Die Zielsetzung der "Divina Commedia"', *Studia Mediaevalia in honorem Raymundi Josephi Martin*, pp. 351–8; and even, in the often curious argument in the essay by G. G. Meersseman, 'Dante come teologo', pp. 190–3, the following clause: 'Certo l'itinerario spirituale di Dante comprende una *metanoia* evangelica...', *Atti del Congresso Internazionale di Studi Danteschi* (Florence, 1965), p. 192.

nature, the biblical tradition of typology fastens on an event of conversion with the aim of effecting another. Acts of God alter existence, or the believer's view of existence, and therefore necessarily come home, when they do come home, to the person who is faced with the experience or addressed by the news of them with a call to a radical re-alignment, with a challenge to change his mind, his way of life, his allegiances, in accord with the new life, the altered conditions, with which he is presented by God. Israel is called to leave Egypt and to leave existence in 'myth', with its intransigent and ingrained conservatism and its terror of 'history', and to enter that 'terrific' history—but to enter with a faith which, built on the past act of God, holds the springs of hope for the future, with a faith in God's power to provide. Similarly, in the New Testament, Judaism and Hellenistic paganism are called; again God's power to transform is invoked; and the power which, in the news of Christ's resurrection, is declared to have overcome sin and death, now confronts man with the call to live up to that victory, to live, now, life eternal. Typology expresses this call by articulating the new situation. It is an existential address from the past or the future action of God to a present which is obscurely—but to faith really—analogous with and caught up in that action. It is the prophet's, or the historian's, or the evangelist's chief way of turning prophecy, or history, or gospel, to challenge. The sheer moral urgency which typology gives to the writings in which it appears ought no longer to be underestimated.

This is the background against which the *Comedy*'s use of typology must be seen. It articulates a similar structure, and reveals similar concerns. But I say 'similar' and do not mean 'identical'. There is a new historical and religious situation by 1300, and one which dictates some alteration of typology's emphasis. Christianity has been adopted nationally and internationally. Men speak of 'Christendom'. The concerns and the structure of Dante's typology differ from the New Testament's by having to respond to this new situation, by having to take it into account. Now it is not a matter of 'becoming a Christian', quite simply. Rather, it is a matter of becoming one truly, of individually appropriating Christianity, of actualizing one's baptism in one's life. To this extent the emphasis-dictating situation is closer to that which the Old Testament's typology confronted. A sentence from Part I (p. 39) can be repeated, quite as aptly, here: 'Only by living up to the imperative could each man affirm the indicative as applying to him, and so become what, by virtue of the act of God, he was already—a member of God's chosen people, living in the new history which God had given him, according to the way which God had shown him.' And just as the Old Testament prophet addresses the word of God's future act too to the present as an imperative, so also does Dante in the *Comedy*. (For this to hold good, to be sure, it will be necessary for us to allow death the status of an act of God—in much the same way as, in discussing eschatological typology, we allow the 'after-life' and eschatology to be termed a period of 'history'. For death, at least in the *Comedy*, is conceived of as leading to a new existence, God-given, and one which is both discontinuous with, and the culmination of, each man's earlier, bodily, existence.) These insights of the Old Testament, which the New Testament, as I have shown, ratifies and begins to adapt to its gospel, Dante develops and presents with such clarity, through the allusive verbal texture and through the very narrative form of the poem, that an elemental aspect of Christian existence is brought, possibly as never before or since, to expression and intelligibility: the aspect of 'subfulfilment', the Christian's subfulfilment of both history and eschatology. If we note how all this is done by means of typology, and by typology perfectly in keeping with the dialectic of typology in the Bible—its theory and practice— we may go on to wonder how else, or at least how better, it could have been done. The figure of Dante, the character in the *Comedy*, takes part in Christ's death and resurrection in a way that looks back and forward, back to the way Christ had shown him, forward to the future Christ promised him; and so doing he stands as a 'sign' which affirms for his contemporaries that the gospel is viable still. The significance of this whole enterprise, for theology, for aesthetics, and for the history of literature, amply justifies my present linking of the *Commedia* with the Bible.

But a word of warning is necessary. It would not be legitimate critical procedure to interpret the *Comedy* immediately into biblical, or biblical-theological, terms. If there is no reason why we should not sometimes translate what the *Comedy* itself shows of its aims, its method, its 'poetic', into such terms (and, indeed, such translation is necessary if the relation between the Bible's and the *Comedy*'s typology is to be clarified), yet nothing exempts us from the need to start from the *Comedy* and justify our translations not from dogma or prejudice but by literary criticism.

But this is a warning which, after all, applies also to other approaches to the *Commedia* and its interpretation. It has not always been paid much attention. Natalino Sapegno speaks of the danger of reducing the *Comedy* to the proportions of a theological *summa*,[1] and on similar grounds to this Mandonnet has justly been attacked by E. Gilson,[2] and Busnelli and Orestano by Bruno Nardi[3]—the *Comedy*'s Thomism, even, still less what might be called its 'Paulinism', is not to be taken for granted.[4]

But a similar, perhaps less obvious, fault is more directly relevant to the question of our approach in this present work. Critics who have specially concerned themselves with the 'allegory' of the *Comedy* have been content chiefly to do so either on the basis of the assumption that Dante's intention was to write what (employing terms derived from *Convivio*, II. 1) is called 'allegory of the poets', or have instead chosen to rely on the *Letter to Can Grande*, of which not only is the authorship not indisputable[5] but in some respects also the meaning, and have therefore seen in the poem an 'allegory of the theologians'.

Neither approach, however, carries conviction when it is applied, as often it is (for example, by Fergusson, Sayers, and to some extent even by more professional Dantists such as Singleton and Montano) from the *Convivio* or *Letter* systematically, or quasi-systematically, to the *Commedia*. The safer, the only correct critical way is the opposite one. The *Commedia* must be interpreted first as far as possible out of itself, out of its own

[1] *La Divina Commedia*, a cura di N. Sapegno (*La Letteratura Italiana, storia e testi*, vol. 4), pp. xxx–xxxi.

[2] See his *Dante the Philosopher, passim*.

[3] See especially *Nel Mondo di Dante*, pp. 353–67.

[4] It is well to remind oneself that Hugh of St Victor, and, of course, Joachim of Fiore, have been proposed as more deeply influencing Dante than Aquinas had done. Cf. S. Bersani, *Dottrine, Allegorie, Simboli, della Divina Commedia*, for the relation between Hugh and Dante, esp. pp. 195–213; and L. Tondelli, *Da Gioacchino a Dante*, for those between Dante and Joachim.

[5] The classic attack and defence are respectively that by F. D'Ovidio in his *Studi sulla Divina Commedia* (1901) and Moore's essay in his *Studies in Dante* (third series) (1903). For recent discussion, cf. pp. 199 f. below.

implications and our own response to its poetry. Then we may see how the *Letter* accords with the poem, and, perhaps then *only*, feel our way towards a view of the possible genuineness of the *Letter*. So with typology. We shall sketch aspects of the poem which seem relevant, discuss them, and see finally how the *Comedy*'s use of typology accords with that of the Bible.

Here, though, one point may be stated as if dogmatically. Nothing in the poem suggests that a consistent allegorization is to be applied from beginning to end, and down to the details. It would be then 'cabbalistic' indeed to attempt to interpret it so.[1]

However, some account of the theory of allegorical exegesis in the Middle Ages being an obvious pre-condition of the inquiry as to whether Dante, in the *Comedy*, makes use of it, it will not prejudice the conclusions of that inquiry if, to avoid later digression, I give a brief outline here.

It may be brief, for ever since the time when the practice of allegorical exegesis came to be considered archaic in both pulpit and commentary[2] it has been a fairly favoured field of historical research. In the nineteenth and early twentieth centuries, it was not only the historians of exegesis, but also the literary historians and critics, such as H. Flanders Dunbar and G. R. Owst, who were doing pioneering work on the topic, and since then it has attracted increasing attention from several sectors. Beside the three full-scale treatments, by C. Spicq,[3] Beryl Smalley,[4] and H. de Lubac,[5] which must be regarded as fundamental, there are a host of shorter contributions from biblical and liturgical scholars, historians and students of

---

[1] Cf. Nardi, *op. cit.* p. 61.

[2] From this time, which begins with the Reformation but was in many milieus as late as the early nineteenth century, come the formal definitions which begin to distinguish allegory from typology for the first time. The following, from J. Gerhard (1582–1637), has become more or less a classic: 'Typus est, cum factum aliquod Vet. Test. ostenditur, praesignificasse seu adumbrasse aliquid gestum vel gerendum in Nov. Test. Allegoria est, cum aliquid ex Vet. vel Nov. Test. exponitur sensu novo atque accomodatur ad spiritualem doctrinam seu vitae institutionem. Typus consistit in factorum collatione. Allegoria occupatur non tam in factis, quam in ipsis concionibus, e quibus doctrinam utilem et reconditam depromit' (*Loci Theologici*, ed. Cotta, 1, 69, cited from G. von Rad, 'Typologische Auslegung des Alten Testament', *EvTh*, XII, 1952, p. 19). From the later end of this period comes the first use of the word 'typologia' (Latin, *c.* 1840), 'typology' (English, 1844).

[3] *Esquisse d'une Histoire de l'Exégèse Latine au Moyen Age.*

[4] *The Study of the Bible in the Middle Ages.*

[5] *Exégèse Médiévale: Les Quatre Sens de l'Écriture* (2 parts in 4 vols.).

medieval literature, among which I can make mention here of only a few that particularly concern themselves with the question of the relevancy of the allegorical treatment of the Bible to the *Divine Comedy*. In his *Dante sous la Pluie de Feu*, A. Pézard provides a useful if summary survey of the exegetical theory; C. S. Singleton, particularly in the first of his collections of *Dante Studies*, and R. Montano, in a series of works of which the essential conclusions are incorporated in his recent *Storia della Poesia di Dante*, attempt to apply it in a fairly thorough-going manner to the *Comedy*; and J. Chydenius offers another account of the theory in *The Theory of Mediaeval Symbolism*, and of its place in the *Comedy* in his monograph, *The Typological Problem in Dante*. With such a profusion of accessible work on the subject it is unnecessary for me to do more than outline the doctrine itself and indicate the features which are most significant for the present study.

The doctrine (so called) of the four senses of Scripture is the one which chiefly concerns our particular subject. It is, admittedly, only a single doctrine in a field in which, in the Middle Ages as now, exegetical doctrines proliferate and merge. But although it is scarcely ever found in its pure form consistently throughout the works of any one author, and was from patristic times always liable to be compounded with a doctrine of the 'body', 'soul', and 'spirit' of the sacred text with which, rationally, it was quite at odds, yet still de Lubac (*passim*) is right to attribute to it a distinct, ideal existence. No doctrine rivalled it in resilience. It runs as a kind of *basso ostinato* through several variant forms, and even where the special threefold *schema* to which we referred was in the ascendancy, the 'doctrine classique' (as de Lubac calls it, acceptably) tended to modify its more speculative excesses.

Thus the single choice of the doctrine of four senses as our chief source for the allegorical hermeneutics of the Middle Ages is not altogether arbitrary. The *ordo expositionis* which distinguishes it (i.e. the order, *sensus litteralis*; *allegoricus* or *typicus*; *tropologicus* or *moralis*; and finally, *anagogicus*)[1] is not only

---

[1] The latter two terms are reversible and sometimes the *sensus anagogicus* is subsumed under '*allegoricus*'. These variations do not, however, materially alter the doctrine. The essential factor is that the *allegoria* comes before the *sensus moralis*. Thus H. de Lubac, *op. cit.* part I, vol. I, pp. 129–69.

the most frequent, but is also, at least in theory, the one possessing the greatest theological potential.[1] It is this doctrine,
besides, which the *Letter to Can Grande* applies to the *Comedy*.

The *locus classicus* for the thirteenth century is in Aquinas,
Summa Theologiae, I, i, 10, and it will be convenient to quote the
major part of the reply straight away:

Auctor sacrae Scripturae est Deus, in cuius potestate est ut non solum
voces ad significandum accomodet (quod etiam homo facere potest)
sed etiam res ipsas. Et ideo, cum in omnibus scientiis voces signi-
ficent, hoc habet proprium ista scientia quod ipsae res significatae
per voces etiam significant aliquid. Illa ergo prima significatio qua
voces significant res pertinet ad primum sensum, qui est sensus
historicus vel litteralis. Illa vero significatio qua res significatae per
voces iterum res alias significant dicitur sensus spiritualis; qui super
litteralem fundatur et eum supponit.

Hic autem sensus spiritualis trifariam dividitur. Sicut enim dicit
Apostolus *ad Hebr. Lex vetus figura est novae legis*, et ipsa nova lex, ut
Dionysius dicit, est *figura futurae gloriae*. In nova etiam lege ea quae in
capite sunt gesta sunt signa eorum quae nos agere debemus.

Secundum ergo quod ea quae sunt veteris legis significant ea quae
sunt novae legis est sensus allegoricus; secundum vero quod ea quae
in Christo sunt facta vel in his quae Christum significant sunt signa
eorum quae nos agere debemus est sensus moralis; prout vero
significant ea quae sunt in aeterna gloria est sensus anagogicus.

We shall have occasion to refer to this statement from time to
time in the following chapters. What is most noteworthy now is
the *kind* of definition of the 'spiritual' senses which Aquinas
offers. It is by content or subject-matter that each sense is
distinguished, and not by hermeneutical method. Untypical in
certain other respects, the passage is utterly typical of medieval
exegetical theorizing in that. And effectively, the distinguishing
content of each 'spiritual' sense turns out to be an historical or
existential situation. The senses are, in effect, senses of history:
'Deus...ad significandum accomodet...res ipsas.'[2] Thus,

---

[1] One might reasonably, over against de Lubac's too sanguine view of the
doctrine's actual achievement in the realm of *heilsgeschichtlich* exegesis, stress the
word 'potential'. For the supporting theology which de Lubac expounds is not
often conspicuous in practice, and often cannot apply.

[2] 'Le sens allégorique, ou sens des choses, c'est essentiellement pour lui le sens
de l'histoire (d'Israël), et dans certaines de ses expressions, telles que *cursus rerum*,
la traduction de *res* par *histoires* s'impose' (H. de Lubac, *op. cit.* II, 2, p. 287, citing
P. Grelot, *Nouvelle Revue théologique*, LXXXIV, 1962, p. 83).

here and throughout the tradition, the *sensus allegoricus* means, in reference to the Old Testament, that the words or events recorded in Scripture are taken as applying to Christ and the Church, that is, to the new dispensation. They are recorded 'pro nobis', for our sake (cf. I Cor. 9. 9; 10. 6, 11), for this is the 'end of the ages', the time of fulfilment, to which the Old Testament points. This, clearly, is the sense which is most obviously related to the traditional scope of typology. Moving on to the next 'sense', as to content the *sensus moralis* speaks for itself; but it is worth remarking that this sense too is addressed to the new dispensation, though as imperative and not as a statement. The way in which this sense may relate to typology we shall suggest, shortly, below. The *sensus anagogicus*, finally, is that which applies the text to the hereafter, and this also (though only, as we should say, when the text in question has to do with an event and one which is confessedly fundamental in salvation history) may sometimes be comparable to the eschatological reference of biblical typology.[1] In cases where the literal sense already refers to present or future existence it would normally, as by Aquinas,[2] be thought idle to refer it back by allegory, or by any means, to a former one.

These are the essential elements of the doctrine, and it is in these elements, if anywhere, that its theological potential must be sought. Its best-known short formulation, the verse usually attributed to Nicholas of Lyra,[3] restates them in epitome:

> Littera gesta docet, quid credas allegoria,
> Moralis quid agas, quo tendas anagogia.

But just as there is no mention in this verse of exegetical method, so also in Aquinas and throughout the period of the doctrine's sway its methodology and rationale were considered very rarely, and then to little purpose.[4] Hence the actual faults in

---

[1] Cf. R. A. Markus, 'Presuppositions of the Typological Approach to Scripture', *CQR*, CLVIII, 48 f.

[2] Cf. *Quaestiones quodlibetales*, VII. vi. 15. ad 5.

[3] But apparently the author is in fact Augustine of Dacia; see de Lubac, *op. cit.* I, 1, p. 23, and 'Sur un vieux distique, la doctrine du "quadruple sens"', *Mélanges Cavallera* (1948).

[4] This is particularly the case previous to the twelfth century. Even so, of course, there are exceptions, the chief of them being, of course, St Augustine's treatment of the subject in Book III of *de Doctrina Christiana*. For the middle ages prior to the twelfth century we quote the opinion of C. Spicq: 'Les considérations générales

practice such as those to which I have occasionally pointed in this essay. For the methods actually used were learned not by rule but by imitation from earlier writers, and were in large part ultimately Hellenistic in origin, radically 'demythologizing' in purpose, 'allegorical' in nature, and, it must be said, arbitrary in application.[1]

But with the faults we are not at present concerned. If its faults were all that there were to be said of the doctrine, the comparison which I have several times invoked would not have been worth while. It is more important to establish whether, and in what sense, despite them, the doctrine might be said to contain genuine theological potential and a genuinely theological rationale. Nobody, I think, who understands this rationale, would deny that it has at least some points of contact with typology, and perhaps with 'applied' typology at that.

For though the methods most commonly associated with the doctrine are only attached to it accidentally by the historical circumstances of the Hellenistic milieu in which Christianity grew up in the early centuries, the essential *schema* of the doctrine is still recognizably Hebraic. And the relating of each 'sense' to a particular context in what we today call 'salvation-history'—or alternatively, and perhaps more accurately, to a particular existential situation[2]—is clearly a development from, if it is not identified with, Hebraic and biblical typology. In this situation it is obviously possible to replace the *schema*'s usual concomitants, the Hellenistic-allegorical methods of late antiquity, with the more dialectical methods which might realize its typological potential. The question is not only, however, 'did such methods exist?' (for it is clear enough from this essay that the methods in question are simply special uses of

d'herméneutique (sont) extrêmement rares' (*op. cit.* p. 17). The treatment of the subject by Raban Maur in *De Clericorum Institutione* is representative of such considerations as there were: it is extremely derivative, emanating in large part from the same *locus classicus* in Augustine (see Spicq, *op. cit.* p. 40). Compare also the article by R. M. Grant in the *Interpreter's Bible*, I, 106–14 and esp. 113 f., and that by A. A. Gilmore, 'Augustine and the Critical Method', *HTR*, xxxix (1946), 149–63.

  [1] On the development of hermeneutics during the twelfth century, however, see G. Paré, A. Brunet and P. Tremblay, *La Renaissance du XIIe Siècle: les Écoles et l'Enseignement*, ch. v; and M.-D. Chenu, *La Théologie au XIIe Siècle*, pp. 159–220.

  [2] I.e. literal sense, man under the law; allegorical or, as I shall henceforth call it in order to distinguish it from literary or Hellenistic allegorizing, *allegoricus*, man under grace; moral sense, man under the imperative which grows out of the gospel's indicative; and anagogical sense, man in eternal life.

analogy), but 'were such methods ready to hand in the period which we are discussing?'

Clearly, the alternative methods to allegory which were to hand were practised only sporadically, but still such methods there were, and, moreover, they were practised. I cite only the most widespread and the most significant, the principle included among the exegetical 'rules' of Tichonius which has been passed on and endorsed by St Augustine,[1] according to which what is said of the Church's 'Head' may often be applied to his 'Body'.[2] The place which this principle held in practice in the Middle Ages is sufficiently vouched for by the place it held in the Old Testament commentary which was perhaps the one most influential throughout the whole period, St Gregory's *Moralia in Iob*. Repeatedly invoked there, it might not be an exaggeration to say that it is one of the principles on which the whole work is based. The legitimacy of the procedure by which Job is initially established as being 'typical' of Christ is of course more than doubtful; but once that step has been taken the further transition to the Church by means of this image of 'incorporation in Christ' is legitimate enough, and often effective:

Igitur quia in ipso expositionis exordio sic persona beati Iob nuntiare Dominum diximus, ut designari per illum caput et corpus, idest Christum et Ecclesiam diceremus: postquam caput nostrum quomodo designatum credatur, ostendimus: nunc corpus eius, quod nos sumus, quomodo exprimatur, indicemus: ut quia audivimus ex historia, quod miremur, cognovimus ex capite, quod credamus, consideremus nunc ex corpore, quod vivendo teneamus. In nobismetipsis namque debemus transformare quod legimus, ut cum per auditum se animus excitat, ad operandum quod audierit vita concurrat.[3]

There is justification here for a *sensus allegoricus* and a *sensus moralis*, for the indicatives and imperatives arise from a faith which takes Christ for both Gospel and Law. There is no denying that this principle closely conforms to the 'applied' typo-

---

[1] *De Doctrina Christiana*, III, 30–7.

[2] *Ibid.* III, 31. This 'rule' has its counterpart, it is worth noticing, in another which concerns the devil and his 'body', the 'wicked' who follow him (*ibid.* p. 37). This, obviously, is analogous to what I have called 'the typology of rejection'.

[3] *Moralia*, I, xxiv, 33.

logy of the new dispensation expounded in the last part; and
how much of the whole doctrine of the four senses can be
justified when this principle is set at its centre and associated
with a second which, taken over from St Paul, was equally a
commonplace of biblical exposition, the principle, namely, that
the whole history of Israel was 'prefigurative' and 'prophetic'
(cf. I Cor. 10. 11),[1] may be judged from the statements of
Aquinas who, not only in the *Summa*, but also, and more fully,
in the Quodlibets, does thus centralize it:[2]

Respondeo dicendum, quod distinctio istorum quatuor sensuum hoc
modo accipi debet...

...Inter omnia autem quae in sacra Scriptura narrantur, prima
sunt illa quae ad vetus testamentum pertinent; et ideo quae secundum litteralem sensum ad facta veteris testamenti spectant, possunt
quatuor sensibus exponi. Secunda vero sunt illa quae pertinent ad
statum praesentis Ecclesiae, in quibus illa sunt priora quae ad caput
pertinent, respectu eorum quae pertinent ad membra; quia ipsum
corpus verum Christi, et ea quae in ipso sunt gesta, sunt figura
corporis Christi mystici, et eorum quae in ipso geruntur, ut in ipso
scilicet Christo, exemplum vivendi sumere debeamus. In Christo
etiam futura gloria nobis praemonstrata est; unde ea quae ad
litteram de ipso Christo capite dicuntur, possunt exponi et allegorice,
referendo ad corpus eius mysticum; et moraliter, referendo ad actus
nostros, qui secundum ipsum debent reformari; et anagogice, in
quantum in Christo est nobis iter gloriae demonstratum...[3]

Some have seen in these statements a criticism, and perhaps
even an envisaged reformation, of the exegetical practices
current up to this time: 'distinctio istorum quatuor sensuum

[1] Of course not everything can be justified by this principle, and allegorizing
can certainly not be. Analogy, conducted on dialectical lines such as I have traced
in the previous chapters, is one thing, but to declare that one event *means* another
tout court is quite different. The 'meaning' of which one *may* speak is strictly only an
'implication for faith'. Failure to recognize this was a radical fault of medieval
exegesis. Even St Thomas speaks, after all, of 'senses' of Scripture and apparently
means that precisely. And a similar failure seriously impairs many of the judgements, though not the unrivalled exposition and scholarship, in de Lubac's *Exégèse
Médiévale*.

[2] I leave open the question how far Aquinas is original in thus centralizing the
principle of 'incorporation'. There is no doubt that it was fairly traditionally
applied in exegesis, but then so after all was much else, which St Thomas *leaves out*
of his dogmatic statements.

[3] *Quaestiones quodlibetales*, VII. vi. 15, ad 5; cf. also, again, *STh.* I. i. 10; and
Commentarium in epistolam ad Galatas, iv. 7.

hoc modo accipi debet.'[1] It is not possible to go quite so far. Aquinas here *adds* very little to the doctrine, and his own practice, as de Lubac points out,[2] is not free of the allegorical procedures which the 'reforming' view of Aquinas would expect him to have disowned. But it is true that his theoretical statements do, to our minds, sort ill with these procedures. For on the one hand Aquinas presents Christ at the centre of what *may now become*, very easily, an historical typology which contains the imperatives and the indicatives,[3] past, present and future, of human existence 'in Christ'. And, on the other, allegorical procedures, to the vindication of which his rationale is irrelevant, are retained in his scriptural commentaries. Perhaps the fact that this rather disconcerting cleavage is polarized as it is is significant—the faults appertaining to the realm of practical exegesis, where the influence of Hellenistic allegorizing was at its greatest, and the 'potential' to the realm of systematic theology, where dialectic is paramount. If the doctrine of the four senses was to become in practice what most recent criticism agrees that in theory it could be,[4] this might well first happen in a realm where the particular allegorical influence in question was more remote than the dialectical influence, and especially in one where dialectics meets history. If it was unlikely to happen in biblical exegesis, where past habits were ingrained, and old interpretations handed on down, it might happen where the necessary focus on history, on the *res gesta*, was not impeded by the counter-attractions of the 'inspired words' of the Bible.

[1] E.g. M.-D. Chenu, *Introduction à l'étude de Saint Thomas d'Aquin*, pp. 217–22. But de Lubac argues forcibly in the other direction (*op. cit.* II, 2, pp. 285–302).

[2] *Loc. cit.*

[3] Compare especially the primary division which St Thomas makes in the just-quoted Quodlibet (*resp.*) between the indicatives and imperatives of typology: 'Veritas autem quam sacra Scriptura per figuras rerum tradit, ad duo ordinatur: scilicet ad recte credendum, et ad recte operandum.'

[4] See, for Aquinas, especially M.-D. Mailhiot, 'La pensée de S. Thomas sur le sens spirituel', *Revue Thomiste*, LIX (1959), 613–63; also, besides the relevant chapters in the books of Spicq, Smalley, and de Lubac, cited above, J. Gribomont, 'Le Lien des deux Testaments selon S. Thomas d'Aquin', *Ephemerides Theologicae Lovanienses* (1946), pp. 70–89; P. Synave, 'La Doctrine de S. Thomas sur le sens littéral des Écritures', *RB*, XXV (1926); T. F. Torrance, 'Scientific Hermeneutics according to St Thomas Aquinas', *JTS*, XIII (1962), 259–89; and the fresh remarks of Miss Smalley in *The Church's Use of the Bible*, ed. D. E. Nineham, pp. 60 f.

CHAPTER 13

FIGURAL REALISM AND THE STATE
OF SOULS AFTER DEATH

APPROACHING the *Divine Comedy*, as we do here, from the
Bible, it is not so much history as cosmology that impresses
itself on the mind. The poem's profound sense of history and
historicality makes itself felt, not necessarily gradually but to a
large extent imperceptibly; one becomes conscious of it rather
by indirect means than immediately. But with the cosmology
the case is quite different. One is aware of it, awake to it, at
every stage, practically, of one's reading: aware, that is, of a
cosmology that is in the highest degree intellectual and articulated, and at the same time wide-reaching, in a way which outside the Christian Middle Ages is scarcely conceivable: for,
apparently at least, the realms of the after-life, eschatological
blessing and woe, which in the Bible are conceived in much
more temporal than spatial dimensions, are here incorporated
in a scheme which brings the spatial dimension very much to
the fore.

The earth is the centre of the cosmos. Around it revolves the
adapted Ptolemaic universe of thirteenth-century scholasticism:
nine concentric planetary spheres embraced in their turn by
the Empyrean, the essential heaven. Beneath the inhabited
(northern) hemisphere hell reaches down in narrowing circles
to the earth's centre, to which Satan fell after being driven from
heaven, and in which now he is fixed for eternity. At the
antipodes to Jerusalem, in the uninhabited south, Mount
Purgatory rises, created by the earth's matter flung upward by
Satan's fall.[1] Seldom, if ever, has the *bête noir* of modern theology, the three-storey universe, been presented as concretely as
here. Hell, Purgatory, Heaven, thus have their apparently
quite objective locations within an organized cosmos. We are
faced not so much with a 'realized' as with a 'simultaneous'
eschatology.

---

[1] *Inf.* XXXIV. 121–6.

Moreover, the objective and concrete, even (let us confess it) *weltanschaulich*, character of the other world is accentuated in the poem. Dante is at pains to bring home its local reality. Purgatory, for example, set as it is 'di retro al sol, (nel) mondo sanza gente' (*Inf.* xxvi. 117)—in the southern hemisphere, that is, unknown and, save for the foolish and fatal journey of Ulysses (described in *Inf.* xxvi; cf. *Par.* xxvii. 82 f.), unvisited —offers, by virtue of this setting, a natural advantage to the poet or theologian who might wish to stress its 'mystical' character.

Since reality tends to be judged by what is known, by stressing Purgatory's 'unknownness', the qualities of it unknown to the human world, he may, without altogether denying its reality, make it still 'unreal' enough to prevent too worldly a view of it and leave it virtually in the province of 'spirit'. Dante, however, does the opposite. There are indeed some stars there 'non viste mai fuor ch'alla prima gente' (*Purg.* I. 24), unseen since our first parents saw them from the earthly Paradise; yet the planetary constellations which we know rise sometimes over those horizons and it is the same sun, though from the north now (*Purg.* IV. 54–7), that lights those shores. The exactness of the geography leaves no doubt as to its all being part of the same world as ours.

Physical features of the landscape of Purgatory support the astronomical carefulness. Dante underlines their relation to what is familiar. In the well-known fifteenth-century picture of Dante and his book, in the Cathedral at Florence, stylization rather disguises the rugged, alpine, character of Purgatory in the poem. But in the *Comedy*, though there is no shortage of mathematics and symmetry, its geometry and arithmetic never interfere with the geographical and topographical realism. The mountainousness of Mount Purgatory is given its due. There are great boulders, fissures, ledges, cliffs. The climb is heavy going. Dante, the pilgrim, being still in the body, pants for his breath, and wishes he had wings (see *Purg.* IV. 24–45): he has to scramble, using hands and feet (*v.* 33); he pauses to ask Virgil a question, or questions Virgil in order to pause (*vv.* 34–6); and, as he feared, receives the answer 'for the moment, straight on up!' And so, the indirect method having failed, Dante resorts to the direct:

O dolce padre, volgiti, e rimira,
   com'io rimango sol, se non restai
(O sweet father, turn and see:
   I shall be left alone if you don't stop.)   (*vv.* 44–5)

and now Virgil agrees: 'Only drag yourself up to that ledge', 'infin quivi ti tira' (*vv.* 46–8). It was a deserved compliment to the credibility of the poet's description of his climb that was made by a nineteenth-century writer of a book on Dante—alpinista![1] It is easy to forget that for fantasy this journey equals anything in Gulliver or von Munchausen. 'Egli immagina', says Parodi, 'il più fantastico dei mondi e lo trasfigura nel più reale.'[2] But it is not fantasy only which is transfigured, it is the domain of the after-life, and we are given no opportunity to forget this, however 'real' it is made.

Paradoxically, or at least unexpectedly, real in the *Comedy*, therefore, is the region of what might be called 'eschatological space'. But it is not only a realism of space that is remarkable. The realism of character is no less; and character, too, is 'eschatological' here.[3]

'Remarkable', that is to say, as much for its presence as for its degree. For character is, after all, not usually associated with spirits; the dimmed and reduced personalities of the 'shades' in the classical underworld harmonize with our own preconceptions of 'ghosts' much more squarely. But 'character' is for us something different. We associate it with being human, and the dead are not properly human at all; not even Dante would call them so.

Apparently, indeed, he wishes to lay some stress on this fact. 'Omo' (uomo) is used directly only of 'man' in general or the living man. The inhabitants of the after-life in the *Comedy* are shades, and they insist upon it. The question comes up in the first canto: man or shade? And Virgil's reply is expressed in

[1] Ottone Brentari, *Dante Alpinista* (Padova, 1888).
[2] E. G. Parodi, *Poesia e storia nella Divina Commedia*, p. 129.
[3] Though, I use the word 'eschatological' here and throughout this chapter in a broad sense denoting the realm of divine salvation and judgement and the after-life generally, it should be noted that the *eschaton*, in the narrower sense (the last judgement, bodily resurrection, etc.) is still to come. Following Aquinas (*STh*, III, Suppl., 69, 2; *SCG*, IV. 91), and, indeed, most of the Fathers, Dante presents the going to judgement as immediately subsequent to death and leaves to the last day only an enhancement of punishment or glory which results from the reunion of body and soul. See *Inf.* VI. 103–11; *Purg.* III. 31–3 (cf. *Purg.* XXV. 79–108); *Par.* XIV. 43–60.

the terms which most emphasize the distinction between him and Dante: 'Non omo, omo già fui' (*Inf.* I. 67). What once were men are souls now, shades without bodies, unable to have full human contact even with one another. Hence the pathos of the situation in which Statius, overcome by exceptional emotion when he learns that it is Virgil who stands before him, forgets himself for a moment and attempts to embrace the other reverently at the feet, and Virgil restrains him gently:

> 'Frate,
> non far, che tu se' ombra e ombra vedi.'
> (Brother, do not do so; you are a shade and see a shade.)
> (*Purg.* XXI. 130–6).

The contrast between life and death is so stressed as to leave no doubt that for Dante death does not mean only a passage from one sphere to another; it is passage and transformation. It is even, as is shown by the recurrence of 'disfatto' and related forms as synonyms for 'dead', an 'unmaking'.[1]

This, of course, agrees in all fundamental respects with the traditional Aristotelian anthropology which Aquinas had re-affirmed and adapted to Christian doctrine. The substantial union of soul and body which makes a man 'man' is dissolved in death.[2] If, in so far as it relates to the body, death is natural, yet with regard to the soul, whose natural condition is to be united with the body, the separation from the body is against nature, so that until the resurrection even a soul which is blessed, though morally perfect, does not make up perfect man, and is, indeed, as to its constitution, *less* than human.[3] Union with the body is not detrimental to the soul but enhances it.[4] St Thomas goes further than Dante when, since the sensitive powers belong to the mortal body, he denies that the 'separated' soul has any access to empirical knowledge through the senses;[5] and he specifically affirms that although the soul retains knowledge acquired in this life it can learn nothing of human affairs after death except by special divine dispensation.[6]

[1] See, for example, *Inf.* III. 57, VI. 42; *Purg.* V. 134.
[2] *STh*, I. 75. 4; *Compendium Theologiae*, I. 154; *SCG*, II. 56, 57, III. 79.
[3] *Comp. Theol.* I. 151, 152.
[4] Disputations, *de Anima* I. ad 7.
[5] *STh*, III (Suppl.), 70. 1; Disputations, *de Anima*, 15.
[6] *STh*, I. 89. 8, cf. 89. 3 and 5.

Dante, however, by his doctrine of the 'airy body' (*Purg.* xxv.
75–108, discussed below) and by allowing even to the damned
some knowledge of earthly history (limited in this latter case to
the comparatively distant future or distant past, as explained
in *Inf.* x. 97–108), in these respects, and in these respects only,
for particular purposes softens the distinction between life and
death. Yet for him, as for St Thomas, the soul is deprived, by
its very situation in a changeless eternity, of certain operations
proper to 'man'. Historical flux and historical action no longer
directly modify the soul's individuality or its future;[1] this being
the case, with very slight qualification, even in Purgatory, for
there too the will is immutable with regard to its ultimate end.[2]
The final decisions have been taken in the course of historical
life and the decisions which remain concern only the choice
between means of attaining what the soul now knows to be
perfect good.[3] The souls in Purgatory are now, from the time
of their death, secure in their destination, and Dante addresses
them,

O anime sicure
d'aver, quando che sia, di pace stato.
(O souls who are sure of reaching, soon or late, the state of peace.)
(*Purg.* xxvi. 53 f.)

Thus the fact of death, as Guardini says, is continually
emphasized in the poem: 'Die Tatsache des Todes wird immer
wieder betont.'[4] The journey of the live Dante, and the
amazement provoked by it in those he encounters, points the
contrast between his state and theirs. Even the dead themselves
are brought by it to a fuller, more existential realization of
death's character as a total sundering from the familiar, human,
historical life of this world. Dante's presence among them brings
recollection, and recollection, in its turn, in Purgatory but
more especially in Hell, again and again produces nostalgia—
instanced by an abundance of phrases, such as 'dolce terra',
'dolce lome', 'dolce mondo', 'mondo pulcro', 'vita serena',
'vita bella', 'vita lieta'.[5] More than this, his arrival as an
ambassador from the world has the effect of prompting the

---

[1] *SCG*, iv. 93. 5.   [2] *Ibid.* iv. 94, cf. iv. 92, 93.   [3] *Ibid.* iv. 95.
[4] R. Guardini, 'Leib und Leiblichkeit in Dantes Göttlicher Komödie', *Anteile*
(Martin Heidegger zum 60. Geburtstag), p. 155.
[5] *Inf.* xxvii. 26, x. 69, vi. 88, vii. 58, vi. 51, xv. 57, xix. 102, respectively.

souls into speech, as though, as Auerbach says, each were 'moved by the awareness that this is its one and only opportunity to express itself'.[1] 'All of them find in the living Dante, who comes to them, an occasion and need to state what they are and to explain how they came to their ultimate destination.'[2] The momentary modification of the otherwise absolute dissociation from life which the meeting with Dante signifies to the dead souls, does not lessen, but rather intensifies, the implied or explicit concentration of their discourse on death. 'Von ihr' (i.e. 'death'), Guardini continues in the essay recently cited, 'wird *alles* umschlossen, was in der Göttlichen Komödie gesagt ist',[3] and this is certainly true of the speeches of the souls in *Inferno*.[4] It is from death that they speak, and they speak of their death and their present situation even when their words are, directly, about their life. For their past life concerns them now chiefly as the process which disposed them to their present situation in death, and it is to events which reveal or typify that disposition that their words characteristically point.

No one, I think, in view of this concentration in the poem on death and the changed constitution which death denotes, would be surprised therefore to hear the work called a *Summa mortis humanae*; and plainly the very rigour of this focal tendency means that, whatever 'character-realism' in this connection implies, there can be no question of a return to (or repetition of) the character as before. If, before death, human character is 'historical', the change it has undergone by death

---

[1] E. Auerbach, *Dante: Poet of the Secular World*, p. 135.

[2] *Ibid.* pp. 139 f. Compare also F. De Sanctis's essay, 'Dell'Argomento della Divina Commedia', ET in *De Sanctis on Dante*, ed. and trans. by J. Rossi and A. Galpin, pp. 11 f. One may quibble with De Sanctis's reading, but he is still mainly correct and splendidly percipient. 'Thus an infinite variety springs to live in a subject which is by its nature narrow and monotonous; there is now a place for everything in life, even the most transitory of its aspects.'

[3] *Art. cit.* p. 155 (my italics).

[4] It is true also of the other two *cantiche*, but to a lesser extent. There too, of course, death modifies all that is spoken by souls, but their own death, their own situation, becomes less and less frequently the main theme of their discourse. The main attention, even when their personal fortunes are the subject, is directed elsewhere. Death to them is the climax of the great transvaluation of worldly values which allows them to look no longer primarily at themselves, at *their* fate, *their* reward, but at God: they speak of their fate now only as a way of speaking about God, as a way of disclosing his grace, and the world's fatal blindness towards it.

may be summed up by saying that now it is 'eschatological';
i.e. it is confronted and modified no longer by history and
contingency but by eschatology and the absolute. Yet in
general critics have not been slow to point out all the same how
realistic is the art by which Dante has made his *personae* seem
vibrant, individual, and, paradoxical though it be, 'live'. And
few would hesitate to accept the justice of the phrase which in
fact has been used to describe the *Commedia*: 'Dante's *Summa
vitae humanae*.'[1]

For however strong Dante's sense of the transformation in
death, he creates too, through the techniques of his poem, a
vital awareness in the reader of the continuity between life and
death which the soul's immortality preserves. The poetic and
dramatic devices by which he transmits this awareness are
legion, and I need indicate only a few of them.

The inhabitants of the 'beyond' retain, first, their individual,
hitherto bodily, features in the 'shade' which the soul's inform-
ing power (*virtù informativa*, *Purg.* xxv. 89) radiates on to its
surrounding air: thus they are visible, and, as we have already
had occasion to notice, having organs, can see, hear, feel (*Purg.*
xxv. 79–108). There is no reason why this deviation from
Thomism, and indeed from dogma in general, should be taken
seriously as theology. Dante was, on occasion, perfectly willing
to depart from Aquinas—Bruno Nardi has shown that he does
so in this same canto and speech (*vv.* 37–78)[2]—or, indeed, from
any of his authorities; but he is unlikely to depart, as he does
here, from them all at once, on a purely speculative matter,
just for the sake of speculation. Instead, as Sapegno well says,
'the idea of an airy body, inconsistent but possessing all its
sensitive faculties, was necessitated by obvious exigencies of
representation and narrative'.[3] It is a case of poetic licence, or,
more specifically, of the application of a principle which, in
relation to scripture, goes back to Origen, Clement of Alexandria, and even Philo,[4] and is expressly utilized and referred

[1] Auerbach, *op. cit.* p. 93.
[2] I.e. in the treatment by Statius of the origin of the human soul. Nardi, *Dante
e la cultura medievale*, pp. 197–9, and *Nel Mondo di Dante*, pp. 364–7, argues that
Dante follows a doctrine of Albert the Great on the generation and formation of
the soul which was expressly opposed by Aquinas.
[3] N. Sapegno, *La Divina Commedia, a cura de N. Sapegno, ad loc.*
[4] See R. P. C. Hanson, *Allegory and Event*, pp. 224–8.

to by Dante in explaining why the souls come to meet him in the various planetary spheres instead of remaining in their place in the Empyrean. According to this principle then, which is technically termed 'accommodation', matters which naturally transcend human perception are suitably expressed metaphorically, in intelligible, often physical, terms:[1]

> Per questo la Scrittura condescende
> a vostra facultate, e piedi e mano
> attribuisce a Dio, ed altro intende.

(So scripture suits its words to human understanding, attributing feet and hands to God but meaning something else.) (*Par.* IV. 43–5)

There is, however, one difference between this doctrine's use in the *Paradiso* and its application to the matter of the soul's 'airy body'. For in the latter case what is signified is not 'something else' ('altro', *Par.* IV. 45) but the very person himself: the person, and not a 'meaning', is revealed to the pilgrim by means of it. Thus, except in Paradise where the forms' radiance veils their features,[2] those whom he knew on earth he recognizes here, and those whom he will know of by repute can be pointed out to him by their appearance. In the valley of princes (*Purg.* VII) Sordello indicates Philip the Bold as 'quel Nasetto' ('small of nose', *v.* 103), while

> quel che par sì membruto e che s'accorda
> cantando, con colui dal maschio naso

(the one who looks so sturdy, keeping time in song with him of the prominent nose) (*Purg.* VII. 112 f.)

is Peter III of Aragon with Charles I of Anjou.

But all the *Divine Comedy*'s realism of character is ultimately based upon this doctrine, this particular example of 'accommodation'. By means of it Dante is able to present character by appearance, gesture, bearing, as well as by the content,

---

[1] *Par.* IV. 24–48. Cf. *STh*, I. iii. 1, and I. i. 9; 'Conveniens est sacrae Scripturae divina et spiritualia sub similitudine corporalium tradere; Deus enim omnibus providet secundum quod competit eorum naturae; est autem naturale homini ut per sensibilia ad intelligibilia veniat, quia omnis nostra cognito a sensu initium habet. Unde convenienter in sacra Scriptura traduntur nobis spiritualia sub metaphoris corporalium...'

[2] Cf. *Par.* VIII. 52–4: 'La mia letizia mi ti tien celato / che mi raggia dintorno e mi nasconde / quasi animal di sua seta fasciato'—Charles Martel ('my gladness hides me from you, for it radiates around me and conceals me like an animal swathed in its silk': cf. also *Par.* V. 124 f., XXVI. 135).

style and tone of speech. And it is not only a means of identification, it is the channel of an otherwise impossible degree of self-disclosure on the part of the shades. Their visibility is itself a step in this direction. Their physical attitude and movement authoritatively suggest their individual nature and quality.[1] Farinata rises 'come avesse lo inferno in gran dispitto' ('as if he held hell in complete contempt') (*Inf.* x. 36), raises his brow a little as he speaks (*v.* 45), and, interrupted, stands unmoved and undisquieted:

> non mutò aspetto,
> né mosse collo, né piegò sua costa.

(his expression did not change, nor did he move his neck or bend his side.) (*vv.* 74 f.)

The shade alongside him contrasts markedly: rising only enough to allow his face to show over the edge of the tomb, he peers about in the vain hope of seeing his son, Guido, there with Dante, weeps as he speaks, and then, assuming prematurely that Guido is dead, falls back: 'supin ricadde, e più non parve fora' ('fell back recumbent and appeared outside no more') (*v.* 72).

Belacqua, whom we meet in a scene (*Purg.* IV. 97–139) which for humour and humanity matches any in the poem, will serve as our last example of this facet of the *Comedy*'s realism. Among those who idly stand in the shade of a boulder in the *Ante-purgatorio* Belacqua alone is sitting:

> E un di lor, che mi sembiava lasso,
> sedeva e abbracciava le ginocchia,
> tenendo il viso giù tra esse basso.

[1] Dante's use of facial and bodily gesture deserves a book, and already in 1902 an excellent one was devoted to it by M. Porena, *Delle Manifestazioni plastiche del Sentimento nei Personaggi della Divina Commedia*. Porena notes (p. 79): 'We have observed a thousand human forms powerfully engraved in the pages of the *Inferno* as highly efficacious interpretors of the psychological attitudes of the damned; and we see still some few in the Ante-purgatorio. But all that remains in Purgatory itself is the odd simple and detached gesture; and one might say that in Paradise there remains nothing.' In the *Paradiso*, however, the expressive functions of gesture are replaced by activities no less expressive, but expressive rather of corporate than of individual attitudes. Porena points out that the intricate groupings of the souls here, as they wheel, dance, form and reform themselves into shape after shape, are the movements of lights, not people; but the movements are still an 'accommodated' expression of the souls' concerns. And he points out, too, how, particularly in the case of Beatrice (but cf. also Mary in *Par.* XXXIII. 40–2), gestural expression persists, though concentrated now in the smile and the eyes (*op. cit.* pp. 96–102).

> —O dolce segnor mio,—diss'io—adocchia
> colui che mostra sé più negligente
> che se pigrizia fosse sua serocchia—

(And one of them, who seemed to me weary, was sitting and embracing his knees, keeping his face low down between them. 'O my sweet lord', I said, 'look at him there, who shows himself more negligent than if he had sloth for a sister.') (*vv.* 106–11)

Belacqua is so much the same man as Dante knew on earth that, when he recognizes him, the poet feels like laughing:

> Li atti suoi pigri e le corte parole
> mosson le labbra mie un poco a riso;
> poi cominciai:—Belacqua...,
> ...dimmi: perché assiso
> quiritta se'?...
> ...lo modo usato t'ha ripriso?—

(His idle movements and terse speech made my lips move towards laughter. Then I began, 'Belacqua...tell me, why are you sitting here?...You've gone back to your old ways, have you?') (*vv.* 121–6)

'Lo modo usato t'ha ripriso?' It is a good question, and one might put it to many a character in the *Commedia* more seriously, perhaps, than it is put here. Belacqua's answer is 'no', as, strictly, in death it must always be. There is no return, no equality even of 'ways' (*modo*) between life and death. No one can undergo death without transformation. But Dante has seen evidence enough in Belacqua's case, as we may in many another, that this question is not unequivocal, and is capable, almost equally, of being answered in the affirmative. Belacqua is very much the same man, though now his excuse for delay is a valid one. That is why Dante, perceptively, has him phrase his denial of the 'modo usato' in terms which, by their juxtaposition of lassitude and self-justification, hark back to the living man:

> ...O frate, l'andar su che porta?
> ché non mi lascerebbe ire a' martiri
> l'angel di Dio che siede in su la porta

(O brother, what's the point of going on? The angel of God who sits at the gate of purgatory would not let me go through to my purgation.) (*Purg.* IV. 127–9)

188

The continuation of Belacqua's speech takes us a step further:

> Prima convien che tanto il ciel m'aggiri
> di fuor da essa, quanto fece in vita,
> perch'io indugiai al fine i buon sospiri.

(First I must wait outside until the sky has wheeled about me as many times as it did in life, because I put off to the end my proper sighs.)

(*vv.* 130–2)

The conception of the '*contrapasso*'[1] which is evidently involved here is well known to anyone who reads the *Inferno* attentively. In principle, at any rate, all the punishments there are conceived as appropriate not only in degree but in mode to the sin. It may be that the punishment involves the sinner in an infliction of the same kind as that which he had inflicted upon others in life: an eye for an eye and a tooth for a tooth. This, fundamentally, is what is represented by the term *contrapasso* in the one place in which Dante uses it: Bertran de Born is condemned as a sower of discord and now carries his dissevered head by the locks:

> Io feci il padre e il figlio in sé ribelli:
> Achitofèl non fe' più d' Absalone
> e di David coi malvagi punzelli.
> Perch'io parti' così giunte persone,
> partito porto il mio cerebro, lasso!
> dal suo principio ch'è in questo troncone.
> Così s'osserva in me lo contrapasso.

(I made father and son rebels towards each other. Achitophel did no more towards Absalom and David by malicious incitements. Because I parted persons so united now I carry my brain, alas, parted from its root, which is in this trunk. So retribution is observed in me.)

(*Inf.* XXVIII. 136–42)

But the *lex talionis* is interpreted with a greater breadth and variety than in this fairly strict though already somewhat figurative application of it. It develops, in the *Inferno*, principally in two directions, the sin now contrasting with the punishment, now analogous with it. The epicures and gluttons, in the first case, are now assaulted through the senses to which they had pandered: there is a foul, cold rain, a putrid smell,

---

[1] Cf. *STh*, II. lxi. 4.

and Cerberus 'who so deafens them that they wish they were deaf' ('Cerbero, che 'ntrona / l'anime sì, ch'esser vorebbe sorde', *Inf.* VI. 32 f.). Similarly, far deeper in hell, in the fourth of the *Malebolge*, the shades of the diviners are contorted and face backward, 'for to see ahead was (now) denied to them' ('perché 'l veder dinanzi era lor tolto', *Inf.* XX. 14). But the other case is far commoner, in which the analogy between sin and punishment is direct and often so vivid that the latter is seen to consist in the perpetual continuance of the sin itself, now transformed to torment through the disintegration of man's proper personality, his free-will lost through being concentrated on the goal of his desires, the 'ben dell'intelletto' (*Inf.* III. 18) lost through intellect's perversion to the service of the passions (*Inf.* V. 29). Here one naturally recalls Francesca da Rimini first. With her lover she comes forward from a background into which at first she merges and against which finally she must be judged: 'la bufera infernal', the infernal tempest which drives the *lussuriosi* hither and thither, up and down, relentlessly, like passion (*Inf.* V. 28–45). But the reflection of the vice in its punishment is as plain as this in other places. The avaricious and the prodigal roll useless weights round the fourth circle, run up against each other, and wheel about quarrelling angrily about the only thing which their contracted vision notices: '"Perché tieni?" e "Perché burli?"' ('Why do you hold?' and 'Why do you throw away?', *Inf.* VII. 30). The law of the *contrapasso* allows wrath, violence against one's neighbour, hypocrisy and other sins to perpetuate themselves with a monotonous intensity which the contingencies of human life inhibited.

Meanwhile the characters are brought to their own kind of life in spite of this 'monotony' which leaves them fixed forever in a single context. It is a paradox that is well worth pondering. Their situation now radically reduces the variety of happenings and therefore elicits from the souls less various reactions than on earth; yet still, as Auerbach in particular has repeatedly emphasized,[1] there is apparently no attenuation of their individuality—rather, the soul's situation seems to assist the individual's self-disclosure. Of course, Dante's journey, which

[1] See especially his *Dante: Poet of the Secular World*, pp. 84–6; essay on 'Figura', in *Scenes from the Drama of European Literature*, pp. 60–76; and *Mimesis*, pp. 166–77.

itself becomes for a brief while part of the dead souls' environment, momentarily modifies this situation, makes it change for
an instant into something which is almost if not quite 'history';
and the effect of this is to produce a broader range of responses
from the 'fixed' wills of the souls in hell, a range which tem-
porarily simulates the variety of human responses on earth.
But that is not the whole answer, though it goes some way. For
in hell even variety of response is still related to the immutability
of the evil will and to the eternity of the soul's retribution: it is
against that background that these responses should be seen for
it is against that background that they are presented.[1] And in
that background, formed by Dante's concept of the *contrapasso*,
the soul is judged for something fundamental and not accidental
in its character; in relation to which the 'accidents' of the
soul's response to the contingent have their meaning.

The *contrapasso*, thus, no less than Dante's journey, assists the
soul's disclosure of its nature—even, indeed, enforces it. In the
concrete symbolism of the 'apt punishment', what was in life
implicitly the organizing centre of a person's actions has become
explicit; and now phrase after phrase epitomizes and drives
home that economy of the soul's judgement, turning it epi-
grammatically into a resonant figure of speech. Bertran de
Born's trope is typical:

> Perch'io parti' così giunte persone
> partito porto il mio cerebro, lasso!

(Because I parted persons so united, now I carry my brain, alas,
parted...)   (*Inf.* xxvIII. 139 f.)

And it is a theme with memorable variations: the violent
against self have rejected human life:

> Uomini fummo, e or siam fatti sterpi,

(Men were we, and are now made trees,)   (*Inf.* xiii. 37)

the sullen are submerged in Styx:

> Tristi fummo
> nell'aere dolce che dal sol s'allegra,
>
> . . .
>
> or ci attristiam...

---

[1] Here, as we shall see in the next chapter, romantic criticism with its concentration on the 'lyrical', 'pathetic', and 'poetic' elements in the *Inferno*, seriously
misrepresented and misrepresents the poem.

(Sad were we in the sweet air which the sun makes glad. . . : now we sadden ourselves.) (*Inf.* VII. 121–4)

The same canto has Virgil saying of the prodigal and avaricious,

la sconoscente vita che i fe' sozzi
ad ogni conoscenza or li fa bruni,

(The undiscerning life which made them foul, now makes them too obscure to be discerned,) (*vv.* 53 f.)

and in canto XII Dante bursts out apropos of the violent against their neighbour:

O cieca cupidigia e ira folle,
che sì ci sproni nella vita corta,
e nell'etterna poi sì mal c'immolle!

(O blind cupidity and foolish rage, which, in brief life, so incites us, and then, in the eternal, overwhelms us so cruelly!) (*Inf.* XII. 49–51)

Here in the principle of the *contrapasso*, then, we have something which, at any rate in the case of the *Inferno*, but to a large degree in the *Purgatorio* also, assists in the revelation of 'eschatological' character. It provides for the objectification of psychological features much as the principle of an 'airy body' allows the shades' physical lineaments to appear and be known. But in the *contrapasso* such objectification is no longer solely for the purpose of recognition, communication, sensation; for, seen in the context of judgement and of the apt punishment belonging to each soul who is recognized, conversed with, seen, by Dante the traveller, the recognition and communication which the 'airy body' permits are now only a part of a new kind of identification in depth. The situation of the soul is on this view recognizable as a translation into objective terms of the *habitus* and leading propensity of the soul in its earthly life: there, this *habitus* was hidden; here, it is revealed. There, the judgements and decisions of earthly existence became, through their repetition, the formative habits of their human subject, through which he committed himself to his personal kind of existence—his *habitus* becoming the invisible axis of his selfhood around which all his actions and sayings revolved.[1] Here, in the soul's eschato-

---

[1] It is interesting to compare with this what J. M. Robinson says in *A New Quest for the Historical Jesus* (p. 68): 'Selfhood results from implicit or explicit commitment to a kind of existence, and is to be understood only in terms of that commitment.' One must, however, take issue with Robinson's assumption that this is 'an

logical situation, on the other hand, the axial *habitus* has become visible, and its speech and actions can now more easily reveal their relationship to it. The soul's context provides a clue that was not accessible in life, and in its light we, and the traveller Dante, may be able to see in the shade's manner, its discourse, and its history, something which otherwise might well be missed, a degree of self-revelation which approaches self-definition, and which implicitly or explicitly confirms the justice of its judgement.

Thus, to take a single example, in the wood of suicides Pier della Vigna tells how slander had unjustly worked against him so that he lost the emperor Frederick's favour, which, before, had kept him in high office. The subsequent imprisoning and still more the contempt in which he was held seemed to him insupportable, and brought him to suicide. Now in Hell's seventh circle, he has become a tree, troubled by the harpies and painfully wounded whenever, as has just happened, a twig is snapped off from his branches.

Several features indicate the man he was, the courtier, lawyer, and poet. He speaks in courteous and measured, but perhaps somewhat too fulsome, terms:

Sì col dolce dir m'adeschi,
ch'i' non posso tacere; e voi non gravi
perch'io un poco a ragionar m'inveschi.

(So much with your sweet speech do you allure me that I cannot be silent; and pray, do not be burdened if I draw out my discourse a little.) (*Inf.* XIII. 55–7)

Once he has recovered from the sudden shock of pain his style is impersonal ('Io son colui', *v.* 58; see I. Brandeis's excellent account,[1] pp. 53 f.), bearing signs of a detachment which contrasts strongly with the immediate cry of pain and appeal for pity which were the first words heard from him (see *vv.*

implication...for biography...of the (peculiarly) modern view of history' introduced by Wilhelm Dilthey. For this 'implication' is, I think, precisely what is involved in the doctrine of the *habitus* which Dante follows in the *Commedia*. Indeed, Robinson's treatment can be seen as an excellent modern translation of that doctrine, especially as he goes on to apply this 'modern' view to New Testament teaching on salvation and judgement and speaks of man's implicit or explicit commitment to 'his blessedness' or (as we may add) to its alternative, a sinful existence culminating in 'woe' (see *op. cit.* pp. 68 f.).

[1] *The Ladder of Vision*, pp. 46–59.

33-6: 'perché mi schiante?...perché mi scerpi? non hai tu spirto di pietà alcuno?' ('Why do you rend me? Why do you tear me? Have you no pity?')). The culmination of his narrative is summed up with fine legal precision: 'l'animo mio... ingiusto fece me contra me giusto' ('my mind...made me unjust to my just self') (*vv*. 70–2); and throughout he indulges his penchant for the neat figure of speech, giving to his lines an excessively stylized, precious and artificial quality which increases the sense of Pier's withdrawal from the immediacy of human contact and intercourse.[1]

Yet all of these features, even those apparently neutral in themselves, serve in the context of suicide and the soul's situation to present the habit of mind which accounted for the act and its punishment. Easily pained, now, by these artificial means, as then, Pier vainly tries in self-defence to detach himself from a world whose terms he cannot accept. As Brandeis notes, even his virtues are twisted to his undoing:[2] having seen, with a jurist's keen insight, the injustice of life, he shrinks from it. He tries to harden himself, but the tree he becomes in hell is still sensitive, and bleeds. His triple protestation of innocence (*vv*. 72, 74 f., 64–7) thus becomes, even though just, a sign too of his refusal to participate and involve himself in life; and when hurt, like the other suicide in this canto,[3] his recourse is the helpless complaint, 'perché mi schiante?' etc., 'why me?'.

And that this refusal and its effects are considered by Dante

---

[1] Sapegno, *La Divina Commedia, a cura di N. Sapegno* on *Inf*. XIII. 25, makes the point in question, listing the accumulation of periphrasis (*vv*. 58–61, 64–6), elaborately varied verbal reiteration (*vv*. 67 f.), antithesis (*vv*. 69, 72) and precious metaphor (*vv*. 55–7). Leo Spitzer points out, and up to a point rightly, that linguistic asperity and syntactical artifices are not, in this canto, peculiar to Piero, nor are they *merely* introduced for the purpose of characterization. (See his article 'Speech and Language in Inferno XIII', *Italica*, XIX, 81–104, reprinted in his *Romanische Literaturstudien*, pp. 544–68, esp. pp. 555–63.) Rather, says Spitzer, these things relate to an 'atmosphere of disharmony which pervades the whole canto'. But in view of what we have said Spitzer's implicit distinction between character and ambience or location will not be found absolute or vital. For, in the *Inferno*, the qualities of places continually reflect the qualities of their inhabitants.

[2] *Op. cit.* p. 55.

[3] Cf. *vv*. 133–5: '"O Giacomo" dicea "da Santo Andrea, / che t'è giovato di me fare schermo? / che colpa ho io della tua vita rea?"' ('O Giacomo da Santo Andrea', he said, 'what good has it done you to make me your screen? What fault of mine was your ill life?'). The parallel confirms the correctness of our interpretation of Dante's intention in the present case.

to be the result of the soul's free decision is made plain at several points in the poem.[1] There is, first, the passage to which both Brandeis and Montano have pointed as shedding light on this canto.[2] In the heaven of Mercury Dante hears tell of Romeo di Villanova who, as to his fortunes, is Pier della Vigna's counterpart: a minister at the court of Raymond Berengar, he was formerly high in his master's confidence; then, brought under false suspicion, poor and old, he went into voluntary exile,

> e se 'l mondo sapesse il cor ch'elli ebbe
> mendicando sua vita a frustro a frustro,
> assai lo loda, e più lo loderebbe.

(And if the world knew the heart he had, while begging his life crust by crust, much as it praises him, it would praise him more.)

(Par. VI. 140–2)

Now, however, Romeo is 'dentro alla presente margarita' (*v.* 127), that is, as the commentator Benvenuto of Imola says, 'intra stellam Mercurii parvam et pretiosam', and it is an emperor, fittingly, who praises him.

But in case the presentational symbol (as in spite of one's aesthetic ideals is often, regrettably, the fact) is barely comprehended until supplemented with the discursive, we have also the clear and explicit statements of Marco Lombardo in *Purgatorio* XVI. There, at the *Commedia's* centre, Dante faces up to a problem which is at its heart, and affirms the absolute justice of the divine judgement: 'the fault, dear Brutus, is not in our stars, but in ourselves, that we are (thus or thus)' (cf. *Purg.* XVI. 67–72, and 82 f.: 'in voi è la cagione, in voi si cheggia': 'in you is the cause, in you let it be sought'). Man does not need to act only as stars or earthly influences prompt him:

---

[1] With what follows we may again compare J. M. Robinson's statements, *op. cit.* p. 86: 'The self is not simply one's personality, resultant upon (and to be explained by) the various influences and ingredients present in one's heritage and development. Rather selfhood is constituted by commitment to a context, from which commitment one's existence arises. One's empirical *habitus*' (by which Robinson means, I think, not *habitus* as we have used it but rather 'one's *original* disposition, one's affections, impulses, inclinations'—compare 'movimenti', *Purg.* XVI. 73, the soul's natural impulses which are prompted by the stars) 'is the inescapable medium through which the self expresses itself, but is not identical with the self, even when one seems to make it so . . . (and) merely drifts with life's tide.'

[2] Brandeis, *op. cit.* p. 56; R. Montano, *Storia della Poesia di Dante,* I, 444.

> Lume v'è dato a bene e a malizia,
> e libero voler; che, se fatica
> nelle prime battaglie col ciel dura,
> poi vince tutto, se ben si notrica.

(Light is given you to distinguish good and evil, and free will, which, if it endures the strain of its first battles with the sky, finally, if well nurtured [by good habits] conquers all.)

(vv. 75–8; see also Par. v. 19–24)

There is, besides, Marco continues, another way of creating an individual's *habitus*, a greater influence than stars or men, which, if in free will one commits oneself to its creative power, turns one's disposition towards salvation and conforms it to God's will. It is the power of God himself:

> A maggior forza ed a miglior natura
> liberi soggiacete; e quella cria
> la mente in voi, che 'l ciel non ha in sua cura.

(In freedom you are subject to a greater power and better nature; and that creates the mind in you over which the stars have no control.) (vv. 79–81)

Marco here refers primarily, doubtless, to the making ('cria') rather than, as in the Pauline passage cited below, the 'remaking' of the human mind. But if it is not a question, strictly, of 'remaking', it accords well enough with the Pauline passage, seeming to imply a *continuing* creation of the mind, so long as it is well guided. The divine power which created the human mind originally, now, as grace, continuously enables you (cf. 'soggiacete' you *are* subject) to overcome the natural influences.[1] Where the pastors fail to guide, there are still laws (*v.* 97), and, as Beatrice develops this theme, there are also the Bible and the sacraments to help you (*Par.* v. 73–8). Grace, if man will freely commit himself to it and submit to its questioning and prompting, will promote another existence within him than the merely natural, the 'new life' of man under election.[2] 'Questo vi basti a vostro salvamento' ('let this suffice you for your salvation') (*Par.* v. 78).

---

[1] Cf. *Purg.* xvii. 127–9, and see K. Foster, *God's Tree*, p. 6, who speaks of these passages in terms of 'an original orientation towards God, which the adult may ignore, but cannot destroy'.

[2] Cf. Rom. 12. 2: 'Adapt yourselves no longer to the pattern of this present world, but let your minds be remade and your whole nature thus transformed. Then you will be able to discern the will of God.'

Now we have dwelt at some length on the rationale of the realism of character in the *Inferno*, and there is no need to treat it as fully with regard to the *Purgatorio* and *Paradiso*. For there the conditions for realism are not fundamentally different. Again, we are in regions where 'character' would be expected to be, and to some extent actually is, modified by having undergone death and by having entered upon a (relatively) changeless existence. Yet, *mutatis mutandis*, the *dramatis personae* in these realms also are 'realistic', and moreover—in a sense still fundamentally that in which it could be said of those in the *Inferno*—they are 'realized': their individual disposition has reached its individual fulfilment.[1] Even those undergoing purgation are 'realized' in this sense, though their 'perfecting', their ethical fulfilment, has not yet come into being or is there only in the way in which it may be in human life, as a kind of pre-echo, an assurance; for they are where they are because the decisions of their life, even if only at the moment of death (cf. *Purg.* v. 101), have committed them there, to the realm of salvation. As surely as character in life can make that critical self-commitment, the character in death will hold fast to it.

Therefore, *mutatis mutandis* again, the *Paradiso* and the *Purgatorio* have their own concrete symbols for the axial centre of a person's existence, their analogues to the *contrapasso*—it was, we recall, Belacqua's situation which initiated our discussion of this principle. In the *Purgatorio*, cornices, and in *Paradiso*, spheres, replace the circles of hell; but still, each in its way, these locations represent visibly the propensities of the souls found within them, and aid the poet in his task of bringing

---

[1] In the *Paradiso*, necessarily, the souls' individuality is less striking. The relativity of earthly judgements has been overcome, and the opinions expressed are fictively presented as absolute; there is no room, on any one subject, for contradiction, and therefore less room for variety: I do not say there is *no* room for the latter, for after all however hard it may be to determine just what Dante meant by it, Siger of Brabant is here with Aquinas (*Par.* x. 133–8). Again, the souls' love and concord bring them together; their characteristic appearance is in harmonious or patterned groups, singing in unison or dancing or moving in time (cf. *Par.* vi. 124–6), and when one soul moves forward to address Dante it is almost always partly as the group's spokesman that he does so. Finally, of course, there are far fewer 'speaking parts' in the *Paradiso* than in either of the previous *cantiche*. Even so there are souls here who are 'vital', for all their perfection, and even partly on account of their perfection: one thinks of Charles Martel's affectionate address, of Cunizza, and, especially, of Cacciaguida, to whom we shall return.

souls' 'eschatological character' into significant relation with human life.[1] For by being in each specific case a kind of symbolic extension of the personality who is here rewarded or punished, these locations cast light back on the living person who, by decisions taken when his will was still mutable, has committed his soul to this place.

'Cast light back': the phrase may stand for the mode and method by which Dante manifests the special historical relationship between the 'shades' and the 'men' they once were. From eschatological existence the 'shades' cast a searching light back on their own historical existence, and perhaps, too, on historical existence in general. Neither equated with, nor wholly distinct from, their living selves, the dead summon up their past life, and expose it more fully than ever before. Despite the great transformation which death brings about, their manifestation here is of such kind that each one is revealed in his situation as the *forma perfectior* of his earthly self, as a self-hood now freed from the contingency of earthly affairs which had hitherto always impeded his total self-revelation.

And this in turn directly confronts us now with the question, in what way this relationship between life and death we have described in this chapter may properly be called typological. We content ourselves here with the few preliminary observations which our treatment can already substantiate. The characters' realism, first, is of a kind which Auerbach, relating it in fact to typology, has called 'figural'.[2] And the facts which we have presented confirm the precision of his term. If the souls whom Dante meets are in the *forma perfectior* of their historical existence this, surely, is equivalent to saying that they realize the existence which their historical lives have prefigured.

---

[1] It is important to notice in passing, however, when we speak of the analogy between the *contrapasso* in hell and the principle of punishment in Purgatory, that although Dante naturally places in each cornice of Purgatory persons of whom the sin punished there was characteristic (thus bringing the scheme of punishment as close as possible to the *Inferno*'s), there is no question of the cornice being in all cases symbolic of the person's *leading* propensity; for the soul is liable to spend time on more than one cornice just as he is liable to have fallen into more than one sin. Moreover, *the* leading propensity of all the souls here is no longer sinful; for they have been led not by nature but grace. *Natural* propensities, therefore, have here to be carefully distinguished from the propensities induced by sanctifying grace.

[2] See 'Figura', *Scenes from the Drama of European Literature*, pp. 60–76; *Mimesis*, pp. 166–77.

Moreover, this 'figural' relationship, with its peculiar success in doing justice to both continuity and change, manifests something which is familiar in another form from our treatment of the Old Testament; for here once again is a dialectic between newness and steadfastness, which is here not ostensibly, to be sure, or directly, concerned with God's action, but rather with human existence. Yet human existence, after all, in Christian belief is directly dependent on the action of God: for Dante no less than for us it has been decisively constituted by the action of the God who, in virtue of that, now justly submits it to judgement. Here again, therefore, we feel ourselves to be in a realm which is at any rate closely associated with what we have understood by 'typology'.

But it is one thing to call a relationship 'typological' and another to call it 'allegorical'; for the relationship which typology embodies is, to our minds at least, a dialectical rather than a directly representational one. One thing does not mean another in typology: it involves it, or has inferences for it, or suggests it, and it does all these things for no other reason than that there is a real, existential, parallel, as well as a certain historical dependency and continuity between the events which typology relates. Allegory, on the other hand (especially as a literary mode), involves not history so much as *sententiae*, spiritual truths rather than unrepeatable happenings, and it generally appears to depend on a devaluation of the 'letter' for the sake of the general truth which the letter figuratively expresses.

The contemporary distrust of the great allegorical onslaught on the *Commedia* associated with Pascoli, Valli and, in his own way, Mandonnet, is in this context wholly explicable; indeed it is wholly correct. And explicable also, in view of the above conception of allegory, is the contemporary distrust of Dante's authorship of the Can Grande letter; for on whatever other grounds this letter may be defended or disputed it has seemed to some critics (most recently Nardi[1] and Hardie[2]) that its allegorical doctrine is positively misleading as a standard by which to interpret the poem. Here, though, it is not so certain

---

[1] *Il Punto sull'Epistola a Cangrande* (Lectura Dantis Scaligera 1960).
[2] See his remarks in *Italian Studies*, XIII (1958), 14 f., and in the *Deutsches Dante-Jahrbuch*, XXXVIII (1960), 51–74.

that these critics are right.[1] It is worth considering the question as it is typically discussed by one of the best of them.

Thus, in the *Lectura Dantis Scaligera* which Nardi gave in 1960 and entitled 'Il Punto sull'Epistola a Cangrande', he finds a discrepancy between the apologetic, defensive tone of the allegorical doctrine in the *Letter* and the outspoken and prophetic literal sense of the poem.[2] The latter, he says, is devalued by the former: implicitly, at least, the *Letter*'s allegorical doctrine decisively compromises a work before which one feels as if confronted by 'a prophetic vision, directly inspired by certain of the prophetic books of the Bible'.[3]

Again, though Nardi does not deny the existence of 'places in the poem which are indeed allegorical' (and he cites 'sotto il velame delli versi strani' (*Inf.* IX. 63) from the scene in which Virgil and Dante, forcibly impeded from entering the city of Dis, await help from heaven) he finds himself forced to deny that such passages are typical of it.[4] And on this account he takes the letter to task, on the one hand for its treating 'the state of souls after death' as the literal subject (for Nardi, the literal subject is the journey of Dante), and on the other for encouraging the allegorizing of this literal subject so as to empty the poem of the personal experience and visionary idealism which bring it close in spirit to Franciscan Joachism and the prophets of the Old Testament. In combination, the two flawed facets of the *Letter*'s *subiectum duplex* reduce the poem, he says, into a kind of 'ethico-theological treatise *De novissimis*'.[5]

Now one cannot but agree with Nardi in his choice between the two alternative readings of the poem which he presents, polarized as they are into 'allegorical' and 'prophetic'. But when one looks at the *Letter* there arise certain doubts. Here, though it will be convenient to quote both paragraphs, it is the second which chiefly concerns us:

[1] Compare, on behalf of the letter's authenticity, F. Mazzoni's studies of the question, the conclusions of which are now widely accepted in Italy: the first (and from our point of view more important) is in *Rendiconti della Accademia dei Lincei*, VIII, x (1955), 157–98; the second in *Studi in onore di A. Monteverdi*, II, 498–516.

[2] *Op. cit.* pp. 23–30.   [3] *Ibid.* p. 24.

[4] *Ibid.* p. 27. Nardi is indubitably right here. There are several passages which cannot but be 'allegory' in the conventional sense, and these are *not* typical of the poem. The wood of error and the beasts in *Inferno* I are obvious examples. But then, is this conventional 'poetic' allegory the kind to which the *Letter* refers? Clearly not.   [5] *Op. cit.* p. 28.

§7. Ad evidentiam itaque dicendorum sciendum est quod istius operis non est simplex sensus, ymo dici potest polisemos, hoc est plurium sensuum; nam primus sensus est qui habetur per litteram, alius est qui habetur per significata per litteram. Et primus dicitur litteralis, secundus vero allegoricus sive moralis sive anagogicus. Qui modus tractandi, ut melius pateat, potest considerari in hiis versibus: 'In exitu Israel de Egipto, domus Iacob de populo barbaro, facta est Iudea sanctificatio eius, Israel potestas eius.'[1] Nam si ad litteram solam inspiciamus, significatur nobis exitus filiorum Israel de Egipto, tempore Moysis; si ad allegoriam, nobis significatur nostra redemptio facta per Christum; si ad moralem sensum, significatur nobis conversio anime de luctu et miseria peccati ad statum gratie; si ad anagogicum, significatur exitus anime sancte ab huius corruptionis servitute ad eterne glorie libertatem. Et quanquam isti sensus mistici variis appellentur nominibus, generaliter omnes dici possunt allegorici, cum sint a litterali sive historiali diversi. Nam allegoria dicitur ab 'alleon' grece, quod in latinum dicitur 'alienum', sive 'diversum'.

§8. Hiis visis, manifestum est quod duplex oportet esse subiectum, circa quod currant alterni sensus. Et ideo videndum est de subiecto huius operis, prout ad litteram accipitur; deinde de subiecto, prout allegorice sententiatur. Est ergo subiectum totius operis, litteraliter tantum accepti, status animarum post mortem simpliciter sumptus; nam de illo et circa illum totius operis versatur processus. Si vero accipiatur opus allegorice, subiectum est homo prout merendo et demerendo per arbitrii libertatem iustitie premiandi et puniendi obnoxius est.

A single reading of these two paragraphs and the questions multiply. First, do the literal and allegorical senses described here really conflict with that literal sense so highly spoken of by Nardi? Secondly, have the alternatives presented by Nardi any connection at all with the 'alterni sensus' spoken of in the Letter? Thirdly, does the literal sense which the letter describes really exclude the visionary journey which Nardi takes to be the poem's proper subject?

The answer to the last question may properly be postponed to a later chapter, but with regard to the first two we can obtain some help directly from the early commentators of the Comedy. According to them, the literal sense of the poem (which, whether or not they write in dependence on the Letter itself,

---

[1] Ps. 114 (Vulgate 113), 1 f.

they take to at least include the *status animarum post mortem*) bears an intrinsic relationship to the subject of the main 'allegorical' (i.e. 'spiritual') sense: the state of souls after death is a figure of their state in this life, i.e. as the letter makes plain, of their state as 'men' when they *were* men and not merely souls.[1] Or rather, as we have seen, the eschatological state of the soul is the *forma perfectior*, the fulfilment of their state in this life. Francesco da Buti writes with exemplary clarity:

Il suggetto di che l'autore parla, si è litteralmente lo stato del l'anime dopo la separazione dal corpo, et allegoricamente o vero moralmente è lo premio o vero la pena a che l'uomo s'obliga vivendo in questa vita per lo libero arbitrio.
(The subject of which the author speaks is, literally, the condition of souls after their separation from the body, and, allegorically or morally, the reward or the penalty to which man, while living in this life, becomes liable through his free decision.)[2]

The part which stands out here as a useful gloss on the expressions of the Can Grande Letter (of which Buti has obviously at least second-hand knowledge) is the phrase 'vivendo in questa vita'.[3] Thus Buti interprets the 'allegory' of the *Comedy* in terms of the historical relationship which we have made the subject of our present discussion. He sees allegory not so much as a means for extracting speculative, unhistorical *sententiae* concerning the justice of God from an otherwise worthless husk of a poem, but rather as a means of impressing on the reader life's real liability to judgement. Again and again Buti makes this perfectly clear, if we read him carefully:

Ciò che dice litteralmente dell'inferno, allegoricamente s'intende de' mondani' [i.e. 'quelli del mondo', those in the world, as on p. 165 of his commentary, and often] che sono viziosi e peccatori.
(That which Dante says literally of Hell is allegorically understood of those in the world who are vicious and sinners.)[4]

---

[1] Elsewhere Nardi has entirely mistaken this point, finding the two senses in paragraph 8 identical (or differing only in that one is general and the other specific—*Nel Mondo di Dante*, p. 60).

[2] *Commento sopra la Divina Commedia* (written 1393), ed. C. Giannini (Pisa, 1858), 1, 6.

[3] Cf. *Letter to Can Grande*, §15: 'Finis totius et partis est removere *viventes in hac vita* de statu miserie et perducere ad statum felicitatis.'

[4] *Op. cit.* 1, 151.

Without implying approval of all the methods used by Buti to draw out the allegory, such statements are surely in principle quite undeniable. What Buti says here of the 'allegory' of the *Divine Comedy* amounts to no more than we ourselves have attempted to show, and without being conscious of using what we would call 'allegory'. Put into modern idiom, Buti is saying only that the souls represent life more vitally than the living themselves for they have had their life brought, by their death, into unmediated confrontation with the just judgement of God. It is hard indeed to see how this interferes with the poem's 'prophetic' character.[1]

And yet this much, when one looks back at the *Letter*, is surely already implied there. With a clarity of distinction, which seems to me wholly Dantesque, the *Letter* has 'souls after death' on the one hand, distinguished from, on the other, 'man' exercising 'free will'. Can this imply only that the two senses differ as 'specific' differs from 'general'?[2] Surely not.

But in this case it seems equally unjust to the *Letter* to see in it an apologetic desire to exalt the allegorical sense at the expense of the literal. The fact that its two senses are distinguished by times, and only by times, like the four senses of the previous paragraph, means that it would be a paradoxical proceeding indeed to go on to attribute to one sense a reality not possessed by the other. For the two are equal and interdependent.

This leads us a step further still. If, as it is with this view, the 'allegory' is constituted precisely by a 'looking back' on human existence from death, is it proper to call it 'allegory' at all? Not, certainly, if we take allegory to mean all that which Nardi means by it. If it were to that 'allegory of the poets' (in which, as *Convivio* II. I, points out, the literal sense is only a *bella menzogna*, 'pleasant fiction') that the *Letter* referred when calling the subject of the poem 'allegorical', it would be a misnomer, quite simply. And, since despite de Lubac's defence of

---

[1] Nor moreover in the body of the commentary does the author find it necessary on account of his allegorical doctrine to devalue the letter and allegorize everything: 'Non fu l'intenzione dell'autore porre ogni cosa allegoricamente, né io intendo ogni parola moralizzare: che sarebbe esporre un altro Dante' ('It was not the author's aim to put everything allegorically, nor do I mean to moralize every word: that would be to expound a quite different Dante') (*ibid.* I, 40).

[2] Thus Hardie, *Italian Studies*, XIII (1958), 14.

patristic exegetical practices[1] they still often seem, to my mind at least, to involve a cursory, if not contemptuous, regard for the 'letter' of history, so would it be a misnomer if its reference were only to such an allegorizing *practice* as Origen's. But is this in fact what is meant?

Clearly, the problem here can be resolved finally only by a more careful investigation of the meaning of *allegoria* and *allegoricus* in Dante's period than Nardi seems to have made. But even the *Letter* itself may show how its own understanding of the term may accord with the *Comedy*'s practice, and so with the poet's intention, the final court of appeal. For there (§7), as in the Middle Ages generally, the 'theological allegory' which is the kind it applies to the poem,[2] defines each sense only (as we have seen) by their historical (or existential) distinction in content. If the one sense (*litteralis*) is Old Testament history, another (*allegoricus*) may be part of the history in the New Testament, another (*anagogicus*) eschatological, and another (*moralis*) (generally) present. But the literal sense of the text may, obviously, already refer to some later period of history, to an existential situation other than that of Israel—that is, to a period or situation which is also the subject of one of the 'mystical' or 'allegorical' senses. In that case, if, as here in the *Comedy*, the literal sense is eschatological, then any other senses there may be must be (so to speak) 'post-figured', rather than 'pre-figured',[3] but they may still be there, as, in the *Comedy*, it is clear that at least one of them[4] is, and intentionally. The *sensus moralis* would still refer to the present life, and the *sensus*

---

[1] See H. de Lubac, *Histoire et Esprit*, and *Exégèse Médiévale, Les Quatres Sens de l'Écriture*. In spite of de Lubac's attempts, in the latter work, at sidelong rebuttal, R. P. C. Hanson's account in *Allegory and Event* of Origen's influential mode of allegorizing is still the soundest and most convincing.

[2] See C. S. Singleton, *Dante Studies I: Commedia, Elements of Structure*; and R. Montano, *Storia della Poesia di Dante*, i, 304–22.

[3] This situation is not altogether new. Eschatological prophecy 'post-figures' (very often) the Exodus or the Creation. In the Gospels, Jesus 'post-figures' Israel. Nor did this situation escape the medieval eye. For example, Aquinas notes that it was fitting that Jesus should have been baptized in Jordan because he thereby fulfilled what the crossing of Jordan prefigured (*STh*, iii. xxxix. 4).

[4] Whether we call this (which, as we have seen, has to do with the life of those living in the world) the *sensus moralis* or *allegoricus* would in strictness depend on whether it was directed as imperative or as indicative. It will be clearer, however, to term the reference to present existence 'moralis', so as to leave 'allegoricus' clear to stand unambiguously for any indirect reference to Christ.

allegoricus to Christ's past life or to life in Christ. Still the mystical senses would be defined by their content, and the content would still be 'historical'. There would still be nothing in the distinction between them to indicate how the mystical senses were to be discovered in, or on departing from, the text. The distinction would only point to the direction, or directions, in which, setting out from the text, they might be sought.

And so far this accords not only with the scholastic but also with traditional (patristic and monastic) habits and views. To recapitulate:[1] the earlier period, as Spicq says, rarely showed interest in strictly hermeneutical problems:[2] sound exegesis was confused with sound doctrine; if the latter were orthodox, the exegesis which mediated between doctrine and text was justified by its results. But even in this situation, whether in spite or because of this disregard for the general problems of exegetical method, the various Hellenistic 'allegorical' methods which were practised (see above, p. 90, for an early example) did not impose themselves on the 'doctrine' or dogmatic statements of the 'three' or 'four senses of scripture'. When, therefore, with the Victorines in the twelfth century, and especially with the great Dominican theologians of the thirteenth, an interest in hermeneutics did arise, the new *magistri in theologia* were able to incorporate the doctrine and its terminology (i.e. *litteralis*, *allegoricus*, *moralis*, and *anagogicus*) without being thereby committed to the doctrine's accidental, if serious, malpractices. The senses were still, by Hugh of St Victor,[3] Bonaventure,[4] and Aquinas,[5] defined by their content. But the typological framework which this content reflected was now much less (though somewhat, indeed) impaired by arbitrariness or by allegorizing. Instead there was a new respect for the 'letter', for history, for sound exegesis. All this is now generally recognized, though by few critics of the *Commedia*. But what has happened in Aquinas' treatment of the four senses of scripture is more revolutionary still, more even (it must be confessed) than Aquinas himself appears to have recognized. In the *Summa*, and

---

[1] With the necessarily brief and generalizing remarks which follow compare the Introduction to this part (pp. 171–8) and the literature cited there.
[2] C. Spicq, *Esquisse d'une Histoire de l'Exégèse latine au Moyen Age*, p. 17.
[3] *De Sacramentis*, Prol. 4; *Didascalion*, VI. 3.
[4] *Breviloquium*, Prol. 4.
[5] *STh*, I. i. 10; *Quaestiones Quodlibetales*, VII. vi. 15.

more fully in the *Quodlibet*,[1] the so-called 'allegorical senses' have for the first time been almost completely detached from the arbitrary methods of 'allegory'. The literal sense is by Aquinas (and before him by Albert the Great)[2] extended, so as henceforth to include all that the human author intended.[3] Meanwhile the other three senses are now comprehensively ordered in a logical interrelation which rests on their mutual relation in the providential action of God.[4] It is possible now, as a consequence of these two facts in combination, to draw out the text's typological inferences, and those of the so-called 'allegorical doctrine', by means of a hermeneutical process which does not include allegory at all. It is possible; and in fact when we look at his treatment of the four senses we find that Aquinas explains them in terms which provide for this only. The 'allegorical' senses as he deals with them all rest apparently only on the providence of God, who has ordered history, as if semantically, to signify his purpose.[5] And their interpretation, given faith, is on that account still akin to the literal interpreting of the words of a human writer: the aim is still to discover the intended meaning of the author. That is why, though he does not call these interpretations 'literal', he can still call them 'senses': 'Auctor sacrae Scripturae est Deus.'

Thus, the 'allegorical' connection between the distinct senses of Scripture has been effectively replaced, though the term 'allegorical' is retained, by a dialectical one. For history here is recognized as in God's providence itself dialectical.[6]

[1] *Ibid.*, and quoted on p. 177 above.

[2] See Spicq, *op. cit.* pp. 208–10.

[3] Cf. B. Smalley, *The Study of the Bible in the Middle Ages*, pp. 292–308; the same author's 'The Use of the Bible in the Middle Ages' in *The Church's Use of the Bible*, ed. D. E. Nineham, esp. pp. 60–2; P. Synave, 'La Doctrine de S. Thomas sur le sens littéral des Écritures', *RB*, xxv (1926), 40–7; T. F. Torrance, 'Scientific Hermeneutics according to St Thomas Aquinas', *JTS*, xiii (1962), 281–5; M.-D. Chenu, *Introduction à l'Étude de S. Thomas d'Aquin*, pp. 200–17; and, of course, H. de Lubac, *Exégèse Médiévale*, ii, 2, pp. 272–302.

[4] See M.-D. Mailhiot, 'La Pensée de S. Thomas sur le sens spirituel', *Revue Thomiste*, lix (1959), 613–63.

[5] *STh*, i. i. 10; *Quodlibet*, vii. vi. 15.

[6] There is no need to stress here what my treatment elsewhere makes plain, that the *particular* view of the divine historical dialectic which Aquinas espouses seems to me unacceptable. Cf. p. 250 n. below, and pp. 94 f., 109 f. and n. above. Associating God's word in history simply with 'meaning' in the sense of 'that which directly represents', Aquinas seems to miss the existential character of the only

And surely, in the *Commedia*, a similar relation has produced closely similar results. In the individual's life and death, which after all form part of history, past and present are recognized as dialectically interrelated; and the expression of their relation is, in the *Comedy*, dialectical in turn. By means of reference and implication, by the language, gesture, and bearing of individual souls, the light of eschatology is cast back on historical life: the future is made to involve the present, the past is fulfilled in the future. In this respect, surely, Nardi is right to call the poem a work of prophecy.

And when we look back once again at the *Letter to Can Grande* now a single phrase seems to stand out: 'duplex oportet esse subiectum, *circa quod currant alterni sensus*'. It is a curious phrase, hard enough to translate, harder still to accept as a natural expression for the operations of the 'allegory' which the 'poets' (or for that matter the pre-scholastic and even scholastic theologians in practice) use—the kind of allegory to which Nardi, and others,[1] understand the *Letter* to refer. 'Around which the alternative senses play' is the hallowed English rendering, and perhaps it is the best. But however we may look at it the phrase is hardly a straightforward one; still less is it a cliché borrowed from the commonplace books of exegetical terminology. In the last resort, perhaps, the dialectical interplay of the *Comedy*'s twofold (historical and eschatological) subject forces its critic, like the author of the *Letter*, to use only indirect and suggestive means to describe the poem's existential structure.

'meaning' which 'events' can have, meaning 'for us'. Meaning in history, in the first sense of 'meaning' can only be seen from outside. What particular events mean to us, or to Israel, or Socrates, on the other hand, is a perfectly legitimate inquiry. Existential meaning—i.e. that which 'means something to' one—is what history is attributed with in the Bible, and similarly in the *Comedy*: the people Dante meets are those who 'mean something to him', the events he records or recalls mean something to him. This is what is meant when I speak of 'history's meaning', or rather, of 'a history's meaning'. A chain of events may, in their happening, or in the recollection or the report (the 'word') of them, set up in me certain chains of thought; they may even suggest to me a line of action for me to take. In somewhat the same way, perhaps, certain scents to a tiger 'mean' food, and may cause him to search out their source.

[1] Esp. R. H. Green, 'Dante's "Allegory of the Poets" and the Medieval Theory of Poetic Fiction', *Comparative Literature*, IX (1957), 118–28.

CHAPTER 14

DANTE AND THE AESTHETES:
THE TYPOLOGY OF DEATH

THE *Letter to Can Grande* is quite decided as to the branch of philosophy to which the *Comedy* belongs: that of ethics.

§16. Genus vero philosophie sub quo hic in toto et parte proceditur, est morale negotium, sive ethica; quia non ad speculandum, sed ad opus incoeptum est totum. Nam si in aliquo loco vel passu pertractatur ad modum speculativi negotii, hoc non est gratia speculativi negotii, sed gratia operis.

In this instance, at least, there is no reason for disputing the letter's agreement with the poet's intention. Even the earlier poems (or some of them), according to Dante's reference to them in the *De vulgari eloquentia* (II. 2), are concerned with *rectitudo*, or, as is also said, with *directio voluntatis*, the 'rightness', or more probably 'righting', of the will; it is hard to deny that the *Comedy* shows a like concern.[1] The seriousness of this aim and intensity of its pursuit make it all but impossible to take the *poema sacro* as merely a representation of what Dante saw or claims to have seen in the 'beyond'. It is rather that this representation itself is to be a means of righting the will, of bringing about change of life. The description of Dante's journey is for us, as in the poem the journey itself is for him, a way of effecting that change.

In nothing is the *Divina Commedia* as close to the Bible as in its 'application' of typology for this purpose. But its typological structure, which has the after-life as the primary narrative subject, is peculiarly its own. The state of souls after death here makes their earthly life seem a prolepsis of their present condition and place. By the same token the world appears in its judged representatives as already submitted to judgement, liable already to reward and punishment ('iustitie premiandi

---

[1] In this connection see C. S. Singleton's excellent remarks in *Dante Studies I: Commedia, Elements of Structure*, pp. 75–7.

et puniendi').[1] And the implication, or application, of this for the reader is that the poem is calling him to realize his own liability in the face of the judgement presented, to expose himself to that judgement, to take stock of it, with anxiety. We are in a realm for which Heidegger's terminology might have been specially created.[2] 'Das Sein zum Tode', though nuanced in its Christian context in such a way as to lay the stress upon its aspect as 'being towards judgement', that is, taking up a responsible stance in view of the judgement, is precisely the theme of the *Comedy*'s 'double subject'. The poem's altogether systematic 'exposure' of the reader to death provides proof of its author's being aware, like Heidegger, that the individual in his everyday life, and man in general (i.e. 'das Man', the impersonal pronoun personified) tries to ignore and evade the reality of death, and has to be awakened to an 'authentic' understanding of the seriousness of his historical existence. And just as for Heidegger the existential realization by the individual that death, and even *his* death, is 'not to be outstripped' makes 'authentic' existence possible, so for Dante; the reader is required to see his own death and his own judgement in the death and judgement of the real people that are represented here; and thus to live according to the promptings of that anticipating insight, that 'fore-having' ('Vorhabe').[3]

The motif itself, 'think on thy latter end', was, of course, a religious commonplace throughout the Middle Ages;[4] and

---

[1] *Letter to Can Grande*, §8. [2] See M. Heidegger, *Sein und Zeit*, II, 1, pp. 235–67.
[3] The distinction between the Christian idea of death, in which death, or man dead (i.e. in the after-life), possesses its or his own kind of being, and that of Heidegger, in which death is 'not-being' or at any rate the 'possibility' of not-being, need not, I think, be stressed in this connection. What concerns us here is 'authentic being *towards* death', which Heidegger finds to exist in 'anxiety' (*Angst*), in which *Dasein* (human being) faces the real possibility of being *Nichtmehr-dasein* or (more obscurely) faces 'dem Nichts der möglichen Unmöglichkeit seiner Existenz' (*ibid.* pp. 265 f.) and which the Roman Catholic, Karl Rahner, speaks of as the act by which (implicitly in his life as well as at the moment of death) man surrenders himself unconditionally in the darkness of death to the incomprehensible decision of God as to his future being (*On the Theology of Death*, pp. 46–54). Significant in relation to our present treatment of Dante (especially in the last section) is what Rahner says on p. 51: 'Man is enacting his death, as his own consummation, through the deeds of his life. Thus, death is present in his deeds, that is, in each and every one of his free acts, the acts by which he freely disposes of his whole person.'
[4] J. Huizinga writes that 'no other epoch has laid so much stress as the expiring Middle Ages on the thought of death. An everlasting call of *memento mori* resounds

even the idea of the good life as a 'fore-having', a proleptic death, is by no means unusual. Gregory the Great had said, 'qui enim considerat qualis erit in morte, semper sit timidus in operatione', and he added: 'Perfecta enim vita est mortis imitatio, quam dum iusti sollicite peragunt, culparum laqueos evadunt.'[1] It is not therefore the counsel itself that is remarkable in Dante, for his counsel is, besides, organically related to the command of the prophets[2] to live eschatological existence, and of St Paul to 'realize' one's own eschatology by dying and rising with Christ. Rather it is the extreme power of this counsel's presentation, and specifically of its presentation through the technique of typology.

For by making his shades 'alive' with their human character undiminished, and with real names, well-known names (cf. *Par.* XVII. 136–8), attached to them, Dante has taken a bold step already. But he has presented them as dead too, inescapably: they no longer have what is essential to *Dasein*, real human being: they are without a future, without, in Heidegger's terms once more, 'something still outstanding which they can and will be'.[3] Their death is the direct subject, and only through death is life seen. But it is seen; life and death are shown as typologically related. And plainly, to the reader, but none the less mysteriously, by this further step Dante has poetically opened the way to a fuller experience of one's own death in the death of others than is naturally possible, or has ever elsewhere been poetically achieved.

Obviously the reader's part in all this is important. To whom much is given much is required, in this case as in others. The reader, or critic, must of course judge for himself the value of 'right will' in the form or forms it takes in Dante's work, and judge the value also of the particular allegiances of Dante. But at least he should always be aware that the *Comedy* does have this serious concern, that its composition, as the Can Grande letter says, both as a whole and in all of its parts, was under-

through life...Since the thirteenth century, the popular preaching of the mendicant orders had made the eternal admonition to remember death swell into a sombre chorus ringing throughout the world' (*The Waning of the Middle Ages*, p. 141).

[1] *Moralia in Iob.* XIII. xxix. 33.
[2] See above, ch. 5.
[3] Cf. *Sein und Zeit*, p. 233: 'Im Dasein steht, solange es ist, je noch etwas aus, was es sein kann and wird.'

taken for practical results ('gratia operis', §16): 'finis totius et partis est removere viventes in hac vita de status miserie et perducere ad statum felicitatis' (§15). It is hard at first, certainly, to take such statements seriously, even if we think they represent the intention of the author. They are after all the kind of statements which are often met in medieval and renaissance prefaces: a kind which we associate with didacticism, and often a didacticism which is wished upon the work— sometimes, as with Tasso's *Gerusalemme Liberata*, after its completion—to suit contemporary literary-critical ideals.

But even in that *genre* these statements are unusually ambitious. For that reason, too, it is hard to take them seriously. For to recognize the *Comedy* as Christian and having moral aims is one thing, but to see it as *essentially* Christian and to take its moral aims as of its innermost nature is another. It is as a poem, primarily, that it exists for us today; and poetry is not often thought of, as the *Letter* thinks of this poem, as (in a sense much stricter and more intense than Osgood's)[1] a possible means of grace, with Christianity and Christian ethics able decisively to modify its whole mode of communication as well as forming a large part of the work's 'subject'.

Yet neither, even in Dante's time, was it easy to think of poetry in these terms. The *Letter*'s statements are no less remarkable for their extreme ambition, in that period.[2] The poets, Alain de Lille and Dante's contemporary, Albertino Mussato, were exceptional in attributing to poetry a close association with theology; but the scholastic theologians repudiated these suggestions of alliance, although these poets did not claim so much as Dante, or the author of the *Letter*, for their work:[3]

[1] For where Osgood seems to mean by the phrase which he takes for his title merely that poetry can be a means to 'spiritual sophistication' (which is not a bad aim, I suppose; cf. *Poetry as a Means of Grace*, pp. 16 f.), the *Letter* can mean nothing less than a means to conversion.

[2] The different approach of F. Mazzoni to the *Letter* provides strong support for the view of it taken here. He shows how the fourteenth-century commentators themselves failed to understand the radical immanence of the 'morale negotium' in the poem. See his article 'L'Epistola a Cangrande' in *Rendiconti della Accademia dei Lincei*, pp. 157–98, and esp. pp. 178–81.

[3] See E. R. Curtius, *European Literature and the Latin Middle Ages*, ch. 12: 'Poetry and Theology', pp. 214–25. This is not to say that the 'allegory of the theologians' was never applied to non-biblical literature. It was sometimes applied to pagan literature—to which it cannot apply, *a priori*—and sometimes (though never habitually or conventionally, despite Stambler, see p. 251 n. below) to modern—

there is no hint, on either side of the controversy, that poetry could be a means of grace. For such a claim to come into existence a new kind of poetry would be needed—and, perhaps, a new kind of reader.

But despite the paradox involved here, and despite the ambiguity of its status, between poetry, theology, allegory and prophecy, the *Comedy* is this new poetry, fusing, for the reader who attends to it, all four. Basically, despite its narrative's compounding of extraordinary occurrence and extraordinary phenomena, it is an existential communication, a communication from and to existence as we know it, and as such it should be taken.

I intend, then, in the remainder of this chapter, to substantiate these claims as they require; and, preferring to concentrate for the moment on the existential character of the *Comedy*, I shall generally leave the relevance of this 'character' to the poem's typology, and vice versa, to be inferred from the flanking chapters. Here, one explanatory word, or one jotting, may be enough. In the *Comedy*, as in the Bible, the existentiality of its address to the readers, the poem's whole urgency and its seriousness, provide the context in which its use of typology should be seen. Typology is used, as it may best be, existentially; it works in the poem, as the fundamentally biblical kind of typology always does, towards criticism, towards revaluation, *metanoia*. For to express 'grace' (i.e. to report an act of grace)— which is the task of such typology—means to express that which will come as a surprise, as the cause of revaluation. And it is so, too, with judgement, which typology also expresses—and which also is a 'surprise'.

We shall see this with Dante the character, through his encounter, in *Inferno* v, with Francesca da Rimini—an episode which all who know Dante know well (and which most of these who write write on), but which also, because of this familiarity and because of its comparative self-containedness, holds out for

where, again, it cannot properly apply so long as the literal sense is pure fiction (the usual case) and the allegorical senses unhistorical in content also. This was a misconception of the theological allegory against which the theologians of the thirteenth century rightly protested. Cf. Aquinas, *Quodlibets* VII. vi. 16; and see H. de Lubac, *Exégèse Médiévale*, II, 2, pp. 182–233. In Dante's case the 'senses' are all historical in reference, even the literal sense of his journey being, as we shall argue below (ch. 15), a mythological or metaphorical interpretation of his personal history.

our purpose one great advantage: it is strangely well able, or liable, to reveal the ultimate tendencies of the various critical standpoints from which the *Comedy* has been judged.[1]

One such standpoint—or perhaps a group of standpoints—is particularly relevant. Its presuppositions are precisely antithetical to those of the *Letter to Can Grande*, and, as I believe the scene itself will show, to Dante's method of poetic communication and his aim. There can hardly be a better name for this standpoint (which is not peculiar to critics) than 'aesthetic', for it seems to have connections with several of the normally divergent meanings of the term. But the precise sense will appear as we proceed.

The standpoint is typified by a wide range of critics, which makes the selection of two somewhat arbitrary. But the two are each representative. First, there is Foscolo, whose tender description of Francesca represents romantic criticism of a kind common in the last century: 'Her fault is purified by the ardour of her passion, and truthfulness beautifies her confession of desire.'[2] But *en passant*, is it truth that is its beauty, or is it that its beauty is taken by Foscolo for truth? This is subjective criticism which tells us more about its propagandist than about Francesca. And second there is Benedetto Croce, who is now, still, more influential, and is more subtle: rightly seeing that Dante's sentiments are not unmixed within this scene, he considers it one of the moments in the *Commedia* when the 'mistero della giustizia divina' contradicts the 'sentimento etico umano'. He can praise Dante for sometimes making us aware of such contradictions—Dante *then* is a poet—and blame him when sometimes he doesn't—and *then* 'ripiglia il moralista' (the moralist takes over) 'e anzi il teologo', while, we infer, the poet stands in abeyance.[3]

These would both serve to represent for us the idea of the aesthete as critic. And they are both open to attack, for by the standards of a more objective criticism, and a steadier regard

---

[1] See B. Curato, *Il canto di Francesca e i suoi interpreti*, for a reasonably thorough presentation of twentieth-century views.

[2] U. Foscolo, *Discorso sul testo della Commedia di Dante, Opere* III, 365.

[3] Cf. B. Croce, *La Poesia di Dante*, pp. 76 f. Similarly D. Vittorini: 'Francesca, while condemned by Dante, the moralist, for having loved Paolo, is redeemed by Dante, the poet, for the nobility of her love' (*High Points in the History of Italian Literature*, p. 79). This is nonsense.

for the poem as it stands, Croce and Foscolo are wrong and wrong precisely here:[1] looked at objectively, Francesca is plausible rather than admirable; she demonstrably—for one can see it in her speeches—subjugates reason to appetite and passion (*Inf.* v. 39); it is her own incomprehension that makes her fate seem so perverse (*v.* 93); and it is surely because of, not in spite of, this passion, this incomprehension, and perhaps this plausibility, that her bid for pity is so strong.[2] Much of our pity for her is the echo of her pity for herself. And similarly, our surprise at her judgement by Dante reflects and is conditioned by her surprise at her judgement by God. We must return to this vital point later. Our present concern is the 'aesthete'.

Yet discussion of the 'aesthete' as critic uncovers only a part of the present relevance of the 'aesthetic': a consideration of Canto v in the light of these criticisms can hardly fail to suggest that Dante himself is *the* 'aesthete', the archetype of these critics. I refer to the '*Dante-personaggio*'; not the poet of the *Commedia*, but the traveller as we find him in this canto.

> Poscia ch' io ebbi il mio dottore udito
> nomar le donne antiche e i cavalieri,
> pietà mi giunse, e fui quasi smarrito.

(After I had heard my master name the ladies and knights of antiquity, pity assailed me, and I was almost lost.) (*vv.* 70–2)

We note first how 'literary' is the quality of the romanticism to which Dante here responds. The lines quoted witness the strength of this response, and considering that what he has had from Virgil is little more than a catalogue of names it is strong indeed. And it seems to me that no other hypothesis so well explains its strength, and fits the facts recorded as this, that the very names, Semiramis, Dido, Cleopatra, Helen, Achilles, Paris, Tristan, evoke for Dante a whole world of romantic literature, and, definitely, literature. The quoted lines themselves drive home the point by the phrase, 'le donne antiche e i

---

[1] F. De Sanctis's reading is preferable. Seeing the sympathy which the *Dante-personaggio* feels, he nevertheless exclaims: 'As if the poet wished to cast the sin in the shade! To say this is to separate what is indivisible; there is not the slightest detail on which "sin" is not clearly stamped' (*De Sanctis on Dante*, ed. and trans. J. Rossi and A. Galpin, p. 47).

[2] Cf. K. Foster's remark, in his introduction to Warwick Chipman's translation of the *Inferno* (Oxford Library of Italian Classics, 1961, p. xiii): 'Dante's Hell is not only a picture of sin as it is...but of sin as it would like to appear.'

cavalieri', with its peculiar redolence of the chivalric romance accentuating once again the 'literary' element in these people's appeal. The nearest equivalent for us is Shakespeare's

> When in the chronicle of wasted time
>   I see descriptions of the fairest wights,
> And beauty making beautiful old rhyme
>   In praise of ladies dead and lovely knights.

For here explicitly, as in Dante implicitly, the romance exists on a 'literary' level; there is no immediacy, only distancing, for the 'ladies' are 'dead' just as Dante's 'donne' are 'antiche'; in properly human terms the poet has no connection with them. And Dante's 'pietà' is conditioned by that distancing; the literature has so filled his head with romantic notions that he is 'quasi smarrito', 'lost', as at first (*Inf.* I. 3).

Nor is that all. We are now faced with a passage of the literature which produces these apparent symptoms of Romanticism. As literature it is excellent: Dante at least attributes to his earlier self good taste. But by the end of Francesca's recitation he is not merely 'quasi smarrito', but absolutely so:

> di pietade
> io venni men così com'io morisse,
> e caddi come corpo morte cade.

(Out of pity I became faint, as if dying, and I fell down, as a dead body falls.)   (*vv.* 140–2)

We can see the stages. Already his call to the lovers is 'affettuoso', tender; and Francesca, when she comes in response to his cry, couches her exordium in a vein of gracious courtly compliment. There are dissident factors—'l'aere perso' ('the black air') (*v.* 89), 'mal perverso' ('perverse fate') (*v.* 93)— and of these Francesca's words take cognizance, treating the facts of her situation, however, as if they essentially did not belong to her, as if she were out of place here. Instead, the manner, the style, of her speech invite us to see the situation as extrinsic to those who are in it, to see them as not of its essence:

> O animal grazioso e benigno,
>   che visitando vai per l'aere perso
>   noi che tignemmo il mondo di sanguigno,

se fosse amico il re dell'universo
noi pregheremmo lui della tua pace
poi c'hai pietà del nostro mal perverso.

(O gracious and benign creature who goes through the black air
visiting us who stained the world with blood, if the king of the
universe were more kindly disposed to us we should pray him for
your peace, because you feel pity for our perverse fate.) (*vv*. 88–93)

The proper setting for this gracious period is the court, or perhaps the walled garden, where the interests of the 'gentle' heart
may be pursued at leisure; and the illusory atmosphere of such
a context is intensified as Francesca continues in the accent of
Guinizelli and of Dante himself, the love poet of the *dolce stil
nuovo*:

Amor, ch' al cor gentil ratto s'apprende...
(Love, that is quickly apprehended by the gentle heart.) (*v*. 100)[1]

With the threefold iteration of 'amor' at the beginning of
consecutive *terzine* the lulling and soothing process is continued
and intensified again. Not surprisingly, Dante, whose part in
the changed situation which her words conjure is, as it were,
already written for him by Francesca (cf. *vv*. 89 f., 93), responds
in the way required of him. 'China' il viso' ('I lowered my
face, *v*. 110):

O lasso,
quanti dolci pensier, quanto disio
menò costoro al doloroso passo!

(Alas! how many sweet thoughts, and what fervour, must have led
them to their sad fall.) (*vv*. 112–14)

And his pitying response is all the more apt, dramatically,
because he is responding to ideals that were at any rate closely
related to, or were actually, or (at the fictitious time of the
journey) are, his own: the whole scene, as Nardi has said, is
'un episodio stilnovista'.[2] And with Dante respond Croce and
Foscolo, though with less reason. But the fact remains, nonetheless, that it is fundamentally a purely 'literary', 'poetic',
'aesthetic', ideal, for Dante as much as for them. It is literary,

---

[1] A line which is obviously intended to recall Guinizelli's poem 'Al cor gentil
ripara sempre amore', and Dante's 'Amore el il cor gentil sono una cosa', key-
poems of the *dolce stil nuovo*.
[2] B. Nardi, *Dante e la Cultura Medievale*, p. 82.

it is of the realm of fancy, but they think it true. And above all, at least for the moment, Dante the traveller thinks it true. *Amor* is irresistible when it comes to the gentle heart: 'Amor...a nullo amato amar perdona' ('Love does not tolerate one loved not to love in return') (*v.* 103).

But there is a change now. The position has been that Francesca acts as romantic (or romanticizing) literature upon Dante, and makes of him, like herself, an 'aesthete'. But in her next speech (*vv.* 121–38) she takes over his present part, or rather, since it is a recollection and in the past tense, she tells how she and Paolo came to this 'doloroso passo' precisely by the means which now lead Dante to the point of tears. 'Noi leggiavamo'—it was literature—'di Lancialotto come amor lo strinse'—and romantic literature at that ('We were reading how love constrained Lancelot') (*vv.* 127 f.). But they took it for life.[1] They translated it, or tried to translate it, into the sphere of existence. And they found that the amorality of the love in the book became immorality in existence. The reason why it is so is not stated. All that Francesca does state is that the book and its author was 'Galeotto', a pandar, a go-between.

But therefore, on the strength of her own 'literary pathos', so has Francesca been a 'Galeotto', to our traveller, our archetypal aesthete. Or at least so she has been if he will not see the parallel between her reaction to Lancelot and his reaction to her. And would not the logic of the situation lead us on, to say further, of Croce and Foscolo, that if they do not see this parallel they make not of her alone but of Dante the poet a pandar, a 'Galeotto'?

From this point the concept of the 'aesthetic' seems to deepen, and to blend with the 'aesthetic' category of Kierkegaard. This 'category', or 'stadium' (to use Kierkegaard's word), denotes a rootless, uncommitted, existence, without fundamental 'seriousness'. 'Rootless' because it does not relate itself in any vital way to its environment, to life as it is, to

---

[1] Plinio Carli points out, in the course of an interpetation of this episode which differs from and yet is related to mine, that 'sospetto', in the line, 'soli eravamo e sanza alcun sospetto' ('we were alone, with no suspicion') means, in all probability, 'suspicion of the effects of this reading'. Cf. his *Saggi Danteschi*, p. 12. And cf. also the essay by Renato Poggioli cited on p. 226 below.

'existence' conceived as (in Heidegger's terms) *In-der-Welt-sein* or *Da-sein*, human 'being in the world', 'being *there*'. This we see in the case of Francesca, and in the traveller's case it is a real danger. And 'uncommitted' because it does not have an end, a purpose, except the illusory one of attaining to a sublime but fancied freedom from ethic or duty, seizing instead only upon the elusive pleasure of the moment. This is seen, in Francesca's case, in the illusory amorality of her 'literary' world.

For the kind of sublimity which Francesca possesses, even in our eyes, consists precisely in her rejection of the ethical, her refusal of responsibility in the world. Francesca made this refusal on earth, and she does so even now, in Hell, speaking in a way which disguises her culpability from her hearers too. For 'she tells the story of her vicissitudes in the most general terms'—in her first speech especially. She words it in the fixed and consecrated formulas of courtly love, 'tending to relate her experience to a generic and impersonal situation, and striving by this means to explain and justify it, to transfer the cause of her first impulse to sin away from the specific responsibility of the individual to a plane where a transcendent and irresistible force is responsible—Love'.[1]

Hence [Sapegno continues] the elaborate structure of her discourse, both from the formal point of view—with its studied internal correspondence and the repeated use, at three points, of a single grammatical subject which does not coincide with the real subject of the actions expressed (and aims, rather, to distract the listener's attention from that real subject: the persons of the lovers)—and also on the conceptual level, on which, by referring each act of the drama to a declared or assumed doctrinal norm, her discourse is transformed into a kind of urgent syllogism, which, from determined logical premises, leads as if by necessity to a foreseeable conclusion, independently of the wills of the particular agents.[2]

Thus this facet too of the 'aesthetic' individual, the evasion of responsibility, is noticeable in Francesca. And certainly, for Dante, it is a moral, not a natural, fault, it is immoral not amoral behaviour; so long as man has his reason he is called to be 'serious', to know good and evil and choose the good as his *telos*, his will's end.

[1] N. Sapegno, *La Divina Commedia, a cura di N. Sapegno*, p. 64 (on *Inf.* v. 100).
[2] *Ibid.*

Here, then, is what today we should call an 'existential category' applying quite well to Francesca and no doubt to others of the inhabitants of Dante's *Inferno*. But the mere presence of existential categories in the poem was never in doubt; for the divisions between the three realms of the after-life, as well as the divisions within them, themselves represent categories of existence: so much our last section showed. Neither that nor even the presence of people who, accidentally, fit into categories created by 'existentialist' thinkers would, by itself, show the poem to be, in the other sense of the word, 'existential' (*existenziell*, that is, as distinct from *existenzial*).[1] And it follows, too, that an interpretation of the poem is not to be called 'existential' merely on account of its using or demonstrating the presence of such categories.

But the *Comedy* does, I believe, demand such interpretation, and our preliminary discussion of 'aestheticism', in terms of both 'critics' and 'categories', may help to make plain that demand.

It is clear, first, that although we may speak of the subjective-ness of the 'aesthetic' interpretation of Francesca, it would be misleading to locate the fault strictly there. It is not subjectivity itself so much as its direction that is wrong. It has fastened on the wrong object, and has failed to take account of the episode's own self-criticism, as it appears, for example, in the soul's context and characterization. The interpretation corresponds, plainly, to something real in the *Dante-personaggio*'s attitude, and it corresponds, too, to Francesca's understanding of herself. But it is not, as it pretends, an interpretation of the scene as a whole, and the actors themselves are only properly understood in that context. Fundamentally, the fault here is not sub-jectivity, but rather a lack of seriousness; the attention given to the poem is 'aesthetic' rather than 'human'. But to this fault ostensibly objective criticism can lead equally.

---

[1] The distinction is expressed by saying that the structure, the analysis, or the characterizing of human existence is *existenzial*; whereas, '"*existenziell*"', on the other hand, is a speaking and listening in terms of one's own concrete concerns' (G. Bornkamm, 'Demythologizing the N.T. message', *Kerygma and History*, ed. C. E. Braaten and R. A. Harrisville, p. 174 n.). In previous contexts I have pre-ferred to let the sense of each usage be understood from the context, rather than imitate the common habit of putting the appropriate German word in place of the normally adequate English one.

Of this J. H. Whitfield sometimes seems guilty. He remarks that all those human passions which one critic (Montano) had indignantly repudiated as gross inventions of De Sanctis are allowed (by the same critic) to return surreptitiously ('but also', says Whitfield, 'maybe triumphantly') 'as the possessions of Dante-character and *Dante-peccatore*'. (Why this is a criticism of Montano it is hard to see.) 'And', Professor Whitfield continues, 'we may be, even if mistakenly, more interested in the peccant Dante than in the end-result.'[1]

Now what Whitfield *says* here is right. One could even go further. We *may* be more interested, and are even (since how many of us do not recognize a part of ourselves in these 'aesthetes'?) *likely*, at first sight, thus to be more interested, because more involved. And we may be forgiven for this—I believe, indeed, Dante intends it. We may be forgiven *if* we repent, if, that is to say, our involvement is only 'at first sight', as with the *Dante-personaggio* it is.

But the tone of Whitfield's remark is not so easy to agree with. The phrase 'even if mistakenly' suggests that the interest he posits here is not an involvement; or rather, that one may persist in one's preference for the peccant Dante without Whitfield's considering it a serious enough 'mistake' to need rectifying. Either, therefore, it is not really so wrong because these 'human passions' are not really so evil as Dante (or Montano) would have us believe; or it is not so wrong because —quite apart from the question whether they are evil or not— Dante does not present, or at any rate he does not attract us to, a viable alternative. In the first case, the criticism of Dante is (theoretically) ethical; in the second (theoretically), literary. In practice, however, Whitfield does not very clearly distinguish them. He contents himself with the mixture, the issue is clouded, and we are persuaded that the human passions of Dante have returned triumphantly indeed. At the end of his lecture Whitfield is able to refer back to near the beginning: 'Did we not see, in starting, that Dante's humility is in *Inferno* I, and is suspect, while his pride is shown in *Paradiso*, and is genuine? This is an opposite paradigm to Montano's.'[2]

Now this is, on the face of it, objective criticism. It is objec-

---

[1] *Essays in the Like and Unlike* (Barlow Lectures on Dante, 1959), p. 14.
[2] *Ibid.* p. 15.

tive, at all events, if one leaves out of consideration the moral element in it—as we shall, for, after all, Whitfield does not commit himself to it. And as such we may deal with this at the same time as we deal with another (again, on the face of it) objective criticism, that of G. Trombatore—a criticism that is (more than Montano's) 'an opposite paradigm' to Whitfield's. Trombatore was not involved with Francesca even at first sight. He saw her, evidently at once, as 'the demoniac woman who employs her fair person, her sensual charms, to bemuse the virtue of the gentle heart and lead it to perdition'.[1]

But this is not what Kierkegaard would call 'inwardness'. It is not even, I should say, sensitive. It misses the point of the episode, and, in a sense, of the *Comedy*—by self-knowledge to see and reject the 'aesthetic' life of Francesca. This deserves stressing: by *self*-knowledge, not merely by knowing the fault of Francesca. Our subjectivity must be involved, and involved by both pity and fear. For we see ourselves in Francesca, as Dante saw himself, and must therefore pity her. And we should also see through ourselves, as we look at her, to what will be our end, if our self-identification with her persists, and are therefore invited to fear. But Trombatore does not pity, and it seems as if Whitfield does not fear. And neither of them so much as seems to realize that it is the *Comedy*'s intention that they should, that the reading that the *Comedy* requires is an active and dramatic one, that the reader is supposed to be changed.[2]

I repeat: it is the *Comedy*, and not my doctrine or my doctrinaireness, that demands this subjectivity, this 'inwardness', and change. Its own 'aesthetic' in the philosophical sense, its own 'poetic', is an existential one. We can see this in action in this same *canto*, where, in rejecting Francesca, Dante plainly rejects too the philosophical aesthetic of the courtly love convention and its poetry, and rejects it as 'aesthetic' in Kierkegaard's sense, because it claims for its elite a freedom from the moral law which governs those outside. And in place of this Dante evolves, and practises, an existential poetic whose aim

[1] Quoted, wrongly, as G. Trombadori, by I. Brandeis, *The Ladder of Vision*, p. 23. The words in question are translated from his *Saggi critici*, p. 77.

[2] See *Par.* XVII. 124–32, which shows that Dante consciously intends to alter his reader through the poem, to offend in order to edify.

is to bring the reader to the point of change, of repentance, the point at which he may (if he will) commit himself to a real ethico-religious Christian existence in the context of a history that has been transformed by grace.

An analogue for this poetic, as it exists in the Francesca episode, can be found in a wholly different kind of work, Thomas Mann's short novel, *Death in Venice*.

Again—to note the more obvious parallels first—it is concerned with a death upon the shores of the Adriatic, and again it is a kind of damnation. Moreover, it is a damnation which is closely bound up with an aesthetic in the strict philosophical sense, and with the deceptive danger of an aesthetic which turns its back upon knowledge—in Francesca's case, the knowledge of good and evil, of individual responsibility, and, in the case of the writer Gustav von Aschenbach, knowledge of the immoral and daemonic tendency of the creative principle. Aschenbach's art is Apollonian, it is all discipline, willed control, ordered and composed, and it celebrates a humanistic moral triumph over the Dionysian abyss: 'explicitly (Aschenbach) renounces sympathy with the abyss, explicitly he refutes the flabby humanitarianism of the phrase: "tout comprendre c'est tout pardonner"'.

And Thomas Mann's own involvement in this is real. As in the *Comedy*, there is an 'appropinquation' or assimilation of the protagonist (and I mean here Francesca) and the author. Francesca speaks like one of Dante's own poems; Dante, as it were, breathes something of himself into her. And Aschenbach's literary output has a palpable relation to Mann's, and his 'aesthetic' is at least one element in Mann's, a possible development of Mann's, as Francesca's is an element and a possible development of Dante's.

Death in Venice is, on one level, the work of that 'possible' Thomas Mann. Its style, like Aschenbach's, is classical, imperturbable, Apollonian, existing in an ordered, if simplified, moral ethos which has no truck with the abyss.

But the story told in the style, the story of Aschenbach, conflicts with the style and with Aschenbach's classical temper, telling of the fever-ridden, hectic dream-world, world and/or dream, which Aschenbach enters as he comes to Venice. And this hectic element, the plague—it is Asiatic cholera, a secret hidden behind the ornate surface of the city—and the moral disorder, the moral and physical *de*composition hidden behind the composed classical style of the esteemed protagonist, these together are the abyss, the swampy jungle of his fitful day-nightmare, and he cannot cope with them, they are outside his scope. But they now fascinate him, aesthetically, and he succumbs to their fascination, hiding from himself the common and clichéd quality of this lure and its fatal 'end', disguising it in the unreal, mythological style of his thought—as Thomas Mann does by the style of the prose.

But there is a difference, despite the 'appropinquation' that signals involvement. Thomas Mann, unlike Aschenbach, is conscious of the 'desperate' direction of the style. By objectifying the danger he is able to elude it. In the realm of Dante poetics we must reckon with the possibility of similar behaviour: as here, when Dante's old style, the *dolce stil novo*, at least in Francesca's first speech, is identified with Francesca's, and *Dante-personaggio* is so 'involved' that he 'swoons'...'di pietade'. It is a deceptive and dangerous style, and Francesca and the traveller are deceived by it. But the poet, like Thomas Mann, rejects it. It has been dramatically re-assumed, but he is now beyond it, and sees through it to its end in despair, in damnation.

It is time to draw threads together and reach a conclusion. The critique of aestheticism is, I believe, for Dante, a means to an end. Here perhaps is the first and fundamental point of comparison between Kierkegaard and Dante. The aim in each case is that of 'becoming a Christian' when all men think themselves Christians, of 'becoming a Christian...when one is a Christian of a sort'. Speaking of the *Concluding Unscientific Postscript* Kierkegaard says, 'this work concerns itself with and sets "the Problem", which is the problem of the whole authorship: how to become a Christian'.[1] And he elaborates this: 'Having appropriated the whole pseudonymous, aesthetic work as the description of *one* way a person may take to become a Christian (*viz. away* from the aesthetical in order to become a Christian), it undertakes to describe the other way (*viz. away*

---

[1] *The Point of View for my Work as an Author*, p. 13.

from the System, from speculation, etc.,[1] in order to become a Christian).'[2]

And Dante asks, 'how may I become a Christian?', and asks his readers to ask it. For this reason Dante the poet deliberately engages us, with his traveller, in the 'human passions' of the *Inferno*, to the end that he may 'find us where we are', and not only find, but show us where we are, to show us with complete moral seriousness what he claims is the teleology of the existence in which we are. 'In quo medio doctrinat nos moraliter in persona sui', as Dante's son Pietro says in connection with another part of the *Inferno*, 'debere aperire oculos mentis ad videndum ubi sumus, an in recta via ad patriam, aut non.'[3] Probably it would be going too far if we said that Dante proposes, by turns, this or that circle, this or that 'state of soul', for us to recognize and assent to as *our telos*, the liable state of our soul. The inspiriting concerns of the poetry are more various, and more complex; the poetry's art, its techniques and channels of access to us, are not so monotonous or so streamlined and (so to speak) super-marketed as that kind of statement suggests. But if the statement can point to a truth deserving of emphasis, a factor which needs facing up to, we may allow it, duly qualified, to stand. For the truth is that the *Comedy* has at least 'such a' deliberately and radically critical tendency as it suggests. The poem does aim, and persistently, to provoke the reader into implicit self-criticism. A. N. Wilder remarks of the stories in the New Testament that 'they "put us on the spot..."' Our consciences must stand and deliver.'[4] It is so, repeatedly, with the *Commedia*. It is assiduous in the attempt to bring us to know ourselves, and to know ourselves, here in the *Inferno* especially, as committed in this way

---

[1] I.e. from empty objectivity; cf. again the *Letter to Can Grande*, §16, quoted on p. 208 above.

[2] *Op. cit.* pp. 41–2.   [3] *Petri Allegherii Commentarium* (Florence, 1845), p. 25.

[4] *Early Christian Rhetoric*, p. 68. The author's context is worth quoting: 'Thus the stories of the New Testament, whether the total story of Paradise Lost and Paradise Regained, or the most minute story like that of the widow who cast all that she had into the treasury...—these stories span our lives and wait our answer. To use a slang expression, they "put us on the spot". The stories are so graphic that we are bound hand and foot. Our consciences must stand and deliver. What is interesting here is the suggestion that it takes a good story to make people realize what the right thing to do is. The road to moral judgment is by way of the imagination! One is tempted to say that aesthetics and ethics are not so far apart in the Gospel as is often supposed. They both have to do with the fitness of things.'

or that to a sinful existence. For such knowledge is one pre-condition for repentance.

Away, then, from aesthetics by showing the end of aesthetics, which, Dante and Kierkegaard agree, is despair: 'Lasciate ogni speranza, voi ch'entrate.' And if the truly desperate are often, like Francesca, quite unconscious of a despair with which they are now unendingly at one, the despair to which Dante introduces us and which he induces in us is one which on the contrary does know and admit its own existence, and from which, therefore, we may be delivered. Away from aesthetics, through despair, to life as a Christian. This is the movement in Kierkegaard's work and the context of his counsel of despair: 'I counsel you to despair...not as a comfort, not as a condition in which you are to remain, but as a deed which requires all the power and seriousness and concentration of the soul, just as surely as it is my conviction, my victory over the world, that every man who has not tasted the bitterness of despair has missed the significance of life.' The *Inferno* illuminates these words, and they in turn light up the *Inferno*, for which they might serve as a motto. 'For here', Dante can say, 'is my victory over the world. I counsel you to despair...if you would wish to join in it with me.' Then, after the victory, despair only remains as something abolished, like the memory of sin after passing through Eunoë.

But if despair is the negative side of the *Comedy*'s existential intention, it needs still a positive side to be presented and shown (as I said somewhat earlier) to be a viable alternative. Despair may be the precondition of repentance, but it does not itself effect repentance. Repentance is made possible only by the sight of something better, of a better way and one within our reach.

For the penitent's self-knowledge is not only what we know when we experience our death and judgement 'conditionally' in (for example) Francesca's: the knowledge of ourselves as doomed by sin.[1] It must include also the knowledge of a future

---

[1] Cf. Benvenuto, *Comentum* (Florence, 1887), I, p. 16: 'Quaedam enim anima est posita in peccatis, et ista dum vivit cum corpore, est mortua moraliter, et sic est in Inferno morali.' The same theme is found in most early commentaries. It is in the context of this belief that the 'aperire oculos mentis ad videndum ubi sumus' of Pietro (quoted above) is seen in its proper perspective, i.e. as a treatment of the poem more as prophecy or parable in the biblical sense than as an allegorical treatise, as a work of poetry designed to bring repentance, to fulfil a 'critical' task.

possibility, one which attracts us more strongly than sin. And if we take the *Letter to Can Grande* at its word, when it says that the aim of the work is to remove the living in this life from misery to happiness, to effect therefore the change of existence which takes place in conversion, it must also be a part of the poem's existential aim to give the reader knowledge of that future possibility, to attract him and direct him towards 'blessing'.

We should expect, therefore, the *Comedy*, like the Bible, to contain alongside the typology of rejection, culminating in despair, a typology of conversion which points, and perhaps directs the will, to salvation.[1]

---

[1] It was only a considerable time after writing the foregoing account of *Inferno* v that I came across the admirable essay by R. Poggioli, 'Tragedy or Romance? A Reading of the Paolo and Francesca Episode in Dante's *Inferno*', in *PMLA*, LXXII, 3 (June 1957), which in some respects anticipates my own findings. The oversight cannot be excused; but it is matter for regret that it appears to have been shared by Italian criticism generally—even the comprehensive survey by B. Curato, *Il Canto di Francesca e i suoi Interpreti* (1962?), making no mention of it. It is to be hoped that the inclusion of an abridged version in the volume devoted to Dante in the 'Twentieth Century Views' series will give Poggioli's essay the wider currency which it deserves.

CHAPTER 15

PROPHECY AND THE TYPOLOGY
OF REDEMPTION

As we should expect, the new knowledge and the new scope of authentic Christian existence—the new, other, possibility for the will's choice—comes to its natural expression in the *Purgatorio* and *Paradiso*, just as in the realms of the after-life which they depict the new scope itself reaches its final fulfilment. For as we have seen, in all three *cantiche* a type of life in death presents itself as the fulfilling, in reward, purgation, punishment, of the soul's historical *habitus*; and as the *Inferno* shows, and vividly, the moral teleology of decisions made for evil, so the *Inferno*'s successors show something at least of the process towards fulfilment and then the very fulfilment itself, this movement and this attainment both issuing from decisions made on earth for good. The address to the reader of this aspect of the structure of the *Comedy* might be the defiant pronouncement found in Deuteronomy: 'See—I have set before you this day life and good or death and evil' (Deut. 30. 15)—a kind of 'take it or leave it'.

Nevertheless, if this were all, the poem would (so far as it is viewed as 'address') consist of nothing more than a series of *exempla*, which, like those in *Purgatorio* (the 'whip' and the 'bit'), though they may encourage a will once resolved, would not often by themselves (as Dante well knows, cf. *Purg.* XIV. 143–7) effect a change in the will's disposition. By however non-didactic means it were presented, it would be *didache* and not *kerygma*: it would in fact be law, not gospel. For to show 'the better way' is one thing; to convince a soul in misery that it is viable is quite another. So here: the fixed wills of the souls permit an echo to be heard of the soul's life while its will was changeable, and in the *Purgatorio* this echo still sometimes recaptures something of the tenuousness and hardship of the movement into Christian existence. But it is only something of the hardship. In the nature of things there is a gulf set between these souls and us. The news of their conversion is less immediately experienced than their present state in bliss or (at least) safety. A certain surprise mingles occasionally with the joy of the Dante-character when he meets someone whom he had known and loved on earth and finds him here and safe (Nino Visconti, for example—'Giudice Nin gentil' of *Purg.* viii—and Forese); but though by such surprises as this the wonder of God's grace is expressed, and its accessibility, a further mediating principle is needed if this accessibility is to be demonstrated to the point of being 'gospel', or if, as the Can Grande letter claims, the presentation is perceptibly and perhaps critically to influence the reader's choice.

This is one main purpose of the living Dante's journey in the poem.[1] The journey itself is the alternative to sin and judgement shown not as a *fait accompli* but as *in fieri*. Gradually, but from the very start and with ever greater clarity, Dante reveals this journey to us as 'salvation coming into being', as the image of conversion. This is 'gospel' in a way the *fait accompli* of the souls in Paradise can never be. Through the tale of how a man, and one such as the Dante whom we see at the beginning, has been enabled to attain to his salvation, salvation's viability for others, or for all, is claimed, is clarified, and is made palpable. At least under this aspect, Dante the character is the reader's representative, the reader's grounds for hope.

Right through the narrative the *Dante-personnagio* is, as any reader will confirm, human, and convincingly. His actions and his words arise naturally and spontaneously out of event and from personality. Moreover, not only in *Inferno* v and i, but right through the poem, at least up to the moment at which Virgil 'crowns and mitres him over himself' (*Purg.* xxvii. 142) and perhaps even after that (cf. *Purg.* xxxii. 9 and *Par.* xvi. 13–15), he is essentially and continually liable to sin. The so-called *Ottimo Commento*[2] makes the dual point, laconically enough, in its '*proemio*':

---

[1] In the *Convivio* (i. 2) Dante mentions the two most manifest reasons which make it permissible for a man to speak of himself. One of these is 'when by a man discoursing of himself the highest advantage, in the way of instruction, follows therefrom to others; and this reason moved Augustine, in the *Confessions*, to speak of himself; for by the progress of his life, which was from bad to good, and from good to better, and from better to best, he gave example and instruction which could not have been received otherwise on such sure testimony.'

[2] *L'Ottimo Commento* (anon., fourteenth century) first published Pisa, 1827.

Ed è da notare, che Dante pone sè in forma comune d'uomo..., e d'uomo, dico, intento nelle sensualitadi di questo mondo, inchinato ad esse: o vero se in forma del libero arbitrio, inchinante alle sensualitadi.

(And it is to be noticed that Dante puts himself in the common like-ness of man..., and of man who is, at that, intent upon the sensuali-ties of this world, and inclined to them—or rather, in view of his free will, *inclining* to the sensualities.)

And again, unlike the souls, Dante's journey figures a process rather than a state, a process moreover which begins and ends in 'our life' ('*nostra* vita', noteworthily, in *Inf.* I. I)—and begins with mortal danger. The threat to Dante's life is both physical and—since he is dying, if the threat is realized, in the *status miserie*, the state of sin—also spiritual. He has lost the straight way (*Inf.* I. 3)—there is no means of telling how,

> tant'era pieno di sonno a quel punto
> che la verace via abbandonai

(so full of slumber was I at the moment of abandoning the true way)

(vv. 11 f.);

and when (*v.* 2) he comes to himself and sees the 'better way', he finds that vice impedes his taking it: he is still in danger, and unable to save himself. When Virgil comes upon him, he is rushing downhill ('in basso loco', *v.* 61), and his cry, with its allusive Latin and the undiscriminating vocative, 'miserere di me..., qual che tu sii' ('have mercy on me, whoever you may be', *vv.* 65 f.), expresses the extreme spiritual desperation of a man to whom the source of his help now is irrelevant so long only as help comes.

Already then, in the middle of life and theoretically there-fore (cf. *Conv.* IV. 23), at the height of his powers, Dante is close to death and threatened by it. The wood is

> lo passo
> che non lasciò già mai persona viva,

(the pass that no-one ever left alive)   (*Inf.* I. 26 f.);

and Virgil describes the she-wolf as

> 'questa bestia' (che)...
> non lascia altrui passar per la sua via,
> ma tanto lo 'mpedisce che l'uccide.

(the beast (which) lets no-one pass this way, but so harasses them that she kills them.)   (*vv.* 94–6)

The gravity of Dante's situation is disclosed by indirect means also. The linguistic connection between the *Comedy*'s first line and the words of Hezekiah—'In dimidio dierum meorum vadam ad portas inferi' (Isa. 38. 10)—is plain. But the relevance of these words, as F. Montanari points out,[1] lies in the fact that there is a closeness of contextual relation too. Hezekiah is also in 'mezzo del cammin di nostra vita' (*Inf.* I. 1). His 'sickness unto death', moreover, has the character of a sentence passed on him by God, not merely a death in the course of nature.[2]

Similarly, Dante, as the reported dialogue between Virgil and Beatrice indicates, has had sentence already passed upon him (*Inf.* II. 96). His saving, then, like Hezekiah's, is a sovereign act of grace, suspending the judgement to which he is liable, and at the last moment snatching him from the gates of hell. Virgil is sent as heaven's instrument of salvation, and Dante's death is postponed.[3]

But the postponement is only of 'essential' death. The 'altro viaggio' ('the other journey') (*Inf.* I. 91) which Dante must take, bears, itself, the closest relation to death: it is, in an almost literal sense, a 'fore-having', a prolepsis. Dante is to experience everything in death except his own death as something finally now bringing his life to an end. An anticipation is substituted for fulfilment.

But the fulfilment which Dante anticipates by this journey is, as is apparent from the manner of its initiation in heaven, no longer the death to which he was hitherto tending. It is a 'fore-having' whose purpose, so far as Dante himself is concerned, is to change his death from death in sin to death in grace, to effect conversion. There is no other way—so far has Dante gone along the 'via non vera' (*Purg.* XXX. 130)—to bring him back upon the 'verace via' (*Inf.* I. 12):

---

[1] *L'Esperienza poetica di Dante*, pp. 164–6.

[2] Cf. Isa. 38. 1: 'Isaias...dixit ei: Haec dicit Dominus: Dispone domui tuae, quia morieris tu, et non vives.'

[3] Compare also the direct reference to Hezekiah in *Par.* XX. 49–54: 'Morte indugiò per vera penitenza' ('He put off his death by true repentance'). Immediately preceding Hezekiah, in this context, is Trajan, who would also appear to be a sort of 'type' of Dante, in that he descended to hell and yet was ultimately saved (in his case, through the prayers of St Gregory, cf. *Par.* XX. 106–17), and this, significantly as we shall see, is also conceived as a 'following' of Christ. See pp. 247 f. below.

> Tanto giù cadde, che tutti argomenti
> alla salute sua eran già corti,
> fuor che mostrarli le perdute genti.

(He fell so far as to be past all remedy save that of showing him the
lost souls.)   (*Purg.* XXX. 136–8)

Et sic auctor noster [writes Pietro] descendit ad infernum iuvenis,
et in medio camini ipsius vitae..., ut eis probabiliter abominatis
moriens non vadet ad essentialem infernum.[1]

Dante is himself exposed to death, and the reader through
him, not, then, ultimately in order to produce despair, but to
make his redemption possible. Repeatedly, in the *Purgatorio*,
we hear this said directly by the *Dante-personaggio*. Casella, for
example, asks him, 'ma tu perché vai?' (i.e. 'why do you go
this way alive?' *Purg.* II. 90) and he receives the answer:

> Casella mio, per tornar altra volta
> là dov'io son, fo io questo viaggio.

(in order to return another time here where I am, I make this journey
now.)   (*Purg.* II. 91 f.)

In contrast to his peril in the Francesca canto (cf. 'caddi, come
corpo morto cade', *Inf.* v. 142) the journey has by this time
taken on the character of an anticipation of salvation rather
than a pre-experience of doom. 'Sono in prima vita', he says
on another occasion, 'ancor che l'altra, sì andando, acquisti'
('I am still in the first life, though, by this journey, I may gain
the other'—i.e. eternal life) (*Purg.* VIII. 59 f.). These phrases
mark a growing optimism about the issue of this journey, an
assurance which modifies the whole feeling of the 'anticipated
death' which the journey involves. And this note, new in its
confidence, if not materially distinct in its meaning from what
was already implied by Virgil's 'a te convien tener altro
viaggio' (*Inf.* I. 91), derives from its location in Purgatory a
significance which makes it apt, too, to the experience of Dante
in Hell. The suffering, the fear, the pity, felt by him there, now
take on the colour which suffering has in this *cantica*: it is
necessary, it is all 'for the sake of' the greater good, the better
way, the *maggior cura* (*Purg.* II. 129) of salvation. Hence Dante's
two exclamations, pointing to the difference between the souls'
sufferings down below and the sufferings inflicted here, cast a

---

[1] *Petri Allegherii Commentarium*, pp. 25 f.

new light back on his own sufferings in the *Inferno*. The latter are now transmuted as their nature is realized as not only temporal and temporary but also 'for the sake of' bringing him to repentance, and hence, ultimately, bliss.

> Ahi quanto son diverse quelle foci
> dall'infernali! ché quivi per canti
> s'entra, e là giù per lamenti feroci.

(Ah, how different are these entrances (i.e. to the cornices) from the infernal ones! for here to the sound of songs one enters, and down there to wild laments.) (*Purg.* XII. 112–14)

Suffering is greeted by song here: to the souls in Purgatory its purpose is known: the moulding of the character into conformity with the will of God. But the reader, like Dante himself in the poem, is struck by the contrast with his own natural reactions. And again, as the poem had implicitly done already in the Francesca canto, by forcing him to respond as the man he is, his natural reaction to the first sight of purgatorial pain is permitted, even expected. But now the poem invites him, by the example of the souls here, to transvalue his values, to see the transforming purpose, the new conformity, the promise of new life, which suffering here involves. And this time he is addressed directly:

> Non vo' però, lettor, che tu ti smaghi
> di buon proponimento per udire
> come Dio vuol che'l debito si paghi.
> Non attender la forma del martire,
> pensa la succession; pensa ch'al peggio,
> oltre la gran sentenza non può ire.

(Reader, it is not my wish that you should be dismayed from good resolve by hearing how God wills that the debt be paid. Heed not the suffering's quality; think of its consequence. Think how, even at worst, it cannot last beyond the great Judgement.) (*Purg.* x. 106–11)

Compare *Purg.* XXIII. 72:

> Io dico pena, e dovrìa dir sollazzo.

(I say 'pain', but should say, rather, 'solace'.)

Dante expects, perhaps, to dismay. But he adds this repeated 'pensa': 'pensa la succession; pensa...!' The changing of values which the poem encourages is a change which Dante himself has undergone in its course.

So the personal value of the journey for Dante becomes, as it proceeds, something which more and more clearly involves the reader as well. And if at this stage the personal value of the journey is all that the *Dante-personaggio* knows ('per tornar altra volta'), it is beginning to be hinted to *us* that by according him this special grace the inscrutable providence of God (cf. *Purg.* VIII. 66–9) may have some deeper purpose, which at least *includes* that of bringing others after him in his tracks.[1]

In this connection it is worth recalling the conclusions of E. Auerbach and L. Spitzer from their work on Dante's 'addresses to the reader'.[2] 'As the announcer of a revelation', writes Auerbach (*Romance Philology*, VII, 1953–4, 276), 'the poet surpasses his readers: he knows something of the highest importance which they must learn from him...The reader, as envisioned by Dante..., is a disciple...' He is called upon 'to follow'. This is where the repeated formal 'addresses', and especially their characteristic imperatives, 'pensa' (*Inf.* VIII. 94, XX. 20, XXXIV. 26; *Purg.* X. 110, XXXI. 124; *Par.* V. 109), and, in other places, 'mirate', 'ricorditi', 'leggi', 'immagini', and so on, take their place. In them one sees Dante's sense of the urgency of this journey of his for his readers too. And we may quote, as Auerbach does (pp. 273 f.), besides the passage from *Purg.* X already cited, especially the address to the reader in *Inf.* XX (*vv.* 19 f.)—

---

[1] It is in this context that we ought to interpret the references to Paul and Aeneas, Dante's precursors in the journey to the after-life. Both were granted these 'extraordinary' privileges, according to the sources (*Aeneid* VI, and the apocryphal expansions of hints in II Cor. 12. 1–5, the *Visio S. Pauli*), for the sake of great missions to Empire and Church. But J. A. Mazzeo, who, with regard to these sources, points the fact out, fails to notice what B. Nardi is aware of (*Dante e la Cultura Medievale*, pp. 282–6), that from the very first (*Inf.* II. 10–36) it is in this connection with 'missions', much more than in connection with 'modes of vision', that Dante treats Paul and Aeneas as 'types' for the journey which he is making. Cf. J. A. Mazzeo, 'Dante and the Pauline modes of vision', *HTR*, L (1957), 275–306.

[2] E. Auerbach, 'Dante's Addresses to the Reader', *Romance Philology*, VII (1953–4), 268–78; L. Spitzer, 'The Addresses to the Reader in the *Commedia*', *Italica*, XXXII, 143–65, and reprinted in Spitzer's *Romanische Literaturstudien*, 1936–56, pp. 574–95. Spitzer correctly points out that Auerbach overstresses Dante's 'authority', as revealed in the addresses. There is nothing, as he says, superhuman about Dante. Dante's 'I' in the poem is 'a poetic-didactic "I" that stands vicariously for any other Christian (cf. again the first lines of the *Commedia*: "Nel mezzo del cammin di nostra vita / Mi ritrovai") for whom, as for Dante, a sudden illumination is possible thanks to the nature of the Christian God' (*Romanische Literaturstudien*, p. 592).

Se Dio ti lasci, lettor, prender frutto
di tua lezione, or pensa per te stesso... !
(If God grant you, reader, to reap fruit from your reading, now think
for yourself...)

—and the sublime passage in *Par.* x which, beginning,

Leva dunque, lettore, all'alte ruote
meco la vista...
(Lift therefore, reader, your sight with me to the spheres)   (*vv.* 7 f.)

makes explicit the message addressed to the reader only indirectly in such passages as *Purg.* XIX. 61–3 and XIV. 148–51,
and then continues:

Or ti riman, lettor, sovra'l tuo banco,
dietro pensando a ciò che si preliba,
s'esser vuoi lieto assai prima che stanco.
Messo t'ho innanzi: omai per te ti ciba.
(Now stay, reader ,on your bench, thinking back to the foretaste you
have had, if you desire gladness before you are tired. I have set the
food before you. Now feed yourself!)   (*vv.* 22–5)

The (to our minds) extraordinarily developed interest in the
processes whereby poetry may influence its readers—in the
lines of force, of action and response, between the poem and the
reader—which such conscious attempts to control the reader's
feelings and thoughts presuppose in the poet, bears fruit
throughout the *Comedy*. In the previous chapter we saw just one
other form of its outworking. And in the breadth and depth of
its application in the *Comedy* this interest must remain remarkable. But at least the fact of its existence can, in historical
terms, be accounted for. The medieval habit of mind by which
poetry is no other than a species of rhetoric, of eloquence, is
enough to explain why this interest is, in itself, by no means
unparalleled in the historical context.[1] A paragraph of the Can
Grande letter may be cited as, in this respect, in the main,
typical of its age—the paragraph, strangely ignored by the
commentators, but still repaying close reading, in which the
writer begins to expound the 'exordium' to the *Paradiso*.

[1] Compare, for example, E. R. Curtius, *European Literature and the Latin Middle
Ages*, ch. 8, pp. 145–66.

§19. Propter primam partem notandum quod ad bene exordiendum tria requiruntur, ut dicit Tullius in Nova Rethorica, scilicet ut benivolum et attentum et docilem reddat aliquis auditorem; et hoc maxime in admirabili genere cause, ut ipsemet Tullius dicit. Cum ergo materia circa quam versatur presens tractatus sit admirabilis, et propterea ad admirabile reducenda, ista tria intenduntur in principio exordii sive prologi. Nam dicit se dicturum ea que vidit in primo celo et retinere mente potuit. In quo dicto, omnia illa tria comprehenduntur; nam in utilitate dicendorum benivolentia paratur; in admirabilitate attentio; in possibilitate docilitas. Utilitatem innuit, cum recitaturum se dicit ea que maxime allectiva sunt desiderii humani, scilicet gaudia Paradisi; admirabilitatem tangit, cum promittit se tam ardua tam sublimia dicere, scilicet conditiones regni celestis; possibilitatem ostendit, cum dicit se dicturum que mente retinere potuit; si enim ipse, et alii poterunt.

If we can once overcome the still latent romantic suspicion of and distaste for a process that attempts to lay bare the workings of poetry and to show them to be as much deliberate as charismatic,[1] this passage can help us to see how profitably 'the art of persuasion' could be harnessed by the medieval writer, and made homogeneous with 'art'.

But in our context there is still more to note. The last phrase, 'si enim ipse, et alii poterunt', is, in context, a little odd. Ostensibly it is linked with the comparatively trivial issue of the possibility of retaining a memory of what he saw, an issue which has more to do with what would strictly be called 'credulitas' than with 'docilitas', which should mean 'docile to receive the instruction imparted by the work', and—since in this work the instruction is, we have just been told, moral and practical, not purely speculative—'prepared to act on such instruction'. But, in that context, the phrase is at least redundant, and it arguably weakens the case. We might expect, if the object is indeed to render the reader more 'credulous' as to the

---

[1] For a modern reader, comments A. Momigliano on the glossings in these paragraphs, 'the frigidity of the scholastic logic by which this poetry is explained and dissolved is amazing...This was the literary criticism of Dante's age: the first commentaries on the *Commedia* witness to it. Criticism was conceived then as an operation of logic..., and poetry as such seems to have been forgotten.' This (which derives from the notes in Momigliano's commentary on *Par.* I. 7–9) seems a little harsh. For a recent discussion of these issues see E. Gilson, 'Poésie et Théologie dans la Divine Comédie', *Atti del Congresso Internazionale di Studi Danteschi* (Florence, 1965), I, esp. pp. 207–11.

possibility immediately at stake, such an argument as we find later, in §28, an argument which is formally this one's reverse: 'if others can, why not Dante?' But in fact the charge of irrelevance attaches more to the issue at stake in this part of the sentence than to the particular phrase which concludes it. When we look back at the paragraph as a whole we see that it is the issue of *credulitas* which is, here, a digression, and that the author, who has been for the moment distracted (presumably by his wish to connect 'possibility' with the 'potei' of the prologue (*Par.* I. 11)) from the question with which the main part of the paragraph really faces him—how far, that is, the 'marvellous matter' ('materia admirabilis') of the *Paradiso* ('presens tractatus') is possible—now only, with the last phrase, returns to it. For to that question (the question, implied by the paragraph, concerning 'docility') the final words as they stand are relevant, and are important—not, indeed, because they justify their own claim or seek, logically, to do so, but because they affirm it, and then carry on with another claim which this time, with the first premised, *is* logical: 'si enim ipse, et alii poterunt'. If Dante could, others may. The marvellous journey is possible, viable; if for Dante, also for others. The phrase, in the setting of the whole paragraph, demands this wide application. The reader may act upon the news Dante has to impart to him, being confident that it is true. For Dante himself has adventured, and has experienced these 'marvellous' things.

Meanwhile, to return to the *Comedy* itself, the *Purgatorio* x passage which I have quoted (p. 232) contains references whose significance for the interpreting of Dante's foretaste of death it would be a pity to miss. It speaks of a 'debt' which is paid by '*martire*' (*vv.* 108 f.), a suffering (or perhaps 'passion') which is undergone in view of an implicitly glorious consequence. These phrases already suggest how one might define the 'conforming' and the 'transvaluing of values' more exactly than I have done so far. The sufferings in Purgatory are not unconnected with the passion of Christ (see *Purg.* XXIII. 73–5), nor is that passion, any more than these sufferings, unconnected with something of which St Paul speaks in the present, in terms of this life: 'We are afflicted in every way, but not crushed..., always carrying in the body the death of Jesus, so that the life of Jesus may be manifested in our bodies. For while we live we are always being given up to death, for Jesus' sake, so that the life of Jesus may be manifested in our bodies' (II Cor. 4. 8, 10 f.; the Vulgate of *v.* 11, which is the most significant for the *Commedia,* reads: 'Semper enim nos, qui vivimus, in mortem tradimur propter Jesum, ut et vita Jesu manifestetur in carne nostra mortali'). The typological back-reference, which not only the sufferings in Purgatory but Dante's whole journey implies, is, in the terms of medieval theory, the dialectically related *sensus allegoricus* of his journey. In our own terms, the journey is a 'subfulfilment' of the Christ-event.

This theme, along with the 'deeper purpose' of Dante's journey as a means of grace, comes to expression in an episode which, for our or any purposes, is among the most significant in the poem. It is the scene (*Par.* xiv. 91–xviii. 51) of the poet's encounter with his ancestor, Cacciaguida, a scene which is set at the centre of the *Paradiso* and elaborated with a breadth of design equalled only by the scene of Dante's meeting with Beatrice in the *Paradiso terrestre.*

In the early part of canto xiv, Beatrice and Dante have finished questioning the theologians; now, having risen from the sphere of the sun to that of Mars, they see (*vv.* 97–102) souls which appear as lights constellated in the form of a cross which so 'shines forth' Christ that no similitude is adequate for its expressing (*vv.* 103–8). Here the lights break into song and sing so sweetly that the poet is rapt and hears only the words, 'Risurgi e vinci' ('Arise and conquer') (*v.* 125). Then all falls silent.

Of these 'lights'—they are 'warriors of God'—one detaches himself and addresses Dante with especial joy (xv. 13–69). It is his great-great-grandfather, Cacciaguida, who, responding gladly (and lengthily) to Dante's questions, speaks of the decline of Florence from his day to the present—its ancient houses destroyed, decayed, or degenerated, its families divided into Guelf and Ghibelline ('O Buondelmonte!', xvi. 140), its nobility passing, the parvenus splitting into further factions. This brings us to the beginning of canto xvii. He foretells then, in canto xvii, 'per chiare parole e con preciso / latin' ('in clear words and with precise speech') (xvii. 34 f.), the fact, and to some extent the course, of the poet's exile, and finally counsels him, as St Peter will do again ten cantos later (*Par.* XXVII. 64–6), and as Beatrice has done (*Purg.* XXXII. 103–5; XXXIII. 52–7), to show all his vision to the world when he returns: 'Tutta tua vision fa manifesta; / e lascia pur grattar dov'è la rogna!' ('Reveal the whole of your vision and let them scratch where they itch') (XVII. 128 f.). And Dante takes it all to heart —with something of a stoic grace, but also, one gathers, with some inner disquietude, for Beatrice finds it incumbent on her to encourage him (XVIII. 4–6). He is now directed to look once more at the once more singing cross, and sees there the souls of Joshua, Maccabeus, Roland and Charlemagne, before being taken up into the next heaven, the heaven of Jupiter where he will meet the souls of 'the just'.

What first stands out as striking in this synopsis is the immediate subject of conversation between Cacciaguida and Dante, which, instead of what might be expected at this stage in *Paradiso* (a placid heavenly discourse, perhaps, on infidels, or courage, or crusading), turns out to be nothing but Florence, than which, as will appear, no topic could be more un-placid or more terrestrial—it is very much, indeed, a topic for Hell. Nevertheless, from XV. 97 to the end of canto XVII, our attention is turned more or less unremittingly back towards Florence, and particularly towards the decline and fall of Florence:

> Fiorenza dentro dalla cerchia antica
> ond'ella toglie ancora e terza e nona,
> si stava in pace, sobria e pudica

(Florence, within the ancient circle whence she still hears the strokes of nine and twelve, was then in peace, sober and chaste.)

(*Par.* XV. 97–9)

Most of the time, in this canto, it is upon this ancient peace that we are directed to look, and it is set against the backcloth of the heavenly peace, 'questa pace' (*Par.* XV. 148), to which, through the last fourteen cantos, we have already been translated; and it seems now as if the first peace has been a 'figure' of the second, as if, alternatively, the first fruits of heaven used to be relished on earth in Cacciaguida's Florence, where the eternal was 'not yet' and yet 'already'. It is not unlikely that

238

this picture was inspired in part by nostalgia;[1] but nostalgia *per se* is unlikely to have so much space devoted to it as this in the poem which Dante himself calls the *poema sacro*. Dante's concern, as appears from the movement of ideas through these cantos, is very much with the present. For the moment we note how Cacciaguida, 'warrior of God' and crusader as he is, delights chiefly in 'peace', despite having been born under the influence of Mars (XVI. 34–9) and in the city whose patronage Mars was so loth to surrender when it was rededicated to the Baptist (*Par.* XVI. 46 f.; and cf. *Inf.* XIII. 143–50). And it is worth noting too that the description of Florence here at peace is pursued by means of an analogy with Rome and Roman traditions (*Par.* XV. 121–9, cf. XVI. 10 f.). Rome was, for Dante, 'sacred history', and the dependence on, and correspondence with, Rome in Cacciaguida's Florence constitutes a typology based still, fundamentally, on faith in the action of God.[2]

But with the next canto an already hinted change of focus takes place. Against the temporal heaven of Mars is set the degenerate city of Dante's own time, which perseveres less and less (cf. XVI. 11) in the imitation of Rome (or heaven!—'quella Roma onde Cristo è romano', *Purg.* XXXII. 102). Luxury has succeeded simplicity; the Florence where Bellincion Berti could be seen going

> cinto
> di cuoio e d'osso, e venir dallo specchio
> la donna sua sanza il viso dipinto

(wearing leather and (a) bone (clasp), and his wife might be seen coming from the mirror without a painted face)   (*Par.* XV. 112–14)

has now disappeared; in its place there is a new Sardanapalus in every home (XV. 107 f.). This luxuriousness is a stressed alteration and a stressed vice; but if one pays canto XVI its due attention one sees that it contains *exempla* of nearly all the vices—luxury, avarice, gluttony, pride, barratry, hypocrisy,

---

[1] R. Montano's indignation at the idea that nostalgia is the chief factor in the description is well justified. But even his account, which is well worth consulting (see *La Poesia di Dante*, III: 'Il Paradiso', pp. 48–54) fails to see the vital significance of these cantos for the interpretation of the Comedy. M. Apollonio's account is, in this respect only, more satisfactory (*Dante: Storia della Commedia*, II, 827–40).

[2] Cf. *Monarchia*, Book II, esp. chh. 2, 4, 9; and see E. Moore, *Studies in Dante*, 1st ser. pp. 26–8.

violence and fraud: it seems as if all the sins of Hell are here, and certainly we are likely to be reminded of those parallel cantos in the *Inferno* (xv and xvi) where also the conversations turn critically back and back upon Florence.

'Laggiù', in those cantos, Brunetto Latini has spoken of the Florentines as 'quell' ingrato popolo maligno' (*Inf.* xv. 61), and adds to these adjectives a few lines later 'avaro', 'invidioso' and 'superbo' (*v.* 68). If we cannot parallel these words here above, the mood is strikingly similar. Brunetto, in the same passage, mentions that 'old report on earth proclaims them blind' (*Inf.* xvi. 67); here, Cacciaguida compares them to a blind bull (*Par.* xvi. 70). Cacciaguida's distrust of parvenus and new arrivals—

> Sempre la confusion delle persone
> principio fu del mal della cittade!
> (always the mingling of peoples was the root of the city's illness!)
> (*Par.* xvi. 67 f., cf. *vv.* 49 f.)

is equalled, in the *Inferno*, by Dante's own indignant outburst:

> La gente nuova e i subiti guadagni
> orgoglio e dismisura han generato,
> Fiorenza, in te, sì che tu già ten piagni.
> (the newcomers and the quick financial gains have engendered pride and prodigality, Florence, in you, so that already you weep for it)
> (*Inf.* xvi. 73–5, cf. *Par.* xvi. 148–50)

—an outburst which is occasioned by a question of Jacopo Rusticucci's as to the truth of reports that Florence's wonted courtesy and valour have quite left her (cf. again, *Par.* xvi. 10 f.). The impression which we receive from such parallels or agreements as these is that Dante is intent on recapitulating the Florence-as-Hell theme of the *Inferno*[1]—or rather, since what we are being shown is not static, a picture, but dynamic, a history, that he is intent on recapitulating the idea of a descent into Hell in terms of Florence, a Florence of which, if, before, as Cacciaguida recollects her, it were true that she felt herself already tasting the 'first-fruits' of redemption, now, certainly,

---

[1] A theme which there is no need to take, with A. Santi (*L'Ordinamente morale e l'allegoria della D.C.*, esp. pp. 90–7), as being consistently (allegorically) intended by Dante's representation of the city of Dis. But that the motif colours moments in his description of the *Inferno* there can be no doubt: the prophecy of woe in such cases points directly, if implicitly, at Florence.

suffers the first-fruits of judgement: a Florence in which the eternal is, in a now wholly unfortunate sense, 'already'.

Florence is, then, judged, and her history hitherto, plainly, is the very reverse of 'redemptive'. Mars (as tutelary deity) has taken a hand in bringing about her decay (*Par.* XVI. 145–7; cf. *Inf.* XIII. 143–50) and, as appears from some lines in this same canto XVI (*vv.* 58–60), the ecclesiastical degeneracy has taken a hand too, but the substance of these speeches agrees with the reading of Marco Lombardo in the *Purgatorio* (again, the parallel canto, XVI), and despite these natural and supernatural influences the blame for evil lies still with the individual, who has the power within him to decide between right and wrong.

These cantos, as appears from their treatment of Florence in decline, constitute an extremely impressive manifestation of Dante's control of historical issues—a control that is 'modern', one would say, much rather than 'medieval', for even the Marxist view would find something in the social and economic explanation of cultural decline here to which its own concerns should not be unsympathetic.

But Florence's is not the only history told in this episode, and the idea of a descent into the Inferno is told in other terms than the social-historical. The descent separated from conformity with the sacred history co-exists in the area of reference of these cantos with references to a descent which is by no means so separated, and which is part of a larger movement which echoes not the *Inferno* alone, but the whole journey of Dante.

Cacciaguida's own history, first: his life is given in only the barest outline—birth, baptism, marriage and death fighting in the crusades (XV. 130–48). The time of his birth is fixed by a reference in the following canto, which relates the event to the Annunciation, as if the angel's promise to Mary lived on past its fulfilment and related also to Cacciaguida's birth:[1]

> Da quel dì che fu detto 'Ave'
> al parto in che mia madre, ch'è or santa,
> s'alleviò di me ond'era grave . . .

---

[1] Similar refulfilments of biblical prophecies, traditionally having the coming of Christ as their scope, in more recent historical times, are striking in Dante's political letters: see especially *Ep.* V (to the princes and people of Italy), *Ep.* VII (to the Emperor Henry VII).

(From that day on which 'Ave' was said, to the time when my mother, who is now sainted, gave birth to me with whom she was laden . . .)

(XVI. 34–6)

That this language is intentional it is impossible to doubt, especially as the actual event of Cacciaguida's birth is narrated with the same evocation; a momentary ambiguity of syntax and the fall of the stress at the beginning of a new *terzina* having the effect of bringing Cacciaguida and Christ into a relationship whereby the former is seen as re-enacting the birth of the latter:

> A così riposato, a così bello
> viver di cittadini, a così fida
> cittadinanza, a così dolce ostello,
> Maria mi diè, chiamata in alte grida.

(To such a peaceful and fair living for citizens, to such a faithful citizenry, to such a sweet lodging, Mary gave me, called on with loud cries.) (XV. 130–3)

And the point of this is driven home:

> insieme fui cristiano e Cacciaguida.

(I became Christian and Cacciaguida simultaneously.) (v. 135)

Of his death, finally, it is said that he came through martyrdom here, to this peace ('e venni dal martiro a questa pace', XV. 148)—which also is a phrase which shows a resemblance to the redemptive history of Christ, and, though Dante's 'martiro' is not so literal, to that of Cacciaguida's 'seed' (XV. 48), Dante.

For Dante himself is subject to the same kind of linguistic resonances from the first time Cacciaguida addresses him:

> O sanguis meus, o superinfusa
> gratia Dei (XV. 28 f.)

—in terms which refer back to the Virgilian Anchises and his Elysean address to Aeneas,[1] but perhaps intentionally also recall the language of sacramental theology. There is no doubt at all of the allusion a few lines later:

> O fronda mia in che io compiacemmi; (XV. 88)

cf. Matt. 3. 17:

> filius meus. . .in quo mihi complacui.

---

[1] *Aeneid* VI. 684.

Dante's role, like Cacciaguida's, like, too, the *Divine Comedy*'s, is to figure the redemptive history of Christ.

And it is on Dante that canto XVII chiefly concentrates, and on his 'scendere e 'l salir', descent and rising, though it is by different steps now than those which the vision as a whole narrates. Of that narrated movement we are, however, first reminded (XVII. 19–23) and then twice more (*vv.* 112–15, 136 f.); but between the first reference and the other two come the clear and deliberate words of Cacciaguida, 'di Fiorenza partir ti convene' ('you will have to depart from Florence') (*v.* 48), and the forecasting of the course of the poet's exile. The juxtaposition of these passages might by itself imply the relation of the narrated story to the story of Dante's life,[1] but in fact the moving passage which stands at the centre of this speech makes the relation plainer still:

> Tu lascerai ogni cosa diletta
>   più caramente; e questo è quello strale
>   che l'arco dello essilio pria saetta.
> Tu proverai sì come sa di sale
>   lo pane altrui, e come è duro calle
>   lo scendere e 'l salir per l'altrui scale.
> E quel che più ti graverà le spalle
>   sarà la compagnia malvagia e scempia
>   con la qual tu cadrai in questa valle.

(You will leave everything most dearly loved; this is the shaft that the bow of exile will first pierce you with. You will find how salt another's bread tastes, and how hard the path which goes down and ascends another's stairs. And that which will weigh most heavily on your shoulders will be the vicious and ill company in which you will fall down into this vale.) (XVII. 55–63)

'Scale', 'scendere e 'l salir', 'valle', 'cadrai'—such diction in such a place seems to recapitulate the whole poem in the terms of exile. Perhaps, too, it recapitulates in terms of Christ. For certainly other lines bring Dante's exile into the same kind of relationship with Christ's death as had previously been suggested by the reference to Christ's baptism. The first reference to Christ's death comes immediately before the exile is

---

[1] Compare especially the similarity of Cacciaguida's statement to that of Virgil already quoted from *Inf.* I. 91—'a te convien tener altro viaggio'—which was, of course, spoken of the narrated journey.

prophesied ('pria che fosse anciso / l'Agnel di Dio che le peccata tolle', *vv.* 32 f.); then (*vv.* 49–51) we hear that the exile is plotted 'là dove Cristo tutto dì si merca' ('where Christ each day is bought and sold'). It is possible, too, that 'ti graverà le spalle' is intended to remind us of the phrase from the gospels already quoted in XIV. 106: 'chi prende sua croce e segue Cristo'. In such a context of allusion the prophecy of Dante's exile has its place; the connotative references are not, as with Florence, of a descent separated from Saviour and Emperor, but of a dying *with* Christ, and it is for this reason possible for Cacciaguida to speak in remarkably joyful terms of his fore-knowledge of these sufferings:

> sì come viene ad orecchia
> dolce armonia da organo, mi vene
> a vista il tempo che ti s'apparecchia.

(as comes to the ear an organ's sweet harmony, comes into my sight the time that is being made ready for you.) (*vv.* 43–5)

For such 'dying with Christ' implies that 'resurgi e vinci' with which our episode began; or at any rate so it seems for some such relationship between 'bitter' and 'sweet' is implied in the whole conversation.[1] We are not far from the spirit of 'these things have I spoken unto you that in me you might have peace. In the world you shall have tribulation, but be of good cheer, for I have overcome the world' (John 16. 33; cf. Luke 6. 22 f.)—a verse which is again brought to mind by Beatrice's 'muta pensier: pensa ch'i' sono / presso a colui ch'ogni torto disgrava' ('alter your thoughts; remember I am close to him who lifts the burden from every wrong') (XVIII. 5 f.), coming so promptly after Dante's tempering in his thoughts 'col dolce l'acerbo' (*v.* 3).

It is from this paradoxical tension, so strong in this part of the poem, a tension that is here bound up with the fundamental historical and eschatological tension between present and future tribulation and present and future (eternal) comfort,

[1] We are reminded once again, by Cacciaguida's joy here, of the sufferings in purgatory, which are 'pain' and 'solace' at the same time (cf. *Purg.* XXIII. 72), because they, too, share in Christ's death with its attendant joy: 'Chè quella voglia alli alberi ci mena / che menò Cristo lieto a dire "Eli", / quando ne liberò con la sua vena' ('For we are led to the trees' which are instrumental in our suffering 'by that same will which led Christ to say "Eli" joyfully when he redeemed us by his blood') (*Purg.* XXIII. 73–5).

that Dante must have drawn that sense of the urgency of his vision for the world and hence of his prophetic calling which inspired, as well as the *Comedy*, the passionately public-spirited letter to the Italian cardinals, with its 'gratia Dei sum id quod sum'. For the indicative involves an imperative, and the knowledge of what 'is' involves a need to act upon it and testify to it. So that it is fitting that here Dante should receive the most elaborate and explicit command to declare his vision that he is to have, at the moment when he learns the worst and the best about his future.

Finally, let me simply point out that the temporal tension with which the episode ends is but an elaboration of what was implied at its beginning. 'Already' but 'not yet' Hell is fulfilled in Florence. Similarly in the *Inferno* persons are presented as fulfilling eternally their most characteristic and individual earthly existences. And on the personal level, just as in cantos XV and XVI the relations of repetitions between Cacciaguida and Christ, and through these cantos and the following one between Dante and Christ depend on the history of redemption that was once for all fulfilled in the Incarnation being brought to effect and repetition in the poet and his ancestor, so the same movement can be traced in the *Comedy* as a whole, and there again the same tension. Indeed, the typological structure of the whole poem is shown to be this tension's image.

The suggestiveness of these cantos cannot be exhausted by the few statements which I may permit myself. Even their relevance to 'typology' will only be sketched at this point.

In the first place, an issue is raised here upon which my whole treatment of Dante's 'applied typology' ultimately depends. It is an issue whose significance has scarcely ever been appreciated by the commentators, though certain of the facts which imply this significance are in themselves quite well known.[1] In the relationship which the Cacciaguida cantos imply between Dante and Christ an image is taken up which has been suggested much earlier. What Dante *does*, in his journey, Christ *has* done. Dante's descent into Hell, and his release from it, is a typological repetition, a 'subfulfilment' of Christ's. Hence the

---

[1] C. Singleton justly complains of the fact. See his essay 'In exitu Israel de Aegypto', 77th Annual Report of the Dante Society, pp. 9–13.

reference to the time of the journey[1] (and especially that in the *Inferno*, XXI. 112–14), which shows that Dante conceived his journey as having begun with a descent into Hell on Good Friday, 1300, and as releasing him from what, at just the point at which the ascent begins, is called the *tomba* of Hell (*Inf.* XXXIV. 128),[2] on the morning of Easter Day. The first line of the *Comedy*, again, has its relevance in this connection: the age which it indicates Dante to have reached, thirty-five ('il mezzo del cammin di...vita') is taken by Dante, as *Convivio* IV. 23 shows, to be the age at which Christ had died.

Dante's 'fore-having' of death is now shown to be more than a purgation-process. It is a 'dying with Christ', taken to an almost literalistic extreme, which revitalizes a phrase grown perhaps over-familiar. The evocation of Christ's having done before him what he now does in the poem is a confession on Dante's part of his dependence on Christ for what he gains from this journey—the 'other life'. The focus here, certainly, has changed since St Paul used the image of dying and rising with Christ. The stressed history here is no longer that of Christ, but the individual follower's, and the Pauline emphasis on the relationship between the believer and his Lord has, moreover, as we have had occasion to notice, been replaced by a stress laid on the relationship between the individual and the general, between this man, Dante, and Everyman, or rather 'whoever' (as Singleton puts it)[3] will go on this journey of redemption, whose viability Dante by these means claims. Yet despite the novelty (in relation to the Bible) of this latter focus, the typology is all there still as historical correspondence and historical dependence and continuity. The one history which the poem narrates includes the prophecy and the recapitulation of others; it is heavy with the marks of these others; one echoes and enfolds, or is echoed and enfolded by another. This is not simply

---

[1] For the complicated question of the time references and the assumed date of the 'journey', see M. A. Orr, *Dante and the Early Astronomers*, pp. 275–88.

[2] Strictly speaking the 'tomba' referred to here is not Hell itself but the cavern which is reached after climbing past the earth's mid-point. Nevertheless, the imagery here is the imagery of resurrection; resurrection and associated ideas recurring in the first lines of *Purgatorio* with a frequency which can only be deliberate. On this point, again, C. S. Singleton's article 'In exitu Israel de Aegypto' should be consulted, and now also his paper 'The Vistas in Retrospect', *Atti del Congresso Internazionale di Studi Danteschi*, I, 296–301.

[3] *Dante Studies 2: Journey to Beatrice*, p. 5.

a method of allegory or simply a form of it, but the expression of history conforming itself through grace to the pattern of Christ's history, or, to reverse the terms, the expression of an effective history (Christ's) whose effect lies in its repetition in and throughout all history. De Lubac's words, explaining the relationship between the moral and the allegorical senses of medieval exegesis (as he conceives it), are expressive in this connection: 'Sommet de l'histoire, le Fait du Christ supposait l'histoire, et son rayonnement transfigurait l'histoire',[1] and as he affirms later, 'le fait de l'Incarnation est d'autant plus magnifié...qu'on en montre mieux le fruit.'[2]

By these images, references, and evocations—that is, by allusive rather than simply allegorical methods—Dante conveys what he sees as the dialectical relation between his 'history' and the redemptive history of the Gospels (a relation which is genuine theologically, it is worth remarking, since the transformation of Dante's life into conformity with Christ depends on the power of Christ's life and death to transform).

Now again the question of 'the four senses of Scripture' and their application to the poem arises. The answer is necessarily a complex and yet, once apprehended, a clear one. Complex, on account of Dante's own physical presence in a narrative otherwise peopled by shades, a presence which reverses the typological situation connected with 'souls after death'. Dante the character only prefigures the after-life which they already exist in—'sono in prima vita / ancor che l'altra, sì andando, acquisti', *Purg.* VIII. 59 f.); the shades post-figure the physical life he still embodies. Literally 'anagogical', their present state implies and echoes the past moral life (the content of the *sensus moralis*) which, for each of them, it presupposes. Dante's present actions, on the other hand, which, if reported other than literally, would be the concern of the *sensus moralis*, imply and pre-echo his future redemption, his 'anagoge' (so to speak), and are its presupposition, its basis and its deciding. So much, from our earlier discussion, is plain: Dante's journey is a type of his future; the souls' state is the fulfilment of their past.

But now we see also that alongside the relation between the predominantly eschatological or anagogical narrative and the

---

[1] *Exégèse Médiévale*, I, 2, p. 520.   [2] *Ibid.* p. 566 n.

sensus moralis (of this life) upon which our treatment has hitherto chiefly concentrated, a third 'sense', the *sensus allegoricus* or *typicus*, shows its presence: the sense whose subject is Christ. This makes itself felt, above all, in connection with the journey of Dante, for the interpretation of which, it cannot be too strongly stressed, it is the single most fundamental factor. But this 'sense', or this analogy, is not confined to that journey; and it would be a little surprising, indeed, if it were. For, at least from the time in which the last chapters of the *Monarchia* and the letter to the Italian Cardinals were written, Dante had come to think of the life of Christ as the single most binding precedent for the guidance of the life of the Church, and, as I think it is reasonable to deduce, of the Church's members.[1] By the same token, conversion is above all a turning to the following of Christ. The fact is written so large in the *Comedy* that we miss it only by its suffering the proverbial fate of woods lost among trees. So, allusions to an analogy with Christ are also poetically and rhetorically active in passages referring to the conversion and lives of others than Dante—in the narratives of St Francis and of Cacciaguida, for example; and a *sensus typicus* reappears, momentarily but suggestively, in the references to Trajan (*Par.* xx. 46–8, 103–17), who, though in a quite different way from Dante, parallels Dante's experience; tardily, by special providence, he too has followed the footsteps of the suffering Saviour, gaining experience both of the infernal and of the heavenly worlds:

> Ora conosce quanto caro costa
> non seguir Cristo, per l'esperienza
> di questa dolce vita e dell' opposta.

(Now he knows how dearly it costs one to live without following Christ, from his having experience both of this sweet life and its contrary.) (*Par.* xx. 46–8)

Thus the subject-matters of all three 'allegorical senses' mentioned in the *Epistle to Can Grande* reveal their presence in the *Comedy*, and, more important, reveal themselves not as

---

[1] 'Forma autem Ecclesie nihil aliud est quam vita Christi, tam in dictis quam in factis comprehensa: vita enim ipsius ydea fuit et exemplar militantis Ecclesie, presertim pastorum, maxime summi, cuius est pascere agnos et oves' (*Monarchia*, III. 15). Cf. *Letter to the Italian Cardinals*, 4: '...per manifestam orbitam Crucifixi currum Sponse regere'.

presences only, but as active and relevant analogies to the protagonist's journey and to the 'state of souls after death'. It would not be difficult to show how Old Testament events also, which are of course the province of the literal sense of 'In exitu Israel', are occasionally invoked by the poet in order to help state or clarify his theme.[1] We must be content to cite only the two or three most important: *Par.* xxv. 52–7, xxii. 94–6; *Purg.* ii. 46–8.

The last of these passages, which quotes the very verse used in the *Letter* in such a context and such a way as makes plain that the literal situation of the souls agrees precisely with the anagogical sense of the Psalm (cf. also the exposition of the 'fourth sense' in *Convivio* ii. 1), prompts me to record my agreement with Singleton[2] as to the special appropriateness of this verse and its 'senses' as defined in the *Letter* to the main themes of the *Comedy*'s narrative. The *Letter*'s phrases speak for themselves: 'nostra redemptio facta per Christum', 'conversio anime sancte de luctu et miseria peccati ad statum gratie', 'exitus anime sancte ab huius corruptionis servitute ad eterne glorie libertatem'. The fact that the literal sense of the *Comedy*, by being located immediately in moral and anagogical regions, differs from that of the psalm leads C. G. Hardie[3] to protest that the *Letter*'s exposition of these senses is 'simplicist and misleading'. But is there really more difficulty in this than in the case of a biblical text which is literally concerned with these fields? The difference lies only in the stress (unusual in the Middle Ages, but not in the Bible) which Dante lays on the need to notice typological back-references as well as forward ones. But even this is not quite unprecedented, as we shall see.

The literal sense of the *Comedy*, however, now needs to be looked at more closely. Here lies the crux of what Johan Chydenius, in the only work devoted to typology in the

---

[1] Cf. Singleton, 'In exitu Israel de Aegypto'.

[2] *Ibid.* pp. 3 and 13.

[3] 'The Epistle to Cangrande again', *DDJ*, xxxviii (1960), 56–8. How, Hardie asks, 'can the Comedy have an anagogical sense as well, when it is already in the literal sense as anagogical as possible?' The answer which I would give is already suggested by what has been said. The *Comedy* is not, in the literal sense, already as anagogical *as possible*, because Dante's journey, being a 'conversio', is at least primarily 'moral', and is anagogical only indirectly through its relation to the 'altra volta' (*Purg.* ii. 91). Similarly, the poem is not as 'moral' as possible, on account of the anagogical character of the souls' situations.

Commedia calls 'the typological problem in Dante'.[1] The 'history', which the literal sense must have for its subject if we are to call the work 'typological', is clearly not, in the *Commedia*, that of the Exodus. But is there a history, properly so-called, at all? There are several problems which here meet, and require solution. For first, though of course it is possible for the *sensus litteralis*, even in the Bible, to be concerned directly with an eschatological, or moral subject, it was Aquinas' opinion that in such cases it would be wrong (but perhaps by this he only means generally 'pointless') to interpret the text by means of back-references into the past.[2] And along with this goes what may seem a more daunting objection to the labelling of the *Comedy*'s subject and method as 'typology'. For where is the 'history' of its literal sense? Are we committed to calling Dante's passage through eschatological regions 'historical'? Even if we prefer to label the *Comedy* 'allegory of the theologians', rather than 'typology', this problem does not wholly evaporate. For as we have argued (and as may also be inferred from Mailhiot's treatment of the subject)[3] Aquinas' senses of Scripture are virtually senses of history, not of words.

[1] See his work of that name, published in *CHL*, xxv. i.

[2] *Quaest. Quodlib.* vii. vi. 15 ad 5: 'In sacra enim Scriptura praecipue ex prioribus posteriora significantur; et ideo quandoque in sacra Scriptura secundum sensum litteralem dicitur aliquid de priori quod potest spiritualiter de posterioribus exponi, sed non convertitur... Illa vero quae secundum sensum litteralem pertinent ad statum gloriae, nullo alio sensu consueverunt exponi; eo quod ipsa non sunt figura aliorum, sed ab omnibus aliis figurata.'

[3] See M.-D. Mailhiot, 'La Pensée de S. Thomas sur le sens spirituel', *Revue Thomiste*, LIX (1959), 613–63, and cf. J. Chydenius, *op. cit.* pp. 41–4. Chydenius correctly observes that there is 'an obvious confusion between the fact of prefiguration and the fact of inspiration in Aquinas' argument against the possibility of works (even historical works) other than the Bible containing the "spiritual senses"' (*ibid.* p. 43). It *is* an obvious confusion, but so far as I know it has not been pointed out save by Chydenius, and as it has some relevance to the argument about whether Dante could use 'allegory of the theologians' in defiance of St Thomas and most of the other authorities, it is worth drawing attention to it. In the relevant texts in Aquinas, little or nothing of the rationale of the senses of Scripture which he presents really depends, as at first seems to be the case, upon 'Deus est auctor sacrae scripturae'. The real premise is 'in eius potestate est ut res ipsas ad significandum accomodet' (cf. *STh*, I. i. 10 *resp.*): it is God's providence, his authorship in history, which provides the theological basis for the 'typology' which is here outlined. This is something which would be clear at once to a poet or historian who had some reason to dwell upon the work of providence in contemporary history and happened to ask himself whether contemporary history, like the Bible, had meaning and purpose and relation with other periods. We know from the *Monarchia* and the political letters that Dante had asked such questions. The Old

Singleton here is evasive. The literal sense of the narrative is for him to be *taken* as true—it is what the poet requires of us.[1] Elsewhere he calls this literal sense the *itinerarium mentis ad Deum* but this is to limit it—even if, as he suggests, we note carefully that 'mentis' does not mean merely 'of the mind' but 'of the soul' and 'of mind and heart', 'for the heart is surely involved'.[2]

For the fact remains that by this phrase, however much one may include in 'mens', something vital is still excluded. Bonaventure's work, *Itinerarium mentis in Deum*, which is the only one Singleton cites in explaining his use of the phrase, is entirely intellectual and affective in scope, and, if we were to interpret Dante's journey entirely in these terms, it would amount to a substitution of something fundamentally abstract for a journey which the *Comedy* makes concrete. If this were the correct interpretation it would be possible only by means of a quibble to distinguish the journey from 'allegory' in the normal sense of the word—an abstracting and generalizing psychological system would be substituted for life and history.

Chydenius, on the other hand, faces the problem correctly, looking for a historical basis about which the *Comedy* elaborates the shape of its fiction. His idea of 'history', however, seems insufficient: it is hardly to be distinguished from 'reality'. And by concentrating rather on 'things' than upon events in his search for the literal truth upon which the *Comedy* 'builds' (the spatial metaphor is, I think, significant) its typology, he virtually prejudges the issue. For the answer is finally imported

Testament prophecies refer on beyond Christ to the present. Similarly, according to texts quoted by Chydenius (*ibid.* pp. 77–86), the history of the recapture of Jerusalem by the crusaders was seen as a further fulfilment of something first foreshadowed by the conquest of Canaan under Joshua, and itself still prefiguring the possession of the heavenly Jerusalem. One thinks, too, of the Joachites. The idea that history, and even personal history, was a part of typological structure was not hard to come across. On this subject see A. Pézard, *Dante sous la Pluie de Feu*, pp. 372–400, quoting many relevant texts from the theological side; also see J. A. Mazzeo, 'Dante's Conception of Poetic Expression', *Romanic Review*, XLVII (1956), esp. p. 241: and M. Bloomfield, 'Symbolism in Medieval Literature', *Modern Philology*, LVI (1958). But nothing in medieval literature or thought would lead one to believe that the *Letter to Can Grande* was written, as B. Stambler thinks (*Dante's Other World*, p. 62) by Dante in a mood of impatience with the 'fourfold method', and Dante certainly could *not* say '*of course* my poem is subject to the traditional fourfold reading'.

[1] *Dante Studies*, I, 94.   [2] *Ibid.* II, 9, cf. pp. 3–12.

from outside and it is the answer required by the 'figures' whose traditional 'typological' meaning Chydenius studies in the greater part of his book: Jerusalem, Paradise, and the Bride. Scarcely anything, then, but the vision of Beatrice is 'typical', for in that vision, which we may be sufficiently convinced really happened, the three 'figures' meet. To do this argument justice, the conclusion certainly follows, for from the understanding of 'typical' from which Chydenius works, scarcely anything could be 'typical' but this vision. Typology has become static, a platonic conception of earthly and heavenly correspondences, instead of historical. Its relations with the historical actions of God, and man's response to such action, has virtually been broken off. As by Singleton's *itinerariam mentis*, or even more drastically, by this view of the *Comedy* the autobiographical substance of the mythologized journey is limited to the sphere of the 'mens'. Biography or autobiography no doubt includes what Singleton calls the *itinerarium mentis*, and it includes, in Dante's case, doubtless also, something which we would call 'vision'—a vision, in all probability, connected with Beatrice—who is also, by the way, an *imago Christi*.[1] But it includes more than this, for events

---

[1] I do not intend, obviously, to offer a total interpretation of Dante's poem; but it may be a just expectation that if typology's place in the poem is as important as I infer I should give some indication of Beatrice's relation to typology. Briefly, it is plain enough that she, like the other souls, is a 'figura impleta', the fulfilment of her own life on earth; and it is plain too that she is, for Dante, both a means of grace and a medium of revelation. But she is certainly not, to my mind, to be generalized on this basis into an allegorical personification of grace or revelation, or theology, or the Church, or even Christ. She is herself; the medium of all these for Dante, perhaps, but not their only embodiment, even in the *Comedy*. In fact she is, precisely, a typological figure. Substantially my own view agrees with that of L. Spitzer, *art. cit. Romanische Literaturstudien*, pp. 593 f. and esp. p. 593 n., according to whom she is revelation (and, I should add, 'grace') in the *individual* form in which it may come to any Christian. And she is also, as Spitzer again notes, not Christ, but an *imitatrix* or *imago Christi* (here Spitzer modifies, correctly in my view, but at the same time builds upon, the work of C. S. Singleton on Beatrice's presentation in the last cantos of the *Purgatorio*; compare especially 'The Pattern at the Centre' in Singleton's *Dante Studies*, I, 45–59, and ch. v, 'The Advent of Beatrice', in *Dante Studies*, II). 'In this respect', Spitzer writes, she is 'the exact counterpart of the *figurae* (or *praefigurationes*) *Christi*, those historical persons born before Christ who foreshadow him.' Cf. also K. Foster, *God's Tree*, pp. 30 f., and especially: 'The "idea" of Beatrice is essentially relative; the relations going two ways, to Christ on the one hand, to Dante on the other. It would be a dangerous over-statement to say that she is to Dante as Christ is to mankind; for she does not replace Christ, she reflects and transmits him' (p. 30).

which encounter man, and man's action in response to events, are in the last resort perhaps what finally constitute 'life'. It is in this sense that Malagoli's phrase, 'una grande sinfonia autobiografica',[1] is a better description of the *Comedy*'s meaning for Dante than either of the attempts at more strict definition which are offered by Singleton and Chydenius.

For if this journey is in fact 'mythologized', it retains still an autobiographical substance with which it never loses contact, and which the 'mythology' serves to interpret. The Caccia-guida cantos, as we have seen, make this certain when they draw a parallel between the narrated journey and the exile. Virgil's words in *Inferno* x suggest the same interpretation: 'da lei (Beatrice) saprai di tua vita il viaggio' ('from her you will learn the journey of your life'). The *viaggio* is a *vita*; the *vita* is a *viaggio*. The journey is a life lived, not just thought of.

Yet clearly something has happened to this 'autobiography' in its transposition into the 'myth' of the poem. Just what has happened, and how, despite its happening, it may remain 'autobiography', is not, however, easy for the modern reader to see—at least, not immediately.

But the early 'Lives' of St Francis provide a helpful perspec-tive. There, undeniably, a historical basis exists for the most part behind each unit of narrative. Whatever may happen in detail, and even whatever may happen in the ordering of the whole, there is always a substratum of actual events and actual human 'living' which the formal or didactic considerations of the writers may sometimes disguise, but not generally hide. Yet these formal and didactic considerations do not normally be-come imposed on the narrative merely because of the aesthetic and didactic character of the author. Very often one senses the aptness of form to content. The saint's life demands a special kind of treatment in order to interpret its effect, and not just mirror its action and its chronology. And it is specially interest-ing in our context that one of the features of St Francis's life which produced such 'stylization', from the earliest 'lives' of the saint increasingly down to the work of Fra Bartolomeo of Pisa at the end of the fourteenth century, was that which the title of Fra Bartolomeo's work precisely expresses: *De*

---

[1] L. Malagoli, *Saggio sulla Divina Commedia*, p. 128. In this connection, see also C. Hardie, 'Dante's Autobiography', in *The Listener*, 7 Feb. 1963.

Conformitate Vitae B. Francisci ad Vitam Domini Jesu.[1] In this latter work—as also in paintings of up to seventy years earlier[2]—the fundamentally theological point in the *imitatio Christi* is brought out by setting event opposite event from the life of Saviour and servant. In the earlier 'Lives' of St Francis, stylization of incident and evocative phrase together do the same work.

If, therefore, as I suggest, the *Commedia*, too, employs stylization and language for the same purpose, there is no more need to assume that this involves a departure from history, than there is in the case of St Francis. 'Nam quis sani intellectus crederet ipsum ita descendisse', writes Pietro, 'et talia vidisse, nisi cum distinctione dictorum modorum loquendi ad figuram?' And he goes on immediately to make the point which justifies the historicality of the *Commedia*'s literal sense which its typological method requires, with a sure instinct extending Aquinas' principle for dealing with metaphors in Scripture: 'Nam non est ipse litteralis sensus ipsa figura, sed id quod est figuratum.'[3] It is Dante's life which is the literal sense, not the figurative journey into eternity. The figuring, the stylizing, of Dante's life, on this view, remains vital, a necessary means of expressing something he felt about it. It is done for the sake of a point of theology, or, better, for the sake of a claim made by means of typology. But the figuring, as such, has no independent existence: it exists not to replace Dante's personal history, but to interpret it. Without the historical basis, the myth would be meaningless; with it, Dante's claim can be made: this, Dante may say, is my own self-conforming with Christ; Christ's truth has become mine, and I believe that my truth points to his.

And if the St Francis legends, or these features in them, help us to see also—as surely they do—the value of the typological back-reference to a history prior to that directly narrated, there is no reason why we should not if we wish to look further back still for assistance in overcoming St Thomas's doubts on this subject[4]—to the features of the New Testament narratives to which we have drawn attention in the previous chapter. There

---

[1] Ed. Quaracchi, 2 vols. 1906–12.

[2] See G. Kaftal, *St Francis in Italian Painting*, pp. 29 f.

[3] *Petri Allegherii Commentarium*, p. 8. Cf. Aquinas, *STh*, I. i. 10 ad. 3; and cf. also M. Barbi's use of the latter citation in *Problemi fondamentali per un nuovo commento della 'Divina Commedia'*, pp. 117–22.

[4] See above, p. 250 and n.

too, in St Paul's journey to Jerusalem, a self-conforming with the life of Christ is presented by indirect means, in phraseology and echo.[1] There too, in the Gospel stories of, above all, the temptation of Jesus, a back-reference exists for the sake of a claim that is existential, both gospel and challenge: the claim that Christ fulfils history. In these narratives too the typology without which such a claim could not be (understandably) presented has attention drawn to it by means of a stylization, by an acted, or at any rate by a biographical, parable recalling past history, by a kind of 'prophetic symbolism'.[2]

And further back still, as this phrase reminds us, the prophets in the Old Testament use typology, not to authenticate their message, but in order to make it intelligible to the listener's pre-understanding of its subject-matter, for the sake, ultimately, of the message's being heard rightly.

Dante's use of typology is akin, therefore, at least in these respects, to the Bible's. The narrative setting is original; and the work itself presupposes a different context in *Heilsgeschichte*, a difference brought about by the passage of time and the flux of historical process. But even the differences in cosmology, anthropology, ontology—all the factors, in short, which go to make up a world-view—do not prevent (and still less does the difference of context) the *Divina Commedia*'s sharing a substantially similar view of existence to that of the Bible. It is this 'view of existence', something distinguishable, it would seem therefore, from a world-view, its feeling for man's historicality, its sense of the immanent and continuous workings of providence, which permits the *Commedia*'s typology to come as close as it does, and uniquely close, to the Bible's. For here, as we have suggested, typology is not catechetic, hardly ever merely didactic, but prophetic, existential, even in its own way 'kerygmatic' in so far as it points to Christ, the fulfilment of history, the perfector and judge of man.

Was Dante, strictly, a prophet, as he is often, at least loosely, called? One thing our discussion permits us to add to the debate.[3] Viewed in the aspect of 'prophecy' the whole *Comedy*

[1] See pp. 150–2 above.   [2] See pp. 105–7, 110 f. above.
[3] So far Bruno Nardi's discussion in *Dante e la Cultura Medievale*, pp. 258–334, is probably still the best introduction to the question. J. Lindblom, who is not by any means prejudiced against the idea of a medieval 'prophet', does not bring

may be seen as, formally, a 'vocation-vision' akin in its nature to those of the Old Testament prophets but here uniquely articulated to contain, itself, the whole sum of the message. And its message is that of the prophets: 'weal' and 'woe', God's grace and judgement,[1] the call to repentance,[2] the call to the new existence[3] which, by God's grace, is made possible.

Dante into his treatment of the nature of prophecy (*Prophecy in Ancient Israel*, see esp. pp. 1–46) but his work provides nevertheless the basis for the discussion of such claims.

[1] Cf. ch. 13.   [2] Cf. ch. 14.   [3] Cf. the account in this chapter.

CONCLUSION

Despite any possible implications to the contrary, the content and proportions of the three parts of this study are not intended to represent the view that the *Divine Comedy* of Dante should or could constitute a third 'Testament', such as that to which the Abbot Joachim of Fiore had looked forward. But these proportions did imply, and now the contents have I hope confirmed, first, that the *Divine Comedy*'s use and understanding of typology has a kind of continuity, if not identity, with the use and understanding of typology in the Bible and, secondly, that in certain respects the *Comedy* may contribute to the fuller comprehension of the dialectics of typology in its biblical and Christian context.

The first, and perhaps the main, contribution of this kind is its depiction, in typological narrative, of the orientation of human existence towards the future, the figural and linear connection between a man's life and his death. The New Testament authenticates this development. It does not actualize it. And even if we can no longer hold to the medieval, or the early Christian, eschatological picture, Dante's depiction must, I think, be allowed to have the power of conveying a sense of existential relevance through this picture, which it is not so easy to shrug off, though, finally, we may gainsay it.

And the *Comedy* also actualizes something which, though in this case it is actualized already in the Bible, is, in the Bible, actualized only quite sketchily: that is, the possibility of a typological narrative which exposes with an ideal clarity the Christian's self-conforming with God's once-for-all past act in Christ. The poem casts a new light of its own, through its presentation of these two typological relations, between present and past and between present and future, upon the question of the Christian's 'subfulfilment' of both history and eschatology (a question which is at the very heart of Christian ethics in the New Testament, and which cannot well be excluded from the subject-matter of typology—on the grounds that it is ethics, or on any other grounds—for, arguably, until it is related to typology it will neither have the intellectual attention it deserves nor reach its right place in the Christian witness). For Dante's journey, representing an anticipation, a foreshadowing, of his death and his salvation, and representing also an echo and an implementing of Christ's giving himself up to man, and hence to death, provides hereby the very image of 'conversion' and 'repentance' as the New Testament conceives them. The whole work 'concerns itself with and sets', as I have already quoted Kierkegaard as saying, 'the "problem"...how may I become a Christian?' And perhaps, as I have argued, the *Commedia* answers it, for Dante, also. Nothing, than this subject-matter, could be closer to the subject of typology in the Bible. The action which is fundamental to both is the action of a 'change of conformities', of the entering upon a 'new' existence which is offered, continuously ('steadfastly'), by the 'wonder-working' God of the Bible.

Thus the *Divine Comedy* corroborates the application of the concept of typology to individual life, and it corroborates the dialectics of its 'application'. And I have also tried to show how here—we may say again, 'as in the Bible'—the message of typology is presented not only as Dante's 'gospel', the gospel 'contemporized' for him, but to us too, as existentially, as directly, and as immediately, as it can be.

Together these three or four points are enough, in my view, to endorse the statement that the nature and scope of biblical typology have in the *Comedy* been rediscovered. Stated thus baldly, this is amazing; but once the fact is established we can see a little deeper into the springs of the *Comedy*'s power and into the rationale of its address, its challenge, to the reader. Yet even at this stage it is only possible to guess at the real explanation for the 'rediscovery' to which the poem bears witness. In its literary-historical context there is no written analogue close enough, not even in the 'saints' lives', for us to be sure that it was from there that the rediscovery stemmed. The nearest source of the typological understanding and method revealed in Dante's poem is probably to be found in the scholastic doctrine of the four senses of Scripture, which has at any rate an implicitly typological structure and a supporting theology linearly descended (though through sometimes unfortunate marriages) from the Bible itself. But if Dante's use of typology as this possible source and the *Letter to Can Grande* suggest, is to be called 'allegory', and 'allegory of the theologians', it is at the same time deeply distinguished from, as well as intimately related to, even *this* kind of 'allegory' as we find it elsewhere. For elsewhere it is the allegory of exegesis, not literature, and bound up too often, too closely, with hellenistic thought-forms and practices. Only in the writing of history—and however stylized and mythologized for the sake of being, from Dante's point of view, understood rightly, the *Comedy* (and some saints' lives) may be, it is history still, fundamentally—could the theologians' 'allegory' be expected to free itself altogether from the hellenistic exegetical concomitants which were at that time, in exegesis, conventional. This is what has happened in the *Comedy*, and so radically does the event distinguish the poem from the exegetical doctrine, that even if, as I believe, the poem's typological structure is expressible in terms of the doctrine, in the last resort the poem breaks out from the doctrine's categories. In this situation it would be better to reserve the term 'allegory' for those features which the work shares with the *Romance of the Rose*, Brunetto's *Tesoretto*, and the *Faerie Queene*; for to call history 'allegory' (even history of the sort we have in the *Comedy*'s basic narrative thread, the descent and rising of its author) cannot but confuse; and when we speak of medieval exegesis of the Bible as 'allegorical' today we are surely referring mainly, even entirely, to its hellenistic methods, methods which the *Comedy* does not share, and to which it can no longer (any more than can the Bible) be subjected. Its own methods and uses are those of the Bible, and especially of the Gospels and Acts. The methods are similarly indirect, in one way or another allusive, but at the same time, at least in their author's belief, dialectically founded; and the uses are still the same as the Bible's, to challenge 'history' with '*a* history' which bears upon it, to present a told history to the concerned mind of the hearer, and to reveal how it may be 'applied' in the hearer's own life. And if the methods and uses are similar, surely the doctrine, the rationale, the dialectic, the theology, is similar too: for on theological dialectic, as I have shown, the uses and methods are founded.

Thus, in conclusion, it may be well to express with such mathematical clarity as is possible what I take that fundamental doctrine to be. We return, then, to the Christian view of Christ's history as the *absolute* norm of divine action and human existence. In that history, God's action and man's answering faith or obduracy come, in the Christian view, to fulfilment. Conformity, or the lack of it, to God's act in Christ is the absolute norm for God's judgement: on the issue of which depends 'eternal life', 'weal' or 'woe'. So, in degree, with regard to Christ's 'representatives', God's acts in the past or the present, their 'word' through prophet or Christian, the 'types', whether pre- or post-figurative, of Christ: they are 'relative' norms on account of their witness to Christ.

But is mathematical clarity, even were it possible, desirable in this region, or apt? The philosophical structures themselves must not be taken for typology's subject. Its subject is surely the history which such structures help to conceptualize and so present for decision. But however adequately these structures represent the Bible's own understanding of history they cannot replace the history itself. The more graphic they are—and they may be graphic:

$$\text{Christ} \left\langle {\text{Israel} \atop \text{Yahweh}} \right. ; \ \text{Christ} \left\langle {\text{past} \atop \text{future}} \right. ;$$

$$\text{Christ's history} \left\langle {\text{salvation} \atop \text{judgement}} \right. ; \ \text{Christ's history} \left\langle {\text{faith} \atop \text{obduracy}} \right. ;$$

—the further do they leave history for a realm of abstraction and speculation. To their very own issues, which are those of our unequatable life and our complex history, these structures can do little justice. Through such media the issues themselves can hardly be heard by the ear of human concern. For this reason are the issues which such structures conceptualize presented—and this too I have throughout tried to show—by the Bible and Dante not as structures at all but as applied and embodied typology, not as philosophical but as existential possibilities. And thus it is ultimately not with regard to the philosophical feasibility of these or any such structures, but with regard to the existential possibility of the critical history for us, as and when it is presented to us existentially, that we are called upon to decide.

So, to summarize, it would always be hard to deny that events have, in some sense, an after-life. But with these events, the crucial events of the biblical history, I have tried to show that we can go further; and to be true to the writers' intention, we must. For at least these events, through typology, demand an afterlife that is their echo, not just their effect, and one which takes place not only broadly, in history, but is also specific, in us. We are called to be part of their after-life.

BIBLIOGRAPHY

MODERN BOOKS AND ARTICLES CITED IN THE TEXT

Albright, W. F. *From Stone Age to Christianity* (2nd edn. Anchor Books; New York, 1957).

Amsler, S. *L'Ancien Testament dans l'Église* (Neuchâtel, 1960).

Anderson, B. W. 'Exodus Typology in Second Isaiah', *Israel's Prophetic Heritage*, ed. B. W. Anderson and W. Harrelson (London, 1962).

—— (ed.). *The Old Testament and Christian Faith* (London, 1964).

Anderson, B. W. and W. Harrelson (eds.). *Israel's Prophetic Heritage* (J. Muilenburg *Festschrift*; London, 1962).

Apollonio, M. *Dante: Storia della Commedia* (2nd edn. 2 vols., Milan, 1954).

Auerbach, E. *Mimesis*, ET (Anchor Books; New York, 1957).

—— *Dante: Poet of the Secular World*, ET (Chicago, 1961).

—— 'Figura', *Scenes from the Drama of European Literature*, ET (Meridian Books; New York, 1959).

—— 'Dante's Addresses to the Reader', *Romance Philology*, VII (1953–4).

Barbi, M. *Problemi fondamentali per un nuovo Commento della 'Divina Commedia'* (Florence, 1956).

Barr, J. *The Semantics of Biblical Language* (Oxford, 1961).

—— *Biblical Words for Time* (London, 1962).

—— 'The Meaning of Mythology in relation to the Old Testament', *VT*, IX (1959).

Barrett, C. K. *A Commentary on the Epistle to the Romans* (London, 1957).

—— *From First Adam to Last* (London, 1962).

—— 'The Bible in the New Testament period', *The Church's Use of the Bible*, ed. D. E. Nineham (London, 1963).

Bartsch, H. W. (ed.). *Kerygma and Myth*, ET (2 vols. London, 1953 and 1962).

Baumgärtel, F. *Verheissung* (Munich, 1952).

—— 'Das alttestamentliche Geschehen als "heilsgeschichtliches" Geschehen', *Geschichte und Altes Testament* (A. Alt *Festschrift*) Beitr. z. histor. Theol., XVI (1953).

—— 'Das hermeneutische Problem des Alten Testaments', *TLZ* (1954).

Bersani, S. *Dottrine, Allegorie, Simboli, della Divina Commedia* (Piacenza and Rome, 1931).

Black, M. *An Aramaic Approach to the Gospels and Acts* (2nd edn. Oxford, 1954).
—— *The Scrolls and Christian Origins* (London, 1961).
—— 'Servant of the Lord and Son of Man', *SJT*, VI (1953).
Bloomfield, M. W. 'Symbolism in Medieval Literature', *Modern Philology*, VI (1958).
Boman, T. *Hebrew Thought compared with Greek*, ET (London, 1960).
Bonsirven, J. *Le Judaisme Palestinienne au temps de Jésus-Christ* (2 vols. Paris 1934 and 1935).
—— *Exégèse Rabbinique et Exégèse Paulinienne* (Paris, 1938).
—— 'Exégèse allégorique chez les Rabbis Tannaites', *RechSR*, XXIII (1933) and XXIV (1934).
Bornkamm, G. *Jesus of Nazereth*, ET (London, 1960).
—— 'Demythologizing the New Testament Message', *Kerygma and History*, ed. C. E. Braaten and R. A. Harrisville (New York, 1962).
Bornkamm, G. *et al. Tradition and Interpretation in Matthew*, ET (London, 1963).
Braaten, C. E. and R. A. Harrisville (ed.). *Kerygma and History* (New York, 1962).
Brandeis, I. *The Ladder of Vision* (London, 1960).
Bright, J. *Early Israel in recent History Writing* (London, 1956).
—— *History of Israel* (London, 1960).
Bruce, F. F. *Biblical Exegesis in the Qumran Texts* (London, 1959).
—— (ed.). *Promise and Fulfilment* (Essays presented to S. H. Hooke) (Edinburgh, 1963).
Bultmann, R. *Theology of the New Testament*, ET (2 vols. London, 1952 and 1955).
—— *Jesus Christ and Mythology* (London, 1953).
—— *Essays, Philosophical and Theological*, ET (London, 1955).
—— *History and Eschatology* (Gifford Lectures) (Edinburgh, 1957).
—— *Existence and Faith*, ET (London, 1961).
—— 'Ursprung und Sinn der Typologie als hermeneutischer Methode', *TLZ* (1950).
—— 'The Significance of the Old Testament for the Christian Faith', *The Old Testament and Christian Faith*, ed. B. W. Anderson (London, 1964).
Burrows, M. *The Dead Sea Scrolls* (London, 1956).
—— *More Light on the Dead Sea Scrolls* (London, 1958).
Carli, P. *Saggi Danteschi* (Florence, 1954).
Chenu, M.-D. *Introduction à l'Étude de S. Thomas d'Aquin* (Paris, 1950).
—— *La Théologie au XIIe siècle* (Paris, 1957).

Childs, B. S. *Myth and Reality in the Old Testament* (London, 1960).
—— *Memory and Tradition in Israel* (London, 1962).
Chydenius, J. 'The Typological Problem in Dante', *CHL*, xxv, i (Helsingfors, 1958).
—— 'The Theory of Mediaeval Symbolism', *CHL*, xxviii, ii (Helsingfors, 1961).
Clements, R. E. *Prophecy and Covenant* (London, 1965).
Cooke, G. A. 'The Israelite King as Son of God', *ZAW*, xxxii (1961).
Croce, B. *La Poesia di Dante* (2nd edn. Bari, 1921).
Cullmann, O. *Christ and Time*, ET (revised edn. London, 1962).
—— *The Christology of the New Testament* (London, 1959).
Curato, B. *Il Canto di Francesca e i suoi Interpreti* (Cremona, 196?).
Curtius, E. R. *European Literature and the Latin Middle Ages*, ET (New York, 1953).
Dahl, N. A. 'The Johannine Church and History', *Current Issues in New Testament Interpretation*, ed. W. Klassen and G. F. Snyder (London, 1962).
Daniélou, J. *Origen*, ET (London, 1955).
—— *Théologie du Judéo-Christianisme* (Paris, 1958).
—— *From Shadows to Reality*, ET (London, 1960).
—— *Message Évangélique et Culture Hellénistique* (Paris, 1961).
—— 'The Fathers and the Scriptures', *Theology*, lvii (1954).
Daube, D. *The New Testament and Rabbinic Judaism* (London, 1956).
—— *The Exodus Pattern in the Bible* (London, 1963).
Davies, J. G. *The Early Christian Church* (London, 1965).
Davies, W. D. *Paul and Rabbinic Judaism* (London, 1948).
—— *Torah in the Messianic Age and/or Age to Come* (Philadelphia, 1952).
—— *The Setting of the Sermon on the Mount* (Cambridge, 1964).
Delling, G. 'Πληρόω', *TWNT*, vii.
De Sanctis, F. *Lezioni e Saggi su Dante* (Turin, 1955).
—— *De Sanctis on Dante*, Essays ed. and trans. by J. Rossi and A. Galpin (Madison, 1957).
De Sanctis, G. B. *L'Unità Poetica della Divina Commedia* (Città di Castello, 1943).
Diem, H. *Dogmatics* (Edinburgh and London, 1959).
Dodd, C. H. *According to the Scriptures* (London, 1952).
—— *New Testament Essays* (Manchester, 1953).
—— *The Apostolic Preaching and its Development* (London, 1936).
—— *Gospel and Law* (Cambridge, 1957).
D'Ovidio, F. *Studii sulla Divina Commedia* (Palermo, 1901).
Dunbar, H. F. *Symbolism in Medieval Thought* (Yale, 1929).

Edgar, S. L. 'Respect for Context in Quotations from the Old Testament', *SNTS*, IX (1962).
Eichrodt, W. *Man in the Old Testament*, ET (London, 1951).
—— *Theology of the Old Testament*, vol. I, ET (London, 1961).
—— *Theologie des Alten Testaments*, vols. II and III (4th ed. Stuttgart, 1961).
—— 'Heilserfahrung und Zeitverständnis im Alten Testament', *TZ*, XII (1956).
—— 'In the Beginning', *Israel's Prophetic Heritage* (J. Muilenburg *Festschrift*; London, 1962).
Eliade, M. *The Myth of the Eternal Return* (London, 1955).
—— *Patterns in Comparative Religion* (London, 1958).
Ellis, E. E. *Paul's Use of the Old Testament* (Edinburgh, 1957).
Engnell, I. *Studies in Divine Kingship in the Ancient Near East* (Uppsala, 1943).
Epstein, I. *Judaism* (London, 1960).
Farrer, A. *A Study in St Mark* (Westminster, 1951).
—— *St Matthew and St Mark* (Westminster, 1954).
—— 'Typology', *ExpT*, LXVII (1956).
Farrer, A. *et al.* *The Communication of the Gospel in New Testament Times* (London, 1961).
Filson, F. V. *The New Testament against its Environment* (London, 1950).
Fitzmyer, J. A. 'The Use of Explicit Old Testament Quotations in the Qumran Literature and in the New Testament', *SNTS*, VII (1961).
Fosbroke, H. E. W. 'The Prophetic Literature', *IB*, I.
Foscolo, U. *Discorso sul testo della Commedia di Dante*, in *Opere*, III (Florence, Le Monnier).
Foster, K. *God's Tree* (London, 1957).
Frankfort, H. *Ancient Egyptian Religion* (New York, 1949).
Frankfort, H. *et al.* *Before Philosophy* (Pelican; London, 1949).
Frör, K. *Biblische Hermeneutik* (Munich, 1961).
Fuchs, E. *Hermeneutik* (Bad Canstatt, 1954).
—— *Zur Frage nach dem historischen Jesus* (Tübingen, 1960).
Fuller, R. H. *The Mission and Achievement of Jesus* (London, 1954).
—— *The New Testament in Current Study* (London, 1963).
Gaster, T. H. *The Scriptures of the Dead Sea Sect* (London, 1957).
Gilmore, A. A. 'Augustine and the Critical Method', *HTR*, XXXIX (1946).
Gilson, E. *Dante the Philosopher*, ET (London, 1948).
—— 'Poésie et Théologie dans la Divine Comédie', *Atti del Congresso Internazionale di Studi Danteschi*, vol. I (Florence, 1965).

Glasson, T. F. *Moses in the Fourth Gospel* (London, 1963).

Goulder, M. D. *Type and History in Acts* (London, 1964).

Grant, R. M. *The Bible in the Church* (New York, 1948).

—— *The Letter and the Spirit* (London, 1957).

—— 'History of the Interpretation of the Bible, I. Ancient Period', *IB*, I.

Green, R. H. 'Dante's Allegory of the Poets and the Medieval Theory of Poetic Fiction', *Comparative Literature*, IX (1957).

Gribomont, J. 'Le Lien des deux Testaments selon S. Thomas d'Aquin', *Ephemerides Theologicae Lovanienses* (1946).

Guardini, R. 'Leib und Leiblichkeit in Dantes Göttlicher Komödie', *Anteile* (M. Heidegger *Festschrift*; Frankfurt a. M., 1950).

Gutbrod, W. (with H. Kleinknecht). 'Law', *BKW*, XI (London, 1962).

Hanson, R. P. C. *Allegory and Event* (London, 1959).

—— 'Studies in Texts, Acts vi. 13 f.', *Theology*, L (1947).

Hardie, C. (Review of D. Sayers, *Further Papers on Dante*), *Italian Studies*, XIII (1958).

—— 'The Epistle to Can Grande again', *DDJ*, XXXVIII (1960).

—— 'Dante's Autobiography', *The Listener*, 7 Feb. 1963.

Harris, R. *Testimonies* (2 vols. Cambridge, 1916 and 1920).

Hempel, J. *Glaube, Mythos und Geschichte im Alten Testament* (Berlin, 1954).

—— (ed.). *Werden und Wesen des Alten Testaments* (Berlin, 1936).

Hebert, A. G. *The Throne of David* (London, 1941).

—— *The Authority of the Old Testament* (London, 1947).

Hesse, F. 'Zur Frage der Wertung und der Geltung alttestamentlicher Texte', *Probleme alttestamentlicher Hermeneutik*, ed. C. Westermann (Munich, 1960).

Hooke, S. H. *Alpha and Omega* (Welwyn, 1961).

Hooker, M. *Jesus and the Servant* (London, 1959).

Hoskyns, E. (with N. Davey). *The Riddle of the New Testament* (London, 1930).

Huizinga, J. *The Waning of the Middle Ages* (Pelican; London, 1955).

Jacob, E. *Theology of the Old Testament*, ET (London, 1958).

James, E. O. *Myth and Ritual in the Ancient Near East* (London, 1958).

Jeremias, J. (with W. Zimmerli). *The Servant of God* (London, 1957).

Kaftal, G. *St Francis in Italian Painting* (London, 1950).

Klassen, W. and Snyder, G. F. (eds.). *Current Issues in New Testament Interpretation* (London, 1962).

Knox, W. L. *St Paul and the Church of the Gentiles* (Cambridge, 1939).

Kohler, L. *Hebrew Man*, ET (London, 1956).

Kummel, W. G. *Promise and Fulfilment*, ET (London, 1957).

Kuschke, A. 'Die Menschenwege und der Weg Gottes im Alten Testament', *ST*, v (1952).

Lampe, G. W. H. 'Hermeneutics and Typology', *London Quarterly and Holborn Review*, Jan. 1965, p. 23.

Lampe, G. W. H. (with K. J. Woollcombe). *Essays on Typology* (London, 1957).

Lightfoot, R. H. *Commentary on St John's Gospel* (paperback; Oxford, 1960).

Lindars, B. *New Testament Apologetic* (London, 1961).

—— 'The Image of Moses in the Synoptic Gospels', *Theology* (1955).

Lindblom, J. *Prophecy in Ancient Israel* (Oxford, 1962).

Löwith, K. *Meaning in History* (Chicago, 1949).

Lubac, H. de. *Histoire et Esprit* (Paris, 1950).

—— *Exégèse Médiévale, Les Quatre Sens de l'Ecriture* (2 parts in 4 vols. Paris, 1959–64).

—— 'Sur un vieux distique: la doctrine du "quadruple sens"', *Mélanges Cavallera* (1948).

Lundberg, P. *La Typologie Baptismale dans l'ancien Église* (Leipzig and Uppsala, 1942).

McCasland, S. V. 'Matthew twists the Scriptures', *JBL*, LXXX (1961).

McIntyre, J. *The Christian Doctrine of History* (Edinburgh, 1957).

McKenzie, J. L. 'The Significance of the Old Testament for Christian Faith in Roman Catholicism', *The Old Testament and Christian Faith*, ed. B. W. Anderson (London, 1964).

McNally, H. *The Bible in the Early Middle Ages* (Westminster, Maryland, 1959).

Mailhiot, M.-D. 'La Pensée de St. Thomas sur le sens spirituel', *Revue Thomiste*, LIX (1959).

Malagoli, L. *Saggio sulla Divina Commedia* (Florence, 1962).

Malinowski, B. *Myth in Primitive Psychology* (London, 1921).

Manson, T. W. *Studies in the Gospels and Epistles* (Manchester, 1962).

—— *The Teaching of Jesus* (2nd edn. paperback; Cambridge, 1963).

—— 'The Argument from Prophecy', *JTS*, XLVI, 1945.

Manson, W. *Jesus the Messiah* (London, 1943).

—— (ed.). *Eschatology* (*SJT* Occasional Papers 2, Edinburgh, 1953).

Markus, R. A. 'Presuppositions of the Typological Approach to Scripture', *CQR*, CLVIII.

Marsh, J. *The Fulness of Time* (London, 1952).

Marzot, G. *Il Linguaggio Biblico nella Divina Commedia* (Pisa, 1956).

Mauser, U. *Christ in the Wilderness* (London, 1963).

Mazzeo, J. A. 'Dante's Conception of Poetic Expression', *Romantic Review*, XLVII (1956).

—— 'Dante and the Pauline Modes of Vision', *HTR*, L (1957).

Mazzoni, F. 'L'Epistola a Cangrande', *Rendiconti della Accademia dei Lincei* (Classe di Scienze Morali e Storiche), VIII, x (1955), 157–98.

—— 'Per L'Epistola a Cangrande', *Studi in onore di Angelo Monteverdi*, II, 498–516 (Modena, 1959).

Meersseman, G. G. 'Dante come teologo', *Atti del Congresso Internazionale di Studi Danteschi* (Florence, 1965), I. 177–95.

Michalson, C. 'Bultmann against Marcion', *The Old Testament and Christian Faith*, ed. B. W. Anderson (London, 1964).

Milburn, R. L. P. *Early Christian Interpretations of History* (London, 1954).

Milik, J. T. *Ten Years of Discovery in the Wilderness of Judaea*, ET (London, 1959).

Momigliano, A. (ed.). *La Divina Commedia, Commento di Attilio Momigliano* (3 vols. Florence, 1945).

Montanari, F. *L'Esperienza Poetica di Dante* (Florence, 1959).

Montano, R. *L'Estetica Medievale* (Naples, 1952).

—— *Suggerimenti per una Lettura di Dante* (Naples, 1956).

—— *La Poesia di Dante* (3 vols. Naples, 1958–9).

—— *Storia della Poesia di Dante*, vol. I (Naples, 1962).

Moore, E. *Studies in Dante* (4 vols. London, 1896–1917).

Morgan, R. 'Fulfilment in the Fourth Gospel, the Old Testament Foundations', *Interpretation* (1957).

Morris, L. *The Biblical Doctrine of Judgment* (London, 1960).

Moule, C. F. D. *The Birth of the New Testament* (London, 1962).

—— 'From Defendant to Judge—and Deliverer', *SNTS*, III (1952).

—— '"Fulness" and "Fill" in the New Testament', *SJT*, IV (1951).

—— 'Fulfil', *Interpreter's Dictionary of the Bible* (Nashville and New York, 1962).

Mowinckel, S. *He That Cometh*, ET (Oxford, 1956).

—— *The Psalms in Israel's Worship* (2 vols. Oxford, 1963).

Muilenburg, J. *The Way of Israel* (London, 1961).

—— 'Preface to Hermeneutics', *JBL*, LXXVII (1958).

—— (*Festschrift*). *Israel's Prophetic Heritage* (London, 1962).

Nardi, B. *Dante e la Cultura Medievale* (Bari, 1942).

—— *Nel Mondo di Dante* (Rome, 1944).

—— 'Il Punto sull'Epistola a Cangrande', *Lectura Dantis Scaligera* (Florence, 1960).

Neill, S. *The Interpretation of the New Testament, 1861–1961* (London, 1964).

Nineham, D. E. (ed.). *Studies in the Gospels* (Oxford, 1955).

—— (ed.). *The Church's Use of the Bible, Past and Present* (London, 1963).

North, C. R. *The Old Testament Interpretation of History* (London, 1946).
—— *The Suffering Servant in Deutero-Isaiah* (2nd edn. London, 1956).
Noth, M. *History of Israel*, ET (London, 1958).
—— 'Die Vergegenwärtigung des Alten Testaments in der Verkündigung', *EvTh*, XII (1952–3).
Orr, M. A. *Dante and the Early Astronomers* (2nd edn. London, 1956).
Osgood, C. F. *Poetry as a Means of Grace* (Princeton, 1941).
Ostborn, G. *Tora in the Old Testament* (Lund, 1945).
Ostlender, H. 'Die Zielsetzung der "Divina Commedia"', *Studia Mediaevalia in honorem...Raymundi Josephi Martin* (Brugis Handrorum, 1948), pp. 351–8.
Oswald, E. *Falsche Prophetie im Alten Testament* (Tübingen, 1962).
Pannenberg, W. 'Heilsgeschehen und Geschichte', *KD*, V (1959).
—— 'Kerygma und Geschichte', *Studien zur Theologie des alttestamentlichen Überlieferungen* (von Rad *Festschrift*; 1961).
—— (ed.). *Offenbarung als Geschichte* (2nd edn. Göttingen, 1963).
Paré, G. *et al. La Renaissance du XIIe siècle: les Écoles et l'Enseignement* (Paris and Ottawa, 1933).
Parodi, E. G. *Poesia e Storia nella Divina Commedia* (Naples, 1921).
Pedersen, J. *Israel: its Life and Culture* (4 parts, London and Copenhagen, 1926 and 1940).
Pépin, J. *Mythe et Allégorie* (Paris, 1958).
Perrin, N. *The Kingdom of God in the Teaching of Jesus* (London, 1963).
Pettazoni, R. *La Confessione dei Peccati* (3 vols. Bologna, 1929–36).
Pézard, A. *Dante sous la Pluie de Feu* (Paris, 1950).
Pfeiffer, R. H. *Religion in the Old Testament* (London, 1961).
Phythian-Adams, W. J. *The Way of At-one-ment* (London, 1944).
Pietrobono, L. *Saggi Danteschi* (Turin, 1954).
—— *Nuovi Saggi Danteschi* (Turin, 1954).
Poggioli, R. 'Tragedy or Romance? A Reading of the Paolo and Francesca Episode in Dante's *Inferno*', *PMLA*, LXXII, 3 (June 1957).
Porena, M. *Delle Manifestazioni plastiche del Sentimento nei personaggi della Divina Commedia* (Milan, 1902).
von Rad, G. *Studies in Deuteronomy*, ET (London, 1953).
—— *Gesammelte Studien zum Alten Testament* (Munich, 1958).
—— *Genesis*, ET (London, 1961).
—— *Old Testament Theology*, vol. I, ET (Edinburgh and London, 1962).
—— *Theologie des Alten Testaments*, vol. II (Munich, 1960).
—— 'Der Anfang der Geschichtsschreibung im Alten Israel', *AKG* XXXII (1944).

von Rad, G. 'Typologische Auslegung des Alten Testaments', *EvTh* XII (1952).

—— 'Les Idées sur le temps et l'histoire et l'eschatologie des Prophètes', *Hommage à Wilhelm Vischer* (Montpellier, 1960).

—— (*Festschrift*). *Studien zur Theologie des alttestamentlichen Überlieferungen* (Munich, 1961).

Rahner, K. *On the Theology of Death*, ET (Edinburgh and London, 1961).

Reardon, B. M. G. 'Philosophy and Myth', *Theology*, LXV (1962).

Reid, J. K. S. *Our Life in Christ* (London, 1963).

Rendtorff, R. 'Hermeneutik des Alten Testaments als Frage nach der Geschichte', *ZThK*, LVII (1960).

—— 'Die Offenbarungsvorstellungen im Alten Israel', *Offenbarung als Geschichte*, ed. Pannenberg (Göttingen, 1963).

—— 'Geschichte und Überlieferung', *Studien zur Theologie des alttestamentlichen Überlieferung* (von Rad *Festschrift*; Munich, 1961).

Richardson, A. *Introduction to the Theology of the New Testament* (London, 1958).

—— *History, Sacred and Profane* (London, 1964).

—— 'Is the Old Testament the Propaedeutic to Christian Faith?', *The Old Testament and Christian Faith*, ed. B. W. Anderson (London, 1964).

Robinson, D. W. B. *The Hope of Christ's Coming* (London, 1960).

Robinson, H. W. *Inspiration and Revelation in the Old Testament* (Oxford, 1946).

—— (ed.). *Record and Revelation* (London, 1938).

Robinson, J. M. *The Problem of History in Mark* (London, 1957).

—— *A New Quest for the Historical Jesus* (London, 1959).

—— 'The Formal Structure of Jesus' Message', *Current Issues in New Testament Interpretation*, ed. W. Klassen and G. F. Snyder (London, 1962).

—— 'The Historicality of Biblical Language', in *The Old Testament and Christian Faith*, ed. B. W. Anderson (London, 1964).

Rowley, H. H. *Israel's Mission to the World* (London, 1939).

—— *The Relevance of Apocalyptic* (London, 1944).

—— *The Servant of the Lord and other Essays on the Old Testament* (London, 1952).

—— *The Faith of Israel* (London, 1956).

—— (ed.). *A Companion to the Bible* (Edinburgh, 1963).

Santi, A. *L'Ordinamento morale e l'Allegoria della Divina Commedia* (Palermo, 1924).

Sapegno, N. *La Divina Commedia, a cura di N. Sapegno* (1 vol. edn. Milan and Naples, 1957).

Sayers, D. *Introductory Papers on Dante* (London, 1954).

Sayers, D. *Further Papers on Dante* (London, 1957).

Schoeps, H. J. *Paul*, ET (London, 1961).

Schweizer, E. *Lordship and Discipleship*, ET (London, 1960).

Singleton, C. S. *Dante Studies. I. Commedia—Elements of Structure; Dante Studies. II. Journey to Beatrice* (Cambridge, Mass., 1954 and 1958).

—— 'In exitu Israel de Aegypto', 77th Annual Report of the Dante Society (1960).

—— 'The Vistas in Retrospect', *Atti del Congresso Internazionale di Studi Danteschi* (Florence, 1965), I. 296–301.

Smalley, B. *The Study of the Bible in the Middle Ages* (2nd edn. Oxford, 1952).

—— 'The Use of the Bible in the Middle Ages', *The Church's Use of the Bible*, ed. D. E. Nineham (London, 1963).

Spicq, C. *Esquisse d'une histoire de l'Exégèse latine au Moyen Age* (Paris, 1944).

Spitzer, L. *Romanische Literaturstudien, 1936–56* (Tübingen, 1959).

Stambler, B. *Dante's Other World* (London, 1958).

Stendahl, K. 'Quis et Unde? An analysis of Matthew 1–2', *BZNW*, XXVI (1960).

Stinespring, W. F. 'Eschatology in Chronicles', *JBL*, LXXX (1961).

Strack, H. L. and P. Billerbeck. *Kommentar zum Neuen Testament aus Talmud und Midrash* (4 vols. in 5, Munich, 1922–8).

Synave, P. 'La Doctrine de S. Thomas sur le sens littérale des Écritures', *RB*, XXV (1926).

Thielicke, H. 'Reflections on Bultmann's Hermeneutic', *ExpT*, LXVII (1956).

Thornton, L. S. *The Form of the Servant* (3 parts, London, 1950–6).

Tinsley, E. J. *The Imitation of God in Christ* (London, 1960).

Tondelli, L. *Da Gioacchino a Dante* (Turin, 1944).

Torrance, T. F. 'Scientific Hermeneutics according to St Thomas Aquinas', *JTS*, XIII (1962).

Trombatore, G. *Saggi critici* (Florence, 1950).

Vallone, A. *La Critica Dantesca Contemporanea* (2nd edn. Pisa, 1957).

Vischer, W. *The Witness of the Old Testament to Christ*, ET (London, 1949).

—— (*Festschrift*). *Hommage à Wilhelm Vischer* (Montpellier, 1960).

Vittorini, D. *High Points in the History of Italian Literature* (New York, 1958).

Voegelin, E. *Order and History. I. Israel and Revelation* (Louisiana, 1956).

Vriezen, T. C. 'Prophecy and Eschatology', *VT*, Suppl. 1 (1953).

Weiser, A. *Introduction to the Old Testament*, ET (London, 1961).

—— (with R. Bultmann). *Faith*, *BKW*, x (London, 1961).

Westermann, C. 'Bemerkungen zu den Thesen Bultmanns und Baumgärtels', *Probleme alttestamentlicher Hermeneutik* (see below).

—— (ed.). *Probleme alttestamentlicher Hermeneutik* (Munich, 1960).

—— *Essays on Old Testament Interpretation*, ET (London, 1964).

Whitfield, J. H. *Essays in the Like and Unlike* (Barlow Lectures on Dante, 1959), *Italian Studies*, Suppl. to vol. xv (1960).

Wilder, A. N. *Early Christian Rhetoric* (London, 1964).

—— 'New Testament Hermeneutics Today', *Current Issues in New Testament Interpretation*, ed. W. Klassen and G. F. Snyder (London, 1962).

Wilkinson, J. *Interpretation and Community* (London, 1963).

Wolff, H. W. 'Das Geschichtsverständnis der alttestamentlichen Prophetie', *EvTh*, xx (1960).

—— 'Zur Hermeneutik des Alten Testaments', *EvTh*, xvi (1956).

Wood, J. D. *The Interpretation of the Bible* (London, 1958).

Wright, G. E. *The Old Testament against its Environment* (London, 1950).

—— *God Who Acts* (London, 1952).

—— 'Archaeology and Old Testament Studies', *JBL*, lxxvii (1958).

—— 'The Faith of Israel', *IB*, i.

Zimmerli, W. 'Verheissung und Erfüllung', *EvTh*, xii (1952–3).

—— 'Le nouvel "Exode" dans le Message des deux grands Prophètes de l'Exil', *Hommage à Wilhelm Vischer* (Montpellier, 1960).

—— (with J. Jeremias). *The Servant of God*, ET (London, 1957).

INDEX OF SCRIPTURAL REFERENCES

18-2

II. NEW TESTAMENT

NAME AND SUBJECT INDEX